Reengineering Legacy Software Systems

Howard Wilbert Miller

Digital Press
Boston • Oxford • Johannesburg • Melbourne • New Delhi • Singapore

Library of Congress Cataloging-in-Publication Data

Miller, Howard W. (Howard Wilbert), 1943–
    Reengineering legacy software systems / Howard Wilbert Miller.
        p. cm.
    Includes bibliographical references and index.
    ISBN 1-55558-195-1 (alk. paper)
    1. Software reengineering. I. Title.
QA76.758.M546 1997
005.1'6—DC21   97–30947
                                                            CIP

British Library Cataloguing-in-Publication Data

A catalogue record for this book is available from the British Library.

The publisher offers special discounts on bulk orders of this book.
For information, please contact:
Manager of Special Sales
Butterworth–Heinemann
225 Wildwood Avenue
Woburn, MA 01801-2041
Tel: 781-904-2500
Fax: 781-904-2620

For information on all Digital Press publications available, contact our World Wide
Web home page at: http://www.bh.com/digitalpress

Order number: EY-W895E-DP

10 9 8 7 6 5 4 3 2 1

Printed in the United States of America

Contents

Introduction

General Information

Despite the positive impact of information systems, organizations continue to focus on the dark side of information technology. They focus on aspects of technology that are missing or on aspects that are less than perfect. Organizations spend a lot of time berating the aspects of the systems that do not work. They berate a system even when it is obvious that it is more expensive to repair or replace it than to live with the alternative. Organizations focus on the increasing cost of technology without looking at the benefits. They look at expenses without analyzing why the benefits do not materialize. If there is a lack of resources, it is assumed that the technology professionals are incompetent.

Part of this dark-side perspective is the belief that there is something wrong with maintaining or enhancing a software system. A larger and larger percentage of information technology resources is being expended on maintaining software systems (40 to 80 percent), and less and less is being spent on developing new systems. It is assumed that this is bad. Yet maintenance is the logical consequence of establishing a critical mass of technology. When a critical mass of technology is reached, it is logical to build on that base. Throwing out technology and starting over without a clear financial return does not make good business sense.

For an organization that has established an information technology architecture, enhancing this critical mass of systems is the most effective way to achieve that architecture. It is a low risk way to make change. It is an opportunity to improve the parts of the system that work. It is a means for identifying the source of problems and implementing a permanent solution. It is low risk because it addresses small chunks of the system. The resource commitment is small, and the consequences of a mistake also are small.

When structured, this enhancement process becomes software system reengineering. The key to reengineering is to focus on the conditions that work well and build on these. Projects are addressed in small chunks, implemented quickly, and evaluated as the source for additional improvement. Successive projects address the new source of improvement. The process is iterative, and the opportunity for return on investment, by means of building on successes, is far greater than spending an equivalent amount on fixing problems.

Organization

Reengineering Legacy Software Systems identifies techniques for planning and implementing software system reengineering. The book is organized into four sections: system reengineering, reengineering techniques, reengineering tools, and a summary.

System Reengineering

The first section addresses the issues surrounding legacy application system reengineering. Chapter 1 is an introduction to the topic of reengineering software systems. Software systems normally are reengineered to incorporate performance improvements or to meet the changing needs of an organization. In pursuit of such improvements, information service organizations need to free themselves from organization concepts and process designs. What is required is a systematic, structured approach that involves input from early analysis to eliminate pathologic conditions and reengineer software applications.

Chapter 2 addresses the topics of information technology change and how software systems parallel this iterative change. Software systems are subject to many influences—business, technical, and human. The result is a systematic structured approach to applying this iterative change thereby improving the ability of an organization to implement information technology. Reengineering techniques focus on the 20 percent of the features of a software system that result in 80 percent of the problems. Twenty percent of the effort is directed at correcting problems, and 80 percent is available to address opportunities. As a result, most of the effort is spent building new and enhanced features with the base of features that work as a foundation.

Chapter 3 introduces the concept of *opportunism*. Opportunism is the logical next step to reengineering software systems. It is an alternative to the problem-solving approach to system development. Chapter 3 analyzes the change process relative to information technology reengineering and identifies methods for selective acceleration of its introduction. Given these methods, it is possible for independent groups to purchase or develop generic systems that minimize future cleanup activities.

Chapter 4 addresses the development of an architecture as an information technology template. Organizations need to build flexibility into their technology architecture. They need to recognize the value of past successes and leverage them with the potential of new technology. This is not a simple task. However, the harmony derived from orchestrating the rich variety of alternatives available through strategic planning can be very rewarding to an organization. Chapter 4 defines the role of the chief information officer as an information technology architect.

Chapter 5 explains how to develop reengineering strategies that maneuver the information technology architecture. Strategies are the catalyst for orchestrating information technology change. Strategies ensure that change is in concert with the information architecture. This chapter identifies a method for developing such strategies.

Reengineering Techniques

The second section addresses techniques for reengineering an information technology architecture that is both flexible and opportunistic. Chapter 6 is an in-depth discussion of the dimensions of quality and how W. Edwards Deming's fourteen points can be used to implement quality in information technology. The future of information technology is bound to the ability of information technology professionals to produce high-quality, low-cost software that meets the expectation of computer users. There is nothing mysterious about achieving this goal; it requires a perpetual commitment to identifying and correcting the source of error. The result is a continuous and measurable improvement in quality and productivity. Techniques for building quality into software cannot be ignored during reengineering.

Chapter 7 emphasizes the need to differentiate projects by size. Reengineering software systems requires that technology professionals return to the basics. This chapter presents a simplified four-step project management procedure that consists of documenting, categorizing and ranking, and structuring projects. It also provides a framework for managing small support projects and a method to assist system development managers maintain an inventory of valid requests. It establishes which requests are consistent with the organization's information technology architecture and helps to formulate reengineering strategies.

Chapter 8 introduces the operational analysis, a reengineering tool that forestalls the need for replacing software systems with new systems. By using the operational analysis before a system reaches maturity, an organization can extend the life of a system. The operational analysis also provides qualitative and quantitative benefits. The qualitative benefits are immediate in the form of better quality utilization and system understanding. The quantitative benefits are acquired when the changes are carried through to fruition.

Chapter 9 is a case study. It shows how software systems change as a result of changes in business strategy. The case study identifies how the operational analysis was used to evaluate systems and identify opportunities for expense reduction and process improvements. The operational analysis identified that the organization was responsive to changing business needs but that it was reactive. The analysis helped identify opportunities to reengineer systems to better position the organization to take advantage of future opportunities.

Chapter 10 presents two additional case studies. These studies clearly differentiate a reengineered software system from conventional software development. The first study describes the design of a system in which timing constraints make it impossible for the organization to specify all of the requirements before the development process begins. The second case study describes the design of a software system for a relatively new function. A group takes on a new mission in which it is clear that an opportunistic approach is required to complete that mission. In this case, designing a flexible system that draws on the experience of computer users results in a design that could not have been achieved otherwise.

Reengineering Tools

The tone of the next six chapters is utilitarian. These chapters address five specific techniques for improving the ability to reengineer software systems. These include client-server technology, object technology, computer-aided software engineering, rule-based systems, and computer center automation.

Chapter 11 addresses the year 2000 as a unique opportunity to reengineer legacy systems. By using the operational analysis to evaluate applications, engineers can identify opportunites to extend the life of the applications and identify mission-critical opportunities for improvement where implementing year 2000 changes.

Chapter 12 targets the reengineering of legacy systems. Organizations need to reengineer their business processes to better utilize the investment they have made in information technology. This does not exclude the use of outsourcing, rehosting, or client-server technology. It should, however, include the reengineering of legacy systems to improve performance and better meet the needs of the organization.

Chapter 13 clears up the confusion surrounding downsizing, re-porting, and converting to client-server technology so that information service professionals can correctly identify opportunities for reengineering software systems to client-server technology on the basis of fact, not rhetoric. In a client-server solution, both the clients and the servers are fully independent computers capable of performing certain processing tasks. The independence and processing power result in a reduction in cost per processing unit while increasing flexibility. It is what distinguishes the client-server environment from other kinds of multi-user systems.

Chapter 14 is an exploration of the use of object technology and its ability to solve business problems. The movement toward wide-scale adoption of object technology in support of a more integrated approach to computing is well under way. Although final results are not available, a clear picture is emerging. Properly staffed, planned, and implemented object technology–based projects demonstrate results superior to traditionally planned and implemented systems in terms of flexibility, user satisfaction, cost, and ability to reengineer software systems.

Chapter 15 discusses the selection and implementation of computer assisted software engineering (CASE). CASE by definition is a technology that applies an automated, engineering-like discipline to computer software design, development, testing, maintenance, and project management. The ability to automate the engineering of software systems facilitates the reengineering of software systems to accommodate business opportunities.

Chapter 16 addresses the selection and implementation of rule-based system technology, another technique for reengineering software. The incentive behind rule-based systems is contained in the attributes of knowledge. Knowledge is perishable, and its longevity is tied to the expert. Rule-based systems seek to pass knowledge to another generation of experts or users and to encourage the growth and expansion of knowledge. Rule-based systems therefore provide the benefit of making knowledge more readily available and software systems easier to reengineer.

Chapter 17 discusses computer center automation. The center provides an opportunity to reengineer the processing of software systems and improve quality and service while reducing human intervention and cost. Computer center automation builds quality into the computer center by helping identify fault points (the points of human intervention) and eliminate the fault points, improving the reliability of software systems and making them easier to reengineer.

Reengineering Summary

The last two chapters of *Reengineering Legacy Software Systems* summarize the software system reengineering philosophy. They tie together reengineering of software systems, the techniques, and the tools into a cohesive approach to the development of computer-based software.

Chapter 18 puts software system reengineering into perspective. The success of reengineering systems is based on the human aspects of information technology. Developing new systems is the solution of choice because it is a durable (if not the most effective) approach to developing and maintaining software systems. Software reengineering is viewed as less desirable than developing new software. Yet most of the benefits from most computer projects are derived from a small number of the features. The real opportunities are derived from reengineering existing systems. Architectures, plans, and strategies are required to reengineer systems when such systems experience a crisis. The critical success factor for harnessing all aspects of reengineering depend on the human factor, not on the technology.

Chapter 19 addresses the issues of using reengineering to establish an enterprise-wide computing architecture. Establishing a strong, sustained link between a computing architecture and a process is a constant challenge. Process reengineering is meaningful only if it promotes the objectives of an organization. Reengineering embeds the corporate vision in each process, making the vision vital to the success of the process. If information service organizations are to continue to play an active role in the effort to control cost and generate revenues, then application system reengineering has to be included as part of the overall enterprise computing architecture.

It is common for software systems to be in a state of disrepair and suffer from the use of outmoded technologies and years of changes at the hands of different personnel who use different programming styles. New software frequently is easier to use, more flexible to modify, and more efficient to operate. Unfortunately, no staffing is provided to bring the systems up to standard. However, the tide is turning, and emphasis is being placed on expense reduction and improved financial performance. As a result, business processes and computer systems are being reengineered. Software systems are moving away from centralized computer centers. Frequently the systems are being rehosted in operating divisions using client-server technology.

When expense is evaluated, it is increasingly apparent that management must seriously consider software system reengineering as an integral component of cost containment and business process reengineering. Furthermore, the increasing popularity of business process reengineering has placed greater pressure on information services to keep pace with similar system reengineering projects. A study done by G2 Research, Incorporated, projected that the computer system reengineering market was expected to double by 1997. Organizations will reengineer legacy systems to make them more cost effective and competitive and easier to maintain and use. This frees resources to support activities associated with business process reengineering.

Part I

System Reengineering

1

Reengineering Software Systems

Reengineering legacy applications to take advantage of client-server technology is gathering momentum. However, the accumulated baggage of 25 years of commercial computing is extremely difficult to discard. The billion dollar investment in COBOL code is keeping client-server technology a one-application-at-a-time affair.

Organizations that converted mainframe-based legacy systems to fourth-generation languages (4GLs) and windowing technology are already realizing much of the benefits of client-server technology. Moreover, most organizations need to reengineer their operating procedures and their application systems before they can hope to shut down mainframe-based applications in favor of more flexible and easy-to-use client-server technologies.

Meanwhile, information system professionals are implementing reengineering plans that could convert 40 to 50 percent or more of mainframe-based applications by the turn of the century. For every application rewritten in a 4GL or application generator, the cost of software maintenance plummets compared with the cost of maintaining COBOL code. By reducing new demands on existing mainframe computers, many users are able to postpone or cancel computer upgrades.

Mainframe computers, however, are not destined to be mothballed in this decade. Mainframes and mainframe-based applications continue to grow at a somewhat slower pace than they did in the past. Client-server technology also continues to grow, and at a rapid pace. The accumulated impact of these strategies, combined with the use of outsourcing and legacy system reengineering, is targeted as the latent demand for computing applications.

The benefits of synthesizing these different strategies are improved organizational productivity and increased competitiveness. However, when the smoke clears, few organizations will be spending less for computing. Instead, they will be spending more. The increased expense will be worth it, because the return on the computing investment will far outweigh it. This chapter is dedicated to the techniques for reengineering computing through the synthesis of these strategies.

1.1 Reengineering Computing

Application systems are reengineered to achieve performance improvements in the following areas:

▶ Time

▶ Cost

▶ Productivity

▶ Quality

▶ Capital

In pursuing such improvements, information service organizations need to be free from the existing concepts of organization and process design. Brainstorming frequently uncovers wildly different procedures for using information technology in ways that increase efficiency and effectiveness.

1.1.1 Exploring Alternative Designs

Exploring work-flow reengineering alternatives involves creativity. It also involves an approach that questions every procedure and principle that currently governs work-flow activities and their approval. Typically, an information service organization investigates and develops alternative work-flow reengineering solutions. It considers information technology applications that may support each alternative. For example, an imaging system for credit transactions and authorizations that works by means of rule-based (expert) systems and work-flow automation may provide one way to handle form processing, routing, distribution, and approval. An alternative is to consider a wide area network (WAN) application tied into the corporate data server to allow immediate approvals and processing on-line by remote sales personnel.

Each solution involves different work-flow activity, staffing, and cross-function support. The intent is not to change or maintain technology models. The intent is to optimize work processes. An information services organization should be continually educating and communicating with fellow team members about the opportunities available for alternative computing designs. The best process design can then be considered before the final selection of a supporting technology. Without this step, the result is typically force-fitting new technologies to existing procedures.

1.1.2 Designing New Processes

The key to successful reengineering is to question why a certain task is done, what are better ways of doing it, who should be responsible, and which information technology best supports the reengineering process. The fundamental elements that must be considered in selecting the redesigned process include the following:

Pattern breaking: Breaking age-old principles and rules. For example, in one company, travel requests must be approved at the unit, departmental, and divisional levels.

Aligning with performance goals: Ensuring that the performance goals set earlier are truly aligned with process outcomes.

Job assignment: Designing work flow around the goals and objectives of the process, not a single task.

Elimination of hierarchies: Replacing bureaucratic hierarchies with self-organized teams working in parallel.

Elimination of identified pathologic conditions: Questioning activities and roles used simply to relay information and whether these can be handled with information technology.

Improving productivity: Moving focus from work fragmentation and task specialization toward task compression and integration.

Appraising information technology: Considering the appropriate computing configuration that can support and enable reengineering.

Reengineering is focused on leveraging time. Processing, transporting, and waiting time can be improved with a reengineered computer process. Vast amounts of time can be saved by eliminating multiple approval levels and noncritical control checks by means of integrating data processing into the work that produces the information, eliminating wait buffers, and integrating multiple tasks.

An important opportunity involves the substitution of sequential activities for simultaneous ones. This reduces the wait time involved in processes and can be achieved by means of applying on-line databases and information networks across the process so that concurrent information access occurs at every node.

Separate tasks within processes should be integrated as much as possible into one job description. This keeps important information from being lost as responsibility transfers across organizational boundaries. In reengineering computing, appropriate information, including immediate feedback on performance, is provided directly to line workers so that problems are resolved immediately. Through the use of computing platforms that support enterprise-wide information access, individual jobs can be designed to conduct parallel tasks and to allow workers to make informed decisions.

1.1.3 Designing for Human Resources

Reengineering computing is not limited to its processes; the computing organizational structure is also fair game. The divisions of an organization should support the processes as much as possible. Reorganizing subunits to minimize unit interdependencies holds potential for reducing costs and improving productivity. Confrontations that consume time and money are bypassed. Minimizing interdependencies between subunits is accomplished by means of improving the alignment of objectives, tasks, and people within a single subunit. When possible, the human resource structure supports a free exchange of information. It also supports refocusing of decisions and actions at the individual and work-group levels.

Inevitably, reengineering may cause a substantial change in organizational structure. Reengineering includes a human resource component that incorporates the following:

▶ Redefinition of job titles and positions affected by changes in cross-function processes

▶ Team-based management techniques, such as establishment of self-motivated teams assigned to specific business processes

▶ Assignments based on the unique skills of an individual

▶ Continual organizational learning through on-the-job training with emphasis on quality, time, and output

▶ Performance evaluation based on team productivity, measured on the basis of group effectiveness

▶ Incentives and reward structures based on group performance and individual contribution to the team

▶ Modification of management structures that require managers to be leaders as well as equals of team members

▶ Continuous reengineering of project communication to all employees who provide feedback on progress

1.1.4 Prototyping

Prototyping is widely used in traditional system development. It produces rapid feedback that helps determine system requirements. Prototyping techniques are extremely useful for reengineering because they can be used to demonstrate proposed redesigns that would otherwise be difficult for people to comprehend.

Computer-aided software engineering (CASE) tools have the capability to develop rapid prototypes. The U.S. Department of Defense adopted a comprehensive reengineering plan that made extensive use of rapid prototyping. The result was a reconfiguration of existing methods and a reduction of command-wide systems from eighty to forty-three. Prototypes provide management with a vehicle to make judgments toward a final process design choice.

1.1.5 Selecting a Computing Platform

Integration, cooperation, ease of migration, adaptability to new technologies, and enterprise-wide information access and sharing are factors that influence the selection of a computing platform to support the reengineered process. The computing base must be able to support communication between corporate systems and decentralized divisional systems. It also must tie suppliers, vendors, and customers by means of WANs. This commonly results in converting mainframe-based systems to local area network (LAN)–based client-server technology by means of object-oriented programming, or it may result in expanding the use of 4GL and windowing technology on a mainframe computer and front-ending it with graphical use interface (GUI) technology. Some experts believe that only an object-oriented infrastructure will allow developers to integrate and implement systems fast enough to meet the reengineering time frame.

The critical need for information sharing and access determines the organizational database design requirements. This may lead to the decision to develop an enterprise-wide information architecture or distributed databases. The computing platform selected must outline the following:

Hardware decisions, such as mainframe computer, departmental computer, or client-server-based configurations.

Software decisions, such as operating system and a data architecture at all levels of system implementation. The platform must detail the appropriate software systems to be implemented at every level, such as development of a decision support system at the executive level with several integrated work-group applications for transaction processing.

Decisions are made about deploying third-party software, in-house software development kits to support applications development, software reengineering plans, documentation, and training plans. The selection of a computing platform for a particular process is always related to the enterprise-wide computing architecture.

1.2 Reconstruction

As with any substantial organizational change, a methodical process is adopted that takes advantage of small-scale pilot projects, user training, and extensive user feedback. When problems arise in this stage of reengineering, the persons involved must retain their commitment to the main ideas generated during process redesign. They must also be amenable to changes that may be required to facilitate the installation. An effort undertaken in the reconstruction stage is the deployment of new systems to support new processes.

1.2.1 Downsizing and Software Reengineering

In some situations, existing systems and technology are replaced entirely with new hardware platforms and application programs. For example, several companies have converted their mainframe-based information systems with more flexible and cost-effective LANs and client-server architectures.

The more common option is software reengineering. Software reengineering is the process of redesigning and reusing existing system code for migration to more effective hardware and software platforms. An important direction in system development is the reverse: reengineering of object code to produce recyclable source code. This source code is then used in forward-engineering techniques involving CASE tools for added capability and restructuring of current systems. Software reengineering can help to improve the reuse, redesign, analysis, and performance of software systems.

Several companies have chosen to radically overhaul current systems with new technologies that provide improved connectivity and cost-performance ratios. Migration to LAN-based client-server technology and groupware applications based on object-oriented design have shown considerable success. Several vendors have groupware products that are based on open systems to allow organizations to develop easily integrated applications.

1.2.2 Reorganization Activities

A crucial element for reengineering success is the design of a new organizational structure consistent with the newly defined process. The human resource organization outlined during redesign must be thoughtfully executed to minimize any disruption of employee morale. The focus on a smooth transition to the new organization design incorporates improvements such as the following:

▶ Subunit reorganization

▶ Job rotation and staff reduction

▶ Empowerment of remaining employees through training and educational programs

▶ Improvement in quality of work life

Empowering workers means placing decision points where work is performed. In essence, this means allowing individual workers to control the process. This basic assumption contradicts traditional bureaucratic theory that states that people doing the work have neither the time nor the inclination to monitor and control their own work performance. Building control and accountability into the work process is accomplished by making those responsible for producing information also accountable for its processing. Properly reorganizing the process and related organizational structure should allow empowered employees to use discretion in judgment and increase the possibility that their work can be a rewarding experience.

Training of personnel in a newly installed process-based environment is critical. The doctrine of reengineering involves the elimination of functional hierarchies and development of organizational structures based on processes. As a result, team-based management techniques are at a premium.

Performance evaluation takes a new twist as team performance rather than individual performance becomes the primary measure of success. Incentives and reward structures must be redesigned according to group performance. Individual reward structures have to be redefined according to the individual's contribution to the team. The changes brought on by reorganization may cause resentment that must be addressed by continual communication between the reengineering team and employees. In the long term, however, the combined people and process changes should produce an organization able to change and learn.

1.3 Monitoring the Architecture

There are two distinct components of monitoring: performance measurement and quality improvement.

1.3.1 Performance Measurement

To determine the success of a reengineering project, new processes must be measured for time, cost, productivity, quality, and capital. These measures are then compared with the processes they replaced. To ensure fulfillment of performance improvements, a wide spectrum of monitoring is used. Several aspects of the organization are continually assessed and controlled. Examples of hard measures include:

Process performance: cycle time, customer service, and quality

Computing performance: software complexity, information rates, downtime, system use, and paper reduction, as through e-mail or an executive information system (EIS)

Productivity indices: for the performance of employees and production and service operations

Monitoring is based on hard measures, such as expense, and soft measures, such as morale and customer goodwill. This multidimensional approach to performance monitoring is essential because of the depth and breadth of the changes caused by the radically reengineered computing process.

This all-encompassing scope of performance monitoring requires the attention and active endorsement of senior management. The new measure for process outcome is directly tied to overall organization performance. If thoughtfully and thoroughly carried out, these monitoring and integration efforts lay the foundation for the continuing success of the redesigned process and further diffusion of the reengineering to other areas of business.

1.3.2 Links to Quality Improvement

Reengineering goals can differ radically from quality programs such as total quality management (TQM) that aim at incremental gains. The fundamental difference between quality programs and reengineering is the focus on continuous improvement as opposed to goals that are set before the reengineering project begins. The monitoring stage provides a fundamental link between the radical focus of reengineering and the continuous incremental improvements of TQM.

Continual monitoring of the reengineered processes is essential, especially in the early stages of deployment. There must exist an efficient feedback loop between monitoring and diagnoses. Such a loop provides an audit of the performance of the redesigned processes and helps identify processes that are candidates for further redesign. It may be necessary to fine-tune certain aspects of the new process and associated computing until acceptable performance gains have been achieved. Reengineering frequently is an iterative process. If the first reengineering project is a success, management may direct the team to focus on another process in need of redesign.

1.4 Conclusion

Corporate management is looking for ways to exploit organizational competencies, to regain competitiveness, and to achieve long-term sustainability. Reengineering computing software applications has captured the imagination of both corporate management and information service leaders. Information service professionals are central to this challenging assignment, and their participation in reengineering is essential.

Although the need for change is recognized, there is no widely accepted execution plan or method available to support such change. The reengineering model presented in this introductory chapter partially fills this void. This plan provides the new generation of system professionals with a framework for integrating mainframe-based technology, client-server technology, outsourcing, and legacy system reengineering into a total computing architecture. The objective of this computing architecture is not to promote or convert to one flavor of computing but to integrate the best available technology to support business processes.

Reengineering computing is not limited to processes; the organizational structure of computing is included. The divisions of an organization need to support the processes. As a result, reorganizing subunits to minimize unit interdependencies reduces expenses and improves productivity. Minimizing interdependencies between subunits is accomplished by means of improving the alignment of objectives, tasks, and people within single subunits. When possible, a designed human resource plan should support a free exchange of information and a refocusing of decisions and actions at the individual and work-group levels.

2

Information System Evolution

As corporate management seeks to optimize organizational performance, one of the methods that is coming to the forefront is computer software reengineering. Management is looking for ways to exploit organizational competencies, to regain competitiveness, and to achieve long-term sustainability. Before embracing software reengineering, however, it is important to understand the nature of computer system change. Computer systems change as a result of business, human, and technology factors irrespective of management's intent. They go through a series of iterative changes—they evolve.

The evolution of computer systems is not smooth. It consists of periods of growth during which changes to a computer application are superficial. These periods of growth are punctuated by periods of turmoil that result in redirection of the evolution of a software system or, more commonly, in creation of a new software system. When left unattended, the evolution of the software system has a high probability of deviating from the direction of the organization.

The most common response to periods of turmoil is to throw out the old computer system and create a new one. The punctuation starts with a flurry of changes or a problem that is resolved by creation of a replacement software system. This creation is a knee-jerk reaction to a crisis in a software system. Over time, the replacement software system is subject to the same cycle. Requirements change, and the software system is repeatedly modified. Another crisis develops, and the response again is creation: problem → creation → problem.

Three categories of factors affect the speed and direction of system evolution: business factors, human factors, and technology factors. By charting the direction of these factors, it is possible to establish an information technology architecture. The alternative to the cycle of problem → creation → problem is to harness the change and direct evolution toward the objective of the organization. *Harnessing change and redirecting evolution* is the definition for software system reengineering used throughout this report. It extends the life of software systems by ensuring that they correspond to the needs of the organization.

2.1 Punctuated Equilibrium

In 1972 Niles Eldredge of the American Museum in New York and Stephen Jay Gould of Harvard University published an article titled "Punctuated Equilibria." In that paper, Eldredge and Gould proposed the theory of punctuated equilibrium. The theory is that species do not change continuously across time but that evolutionary change happens suddenly, as does a punctuation point in a sentence. The equilibrium part of the theory implies that most of the time species are not evolving. Environmental conditions are stable, and the stable conditions do not allow change. *Punctuation*, on the other hand, refers to the sudden change experienced after what can be long periods of stability.

The theory of punctuated equilibrium therefore suggests that there are periods of little or no change that are punctuated by sudden and sometimes catastrophic change. Most species change little from the time they first appear until they disappear, but their elapsed period of existence may vary considerably. Further, the faster the metabolic rate of a species, the shorter is the elapsed period from appearance to disappearance. Most species of clam, for example, experience relatively little evolutionary changeover millions of years, whereas mammals are just the opposite. After I read the article "Punctuated Equilibria," it became evident to me that a direct parallel exists between these concepts and the information technology life cycle.

2.2 System Evolution

In September 1986, I wrote an article published in *Computerworld* that drew a parallel between the concept of evolution and the system life cycle. This was my first attempt at drawing a cross-disciplinary parallel between evolution and information technology. The premise was that at some point in the life cycle of a system, factors external to the system affect it in a manner that the system cannot accommodate, producing change. The periods of evolution are governed by the following four rules, modeled on Darwin's theory of evolution (Figure 2.1), that determine the speed and direction of the system evolution:

1. A system is not static; it is always evolving and changing. New systems or subsystems are emerging while others are becoming obsolete.

2. The process of evolution is slow but continuous. It does not operate at a constant speed; it is subject to acceleration and deceleration. However, substantial sudden change is almost nonexistent.

3. The rule of common descent: similar systems are related in concept and descend from a common origin. This concept is especially evident in areas such as computer architecture, operating systems, database systems, and manufacturing systems.

Figure 2.1 *The Four Postulates of Evolution*

The Four Postulates of Evolution

1. The first was the postulate that the world is evolving. Species change continuously, new ones originate and others become extinct.
2. The second concept was the postulate that the process of evolution is gradual and continuous; it does not consist of discontinuous saltations or sudden chances.
3. Darwin postulated... that similar organisms were related from a common descent.
4. Darwin's fourth sub-theory was that of natural selection, and it was key to his broad scheme. Evolutionary change... is not the result of any mysterious Lamarckian drive, nor is it a simple matter of chance; it is the result of selection. Selection is a two step process.

   • The first step is the production of variations. In every generation, according to Darwin, an enormous amount of variation is generated.

   • The second is selection through survival in the struggle for existence. In most species of animals and plants, a set of parents produce thousands if not millions of off-springs. Darwin's reading of Thomas Malthus told him that very few survive. Which ones would have the best chance of survival? They would be those individuals that have the most appropriate combination of characters for cooperating with the environment including climate, competitors and enemies; they would have the greatest chance of surviving, of reproducing and of leaving survivors and their characters would therefore be available for the next cycle of selection.

Quoted from Ernst Mavr, "Evolution," Scientific American, September 1988.

4. The rule of compromise: system evolution is the result not of shrewd design but of a long series of compromises. This compromise is a two-step process, as follows:

▶ The first step is recognition and introduction of variation in a system to satisfy user needs. No two systems are ever installed in exactly the same way.

▶ The second step is improvement through selection. Of the thousands of variations in the way a system is used, certain variations demonstrate themselves as having more value than others. These characteristics are selected and carried forward as the system evolves.

As both the age and size of a system increase, a phenomenon occurs—the prolonged growth results in corresponding change, an evolution. Smooth evolution is not inevitable. It cannot be assumed that system growth is linear. This model for system evolution suggests that there are periods of little or no change punctuated by sudden and sometimes catastrophic change.

Most computer-based systems experience slow and superficial change from the time they are first installed until they disappear. However, the elapsed life expectancy for a computer-based system may vary from years to decades. The faster the rate of change, the shorter is the elapsed period from appearance to disappearance. Most financial systems, for example, experience relatively little evolutionary change over years, whereas a marketing or manufacturing system behaves the opposite way.

The three factors that affect the speed and direction of system evolution are business factors, human factors, and technology factors.

2.2.1 Business Factors

Most organizations view information technology as a cost of doing business. There are few examples of the strategic use of information, and the same few examples are cited over and over. There is a tendency to invest heavily in information technology when business is thriving and to reduce expenses when business is slow.

The irony of this situation is that the process is self-defeating. Information technology is best introduced during a business decline. During prosperity, the focus of an organization is on meeting the demands of its customer base. The organization assumes that what it is doing is correct; it has made the organization prosperous, and it wants more of the kind of information it associates with success. Furthermore, new information technology usually has a long lead time. The promise of new information technology and the long lead time associated with it becomes a source of frustration. A period of prosperity is the wrong time to look at introducing new information technology, because the perspective of the organization is wrong. The perspective of the organization is to accelerate the way information has been processed in the past.

When business is poor, an organization usually has a better perspective on where information technology will benefit. The focus is almost always on reducing cost and generating revenue. Business slumps are usually industry-wide. This is an opportunity to make the lead time work for the organization, to introduce technology when the competition is not, and to have that technology in place when it is needed. It takes courage and business skill to invest when business is poor, but this is the stuff that makes business legends.

The moral is that no matter how good the technology, it has little chance of success if business conditions do not foster its introduction.

2.2.2 Human Factors

A simple maxim of information technology best summarizes the human factor. No matter how good the information technology, if people do not want it, it will not work. Further, no matter how poor the information technology, if the people want it, it will work. If people want cars that talk to them or if they view automatic teller machines as convenient, they will use them. If people do not want to do end-user computing or do not believe it enriches their jobs, they will not do it. If people do not want to use personal computers because they fear them, they will not use them. There are countless examples of brilliant technology that did not work because the marketplace did not accept it.

This maxim is often overlooked in the rush to implement new information technology. As with business factors, it is an opportunity waiting to be exercised. By using any opportunity available to educate staff members in the use of information technology, an organization enriches their jobs, and the staff develops a technology perspective. The objective is for them to view information technology as exciting and job enriching, not as threatening.

The moral is that no matter how good the technology, it has little chance of success if people do not embrace it.

2.2.3 Technology Factors

Organizations are becoming comfortable with information technology and are coming to expect technologic change. By almost any realistic measure, the successful track record for implementing innovative information technology, despite immense uncertainty and low odds of success, is a noteworthy achievement. As new information technology is implemented, the uncertainty and odds of failure lessen, but the lead times for acceptance and implementation continue to be long. As a result, practitioners of information technology have learned the following bitter lessons:

► The selection criterion for information technology is "good enough" and not "best possible." Seeking the best possible alternative tends to exaggerate the lead time for implementation and promotes frustration. The correct approach is the 80/20 rule: 80% of the results are realized from 20% of the investment. "Good enough" is derived from experience of what we have learned to accept or expect, rather than from rational evaluation of requirements. Requirements tend to be derived from experience rather than needs or capabilities.

► New information technology is not always successful, but to be valuable it does not have to be successful. Over the years many dead-end devices have been introduced that paid a financial return and furthered the technology in a manner that almost no other approach could.

► Murphy's Law always applies. During design, the positive effect of information technology is immediately apparent and the negative is not. The negative is, however, immediately apparent upon implementation.

► Extending existing information technology is almost always superior to introducing new technology. The key to success for new technology is to introduce it on a small scale and extend it.

► Developing standards and precision is a prerequisite. If standards and precision are not present, information technology will not create them. A good apple in a basket of bad apples will not make the other apples good, but a bad apple in a basket of good apples will make the other apples go bad.

The moral is that expectations and the use of information technology have to correspond with the way technology actually evolves.

2.3 System Creation to System Evolution

Evidence from numerous case histories supports periods of little or no system evolution. These periods are clearly punctuated with periods of turbulence that result from business, human, and technologic incursions into the stability of an organization. Such infringement results in a system crisis, a serious upheaval, that results in elimination or replacement of a system. During this crisis, the user organization does one or more of the following:

- ▶ Outgrows its present system

- ▶ Identifies an opportunity for cost reduction

- ▶ Requires faster, more accurate, more detailed information

- ▶ Experiences a change in operating personnel

- ▶ Experiences a change in technology

- ▶ Determines the system is no longer efficient

- ▶ Discovers that the software is not supported by its supplier

Despite the reason, the result is usually the same. A completely new system is designed. The task is tackled with the optimism that the ills of the existing system can be overcome. The designers believe they are developing a lasting, durable application that will withstand the test of time. Because there is no such thing as a utopian system, the system design often takes multiple person-years, ends up behind schedule or understated, is implemented in an atmosphere of trauma, and goes through multiple specification iterations while causing turnover of users and management information services (MIS) development staff.

This information technology development scenario consists of a project life cycle that starts with a crisis or a problem statement. The problem statement is translated into software design, development, or selection and finally into a working application software system. After installation, the software system is altered until the numbers and complexity of the alterations increase, and the software is perceived as no longer capable of accepting the changes necessary to support its mission. This is the problem scenario: it starts with a problem statement and ends with a problem statement. It starts with creation and ends with creation.

2.4 The Evolution Alternative

The evolution of computer systems is not smooth. Evolution is an iterative process that consists of periods of growth. During growth periods there are few or no changes to a computer system. These periods of smooth growth are punctuated by periods of turmoil that result in redirection of the evolution of the software system or creation of a new software system. The faster the rate of change, the shorter is the elapsed period from appearance to disappearance of the system. The rate of change is the determinant for selecting a solution to a problem statement, either creation or evolution.

When the application software system is perceived as being worn out and the creation alternative is chosen, all the features of the system are replaced, both good and bad. In most instances, however, only 20% of the features of the computer system represent 80% of the problems (Figure 2.2).

In the creation alternative, only 20% of the replacement effort is expended on the problem features, 80% is expended on replacing the problem-free features, and no effort spent on improving the portion that works. The solution to this ineffective distribution is to apply 20% of the staff to correcting the problem features, which in most instances represent 80% of the problems, and to apply the other 80% of the staff to improving the features of the software system that work. This distribution of staffing harnesses the evolution of the computer system by eliminating problems and improving the features of the computer system. However, improving the features of a software system and resolving problems are not the only form of evolution. During periods of high change, creation is a valid solution to problems. It is possible and even desirable to create such an iterative system.

2.4.1 Harnessing the Change

As the age of a system increases and the changes become compounded, there is a degradation in both the ability of the computer system to meet the needs of the computer user and the ability of the information technology group to continue to make changes to the computer system. On one hand, the number of problems increases, and on the other, it becomes more difficult to correct the problems and to make the improvements. One of the most common mistakes is to assume that these conditions result in no alternative but to replace the system, creating a new system.

Figure 2.2
Distribution of
Problem Features

WRONG	ADEQUATE	IMPROVEMENTS
20%	60%	20%

In most computer systems, 20% of the features are a problem, 60% meet the expectation of the computer user, and an additional 20% provide an excellent opportunity for high-return improvement. The computer user, however, usually equates inability to make improvements to a system with problems, making the status of the system appear far worse than it is.

In many cases, this is not true. New development is commonly viewed as desirable, and software system correction and enhancement are viewed as undesirable. Correction and enhancement are performed in response to the requests of the computer user. They are performed in response to daily problems, changes in the law, and perceived opportunities for improvement. In most cases, there is no established direction for the changes to the application system. No one identifies where the organization wants the application system to be next year, or the year after. As a result, changes are uncoordinated. The design of the software system becomes disjointed, and performance deteriorates.

Where there is a direction, the changes are evaluated in relation to the direction, opportunities for improvement are evaluated for return on investment, and the change is aimed at the objectives of the organization.

2.4.2 Creating through Change

Successful change demonstrates that learning is gradual, as shown by the following observations:

▶ Computer users do not accurately specify requirements until they see the results of their earlier specifications.

▶ It is easier to modify than to create.

▶ Improvements have a greater chance of success than do new designs.

▶ Implementing high-return features improves the success of a software system.

Software creation and *software change* are not contradictory terms. Change is simply a slow period in the overall creative process. Nor are creation and change mutually exclusive. It is both possible and desirable to create an iterative system.

If an organization develops a direction for its technology and if it develops a direction for change, it is possible to break the development into small chunks that will deliver a usable product. Limiting the scope of each chunk makes it possible to deliver a usable product quickly, with little financial investment. Through gradual learning, computer users can specify improvements. High-return improvements are worked into the design by means of incorporation of the changes into the next small chunk. The result is a successful system that evolves over time.

2.5 Reengineering Change

The direction of almost every software system developed is in some way determined by the past. Once an organization understands the concepts and the factors that influence the change of a software system, it becomes possible to harness the direction of evolution. It is possible not only to determine the direction of the evolution of an existing base of software systems but also to reengineer current software and create new software in an evolutionary manner. The technique for reengineering evolution is to establish an architecture, strategies, and supporting technology.

2.5.1 Architecture

Organizations can no longer choose a hardware vendor and simply evolve through that vendor's technology. The increasing number of innovative solutions in support of organizational objectives cannot be ignored. Information technology is akin to a symphony in which hardware, software, and turnkey solutions are like instruments. The architecture is the orchestration of these instruments. The composition of the orchestra changes with the business objectives of an organization, the availability of technology, and the receptivity of the staff.

Business, technology, and human factors affect the speed and direction of the evolution of computer-based systems. Organizations need to build an architecture on these factors as a template for evolution. This architecture has to be flexible. It has to allow the organization to recognize the value of past successes and leverage them with the potential of new technology. This is not a simple task, but the harmony derived from orchestrating the rich variety of alternatives available through strategic planning can be rewarding to an organization.

2.5.2 Strategy

The second step is to develop a set of strategies for implementing the information technology architecture. The strategy should include a heavy dependence on directing the evolution of existing software systems and on the development of new software by means of evolutionary techniques.

Organizations can direct the evolution of existing software systems by directing their maintenance and enhancement. An organization needs to establish a direction for the software system, identify the requested maintenance and enhancement, and specify the improvements. Implementation is achieved through a long series of small projects, sometimes called *chunks*. As new changes are requested, they are tested against the direction for conformance. The organization becomes comfortable knowing that changes are moving the software systems in the desired direction.

When it is necessary to create new software systems, an organization needs to create them with an evolutionary strategy. The new software system is created in small chunks that deliver usable products quickly. As portions of the new system are designed and implemented, other portions become clear. Learning is gradual, and users cannot accurately specify system requirements until they see them. Frequently, it is necessary to go back to change some of the earlier designs as direction changes. Nobody is clairvoyant, and allowing room for software system improvement ensures a greater chance of success than does trying to identify every feature of a software system. It is usually easier to improve or modify an existing software system than it is to specify all of its features with no prior knowledge.

The strategy should be based on implementing quality into all aspects of information technology. The future of information technology is closely bound to the ability of information technology professionals to produce high-quality, flexible, low-cost software that meets the expectations of computer users and of the computer center. There is nothing mysterious about achieving this goal; it requires a never-ending commitment to identifying and correcting the source of error. The result is a continuous and measurable improvement in quality and productivity.

An organization needs to implement a strategy that supports segmenting projects into small pieces or chunks that are quickly developed and evaluated by users. Implement the product quickly and try it out with computer users. The small chunks become prototypes that give computer users a chance to "fly before they buy" and to change their minds before they make large investments. Use of small chunks allows software products to be tested and implemented quickly before barriers are developed. Chunking incorporates all the principles for successful evolution: it allows easy modification, learning is gradual, users see the results of requirements, and the software is easy to test.

2.5.3 Technology

The single factor that inhibits expansion of information technology is software development itself. Software development is both laborious and error-prone, and the result is software systems that are rigid and difficult to change. An ever-increasing proportion of software development personnel must be expended on maintaining these software systems. Information technology has not redirected the technology to automating itself.

One of the solutions to this problem is computer-aided software engineering (CASE), which is a highly flexible software development environment. The objective of CASE is automation of the software engineering process. CASE is a relatively new acronym. It has become recognizable to system and data-processing professionals only in the last five years, although its roots extend well back into the 1970s and are evident in many of the products marketed as CASE tools. CASE is a technology that applies an automated, engineering-like discipline to the specification of computer software system design, software development, testing, maintenance, and project management.

Two aspects of CASE make it good for the evolutionary environment. First, CASE facilitates evolutionary creation by means of automating the creation requirements, design, and software in a reusable manner. Second, CASE has a feature called *reverse engineering* that allows software systems to be translated into requirements and design. It becomes significantly easier to control the evolution of existing software systems.

The second solution is rule-based—a discipline that creates computer software to emulate the way people solve problems. Rule-based systems is a broad concept that encompasses a number of different disciplines, but it is typically equated with expert system technology. Experts can solve difficult problems, explain the results of a solution, learn from problem solving, explain the relevance of a solution, and most important, know when they do not know. Like human experts, a rule-based system gives advice by drawing on its own store of knowledge (rules) and by requesting information specific to the problem at hand.

There are several incentives for replicating the expert. Knowledge is a perishable and scarce commodity that is difficult to apply, distribute, and accumulate. Knowledge is vague, inconsistent, and widely dispersed. Expert systems preserve, clone, and apply knowledge. Rule-based systems distribute knowledge and encourage its growth. They make knowledge more precise and systematic and collect it into a knowledge base.

Rule-based systems, like CASE, offer two avenues for extending evolutionary systems. Expert systems are applicable to replicating the high degree of expertise required to develop software systems. Rule-based systems are valuable for leveraging the base of an installed system. They are an opportunity to build on the base of systems already installed. They are more readily available and easier to install with client-server technology.

2.6 Conclusion

The benefit of an evolutionary strategy for software reengineering is the improved ability of an organization to implement the information technology that has the most immediate return for the organization. Evolutionary systems are iterative; they focus on the 20% of the features of a software system that result in 80% of the problems. In an evolutionary strategy, 20% of the information service effort is directed at correcting problems, and 80% is available to address opportunities. Most of the effort is spent on building new and enhanced features on the base of features that already work.

The evolutionary process is achieved by means of first establishing an overall computing architecture. The architecture defines the business, technologic, and human directions of the organization. The second step is to establish a set of strategies for implementing an evolutionary approach to software system development. The last step is to automate the software development process by use of CASE, rule-based systems, and object technology techniques. These technologies are easier to install and use in a client-server environment.

3

Opportunism and Reengineering

Information technology is changing rapidly. In many organizations, for example, it is no longer necessary for users to wait for the information service department to satisfy their needs. Hardware costs are so low that any group can install a personal computer and develop or purchase its own system.

As a result, many diverse systems are popping up all over organizations. Each system is generally developed independently of existing or planned systems. There is no common development method, no standard procedures for documentation, no standards for handling data, and little or no security. Although each independent system serves its purpose, there is no uniform selection procedure to ensure the most effective use of resources and the systematic development of organizational data.

Building independent systems may work well in the short term, but such actions lay the base for a huge long-term problem. Inevitably there is a need to interface some of these independent systems, to compare the data in one system with that of another, or to consolidate independent information. At that time, someone has the difficult and expensive job of converting these systems to make them compatible. The unmanaged information technology change of today is generating a mess that will be expensive to clean up tomorrow.

It is ironic that the rapid introduction of information technology is not only good but essential for maintaining a competitive position in a service-based economy. Therefore, it is essential to have an enlightened technology objective. Describing such an objective helps an organization to identify methods for selective acceleration of the introduction of information technology and to minimize the negative effect of change.

This chapter analyzes the change process as it applies to reengineering information technology and identifies methods for selectively accelerating its introduction. Given these methods, it is possible for independent groups to purchase or develop generic systems that minimize future cleanup activities.

3.1 Understanding Change

3.1.1 Continuous Change

Change is the norm in most organizations. Business cycles and management philosophies change, demographic factors shift, sales and profits increase or decline, employees come and go, technology is introduced, and technology becomes obsolete. The speed and duration of change may vary considerably, but nevertheless change is continuous.

Some changes occur quickly, whereas others are almost imperceptible, occurring over a very long time. Archaeologists have traced the evolution of the Egyptian pyramids from small mud-brick structures to the mammoth stone monuments that we all recognize. In the third Egyptian dynasty, 2800 to 2700 B.C., a catastrophe occurred that altered this evolution for one hundred years: the Medium Pyramid collapsed. As a result of this failure, the Egyptians altered the design of the Bent Pyramid; the angle was changed from 52 degrees to 43.5 degrees about halfway through construction, producing its unique bent profile. The Egyptians incorrectly assumed that the collapse of the Medium Pyramid was caused by a design flaw and proceeded to construct the Red Pyramid with an angle of 43.5 degrees. A technologic failure altered the direction of Egyptian construction for one hundred years.

There is no way to stem the ebb and flow of change, but it is possible to create an environment that is receptive to the change and recognizes it as an opportunity. By means of charting and measuring the impact of the change, it is possible to isolate opportunities to achieve organizational objectives. The advanced age of the population, for example, offers the opportunity to create products and services aimed at older people and reduces the opportunity to market products aimed at younger people.

3.1.2 Controlling Change

Some types of change are easier to control than others. Some aspects can be controlled and others cannot. For example, business cycles are difficult if not impossible to control, but profits can be sustained and even improved despite these cycles. A stable workforce is impossible to maintain; employees retire, get sick, are promoted, and so on. Despite these forces of change, it is possible to manage turnover and avoid a crisis.

Accepting that some change can be easily managed and other change cannot is essential to the concept of reengineering. If change is perceived as inevitable, no direction is possible. Perceiving change as capable of manipulation, however, sets the stage for directing the change. Accepting the concept that change can be managed is only part of the story. Easily managed change must be differentiated from change that is too difficult and time consuming to implement. True innovation is achieved by means of directing energies at manageable change not by means of wasting energy on unmanageable change.

3.1.3 Some Change Works

Some change works and other change does not, but all change, whether it works or not, creates an opportunity. When the foundation of the Carlisle Cathedral began to sink, the architects suspended work. Finding that the vaults had settled only several feet below the intended level, the architects carried on as if nothing had happened. The result was a change that worked—an excellent example of the skewed Norman vault. The principles are as follows:

▶ If the change works, it is usually followed by a period of stabilization. This period is short or long depending on the nature of the change. After the period of stabilization, the change process is ready to start again.

▶ If the change does not work, the change process is immediately terminated. The process either reverts back to its prechange condition or remains in its new, less favorable condition. In either case, the change process is ready to start again.

The danger with change is on the failure side. Successful change is an incentive for additional change. With unsuccessful change, the tendency is to revert to the prechange state and do nothing further or, even worse, to accept the unsuccessful postchange condition.

In 1225, construction of the 158-foot-high Beauvais cathedral was started. This ambitious structure was to become the tallest cathedral ever constructed. In 1284, however, the nave of the cathedral collapsed. Modern analysis has determined that the architectural design for the cathedral was correct but that the nave collapsed because of an unstable site. A design problem was assumed, and even though the design could have been realized, no taller cathedral was ever attempted.

The failure scenario is unfortunate. The insight gained from an unsuccessful attempt usually improves the likelihood of success for the next change. The correct approach is to promote and reinforce change while downplaying the impact of unsuccessful change.

3.1.4 Change Is Not Equal

Some changes have a more positive impact than others, and some fit the objectives of the organization better than others. Some changes, even when positive, conflict with or are redundant with others. Some positive changes combined with other positive changes have a negative impact. It is therefore desirable to optimize the positive and minimize the negative impact of change. When possible, it is desirable to direct focus toward the positive impact of change to achieve the high-return objectives of the organization.

3.1.5 Capacity for Change

The opportunity for directed, positive change almost always exceeds the resources available to effect that change. This condition is especially true in information technology. The demand for new technology always exceeds both the capability of vendors or service organizations to satisfy the demand and of the recipients to afford or use the technology. For example, software cannot be produced fast enough to satisfy all the requested applications. The demand for software also exceeds the ability of the requesting organization to incorporate it into their operating procedures and still achieve their day-to-day mission.

3.2 Information Technology Change

In my capacity as information technology executive, I was once asked, "How do you select new information technology for your organization?" I answered that I do not select new information technology. I identify requirements and select the best technology solutions available using proved, cost-effective technology.

After thinking the question through, I realized that my scenario for implementing information technology was a problem-solving scenario. If something innovative came along, assuming I recognized it as such, I would have no easy way of interjecting it into the organization. The ability to recognize and implement such opportunities requires a different information technology development scenario.

3.2.1 Problem Scenario

The most common information technology development scenario consists of a project life cycle, which starts with a statement of requirements or a problem statement. The problem statement is translated into software design, development, or selection and then into a working application software system. After installation, the software system is altered until the numbers and complexity of the alterations increase and the software is perceived as no longer capable of accepting the changes necessary to satisfy its mission (Figure 3.1). This is the problem scenario; it starts with a problem statement and it ends with a problem statement.

The problem scenario of information technology development has the following fundamental shortfall:

Excellence is not achieved by resolving problems. The best that can be achieved from problem solving is a rise to adequacy.

The problem-solving scenario, although sometimes necessary and always well intentioned, is a reactive strategy. It is limited to resolving problems and replacing functions that work. When the application software system is perceived as being worn out, all functions of the system, good and bad, are replaced. In most instances, however, only 20% of the functions of the system represent 80% of the problems. Therefore, only 20% of a replacement effort

Figure 3.1 *Implementing Information Technology*

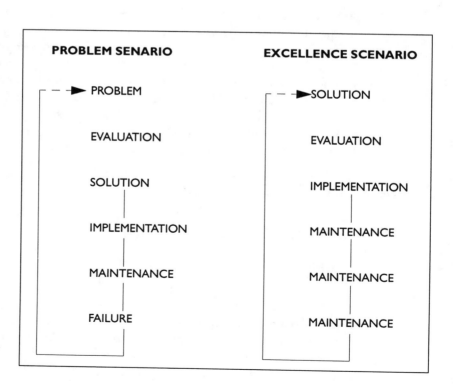

is expended on resolving problems; 80% is spent replacing the problem-free portion; and no effort is spent improving the overall application system.

The division of labor in the problem-solving scenario makes it almost impossible to improve the functions that work. Excellence is achieved by improving something that works. Improving something that works results in raising the quality level from adequate or good to good or excellent. The problem-solving scenario therefore makes it almost impossible to achieve excellence.

3.2.2 Excellence Scenario

The alternative to the problem scenario is the excellence scenario, an opportunistic approach that emphasizes the search for and installation of technology that furthers the objectives of the organization. In his book *Innovation and Entrepreneurship*, Peter Drucker states that "systematic innovation . . . consists in the purposeful and organized search for changes and in the systematic analysis of opportunities such changes might offer for economic or social innovation." Similar themes can be extracted from books like *In Search of Excellence* and *The Change Masters*.

The excellence scenario has an entry point for introducing change different from that of the problem scenario. The excellence scenario starts with a solution, which is translated into software design, development, or selection and then into a finished-application software system. After installation, the software is maintained until the next opportunity for improvement is perceived (see Figure 3.1). The objective of the excellence scenario is to leverage an existing achievement to a new level of excellence. In effect the excellence scenario is, "Anything that can be done, can be done better" or "If it works, fix it." It is not, "If it works, don't fix it."

3.3 The Search for Opportunities

3.3.1 Information Technology Change

Stability

Two types of change processes have been discussed. One results from problem resolution and the other from the response to opportunities. Problem resolution has a magnetic effect that allowed to continue attracts and consumes all the energy of an organization. The priority of the organization becomes resolution, resolution to the exclusion of opportunity and the achievement of the objectives of the organization. This is bad change. Good change is change directed at the opportunities to implement new information technology in support of the objectives of the organization. Because the impact of problem resolution is devastating, the prerequisite for good change is an existing stable environment with a minimum of problems.

Opportunity

Change is the norm. Opportunity for change exceeds the capacity to absorb change, and some change has a higher return than other change. These characteristics suggest that organizations continually have high-return opportunities to implement information technology and that these opportunities are camouflaged by many other less valuable opportunities. The innovative organization is the one that has the facilities to seek out and implement the high-return opportunities for information technology change.

3.3.2 Isolating Opportunities

Most successful information technology innovations exploit the change condition. The very source of information technology opportunities is change, and focusing on this change is equivalent to focusing on opportunity. The change, either internal or external, provides an opportunity to enhance an existing technology, extend its life, or create new value. The person most qualified to achieve this goal is the chief information technology officer. The chief information technology officer has a base of experience, a management perspective, and the opportunity to implement change that is unequaled in the organization.

Internal

Internal change is primarily, but not exclusively, visible to people within an organization. In some cases external consultants or even visiting management recognize unseen opportunities. The opportunities are found in the unexpected, the inconsistent and within the requirements and the structure of the organization. Note the following:

▶ Unexpected successes, failures, or events provide an opportunity. These conditions place unusual demands on an organization, demands that are not typically achieved through planning. Recognizing such events is easy, but isolating the benefits and perpetuating them requires a conscious effort. In one organization, the unexpected success of a new service required a new approach to evaluating marketing information. A new facility for viewing and analyzing the information was developed. Later it was found that the same techniques were equally successful for analyzing other new services and for reevaluating existing services.

The inconsistency between what actually happens in an organization and what is assumed to happen is another source of opportunity. In one organization it was assumed that there was not sufficient computer capacity to support on-line processing. Batch processing became an acceptable alternative. Further evaluation showed that the batch processing was the cause of the capacity problems. By shifting the batch to off-peak periods and converting the batch to on-line processing, the organization created a more productive environment. The inconsistency between actual and assumed factors led to identification of an opportunity that furthered an objective of the organization.

The requirements of an organization are another source of opportunity. Every organization has a long list of well-recognized requirements that go unaddressed. These requirements are typically an untapped source of opportunity. This is seen, for example, in the case of an organization that had a high volume of requests for information in which selection of data was so complex that only skilled professionals were capable of supplying the information. By using simple artificial intelligence tools, the organization simplified this function, and valuable professional staff were redirected into other projects. By viewing this requirement as an opportunity, the organization was able to further its objectives.

Structural changes in organizations, industries, or markets provide opportunities for introducing new technology. Changes in staff are the most common examples of this phenomenon. Hiring someone who is receptive to new technology or familiar with a technology can completely alter the destiny of an organization. For example, the banking industry was altered markedly by the introduction of the automatic teller machine.

External

External changes are changes generic to all organizations. They are visible to anyone who takes the effort to recognize them. Because there is no direct cause-and-effect relation between the change and the organization, these changes can go unnoticed for long periods. External changes include environmental, attitudinal, business, and technologic.

Environmental changes such as demographic factors, pollution, erosion, and climate can provide opportunities that are easily missed. A declining birth rate in developed countries coupled with a shift to information- or service-based industries has produced renewed interest in office productivity. The availability of office productivity tools creates opportunity for organizations even when they are not seeking new opportunities.

A change in *attitude* is an outstanding opportunity. Change is personal—it affects lives, it produces unfamiliar conditions, and it is often viewed as threatening. Changes in attitude therefore offer an opportunity to introduce technology when attitude shifts produce a receptive environment. A positive climate has developed around personal computers. As a result, it is much easier to introduce office automation today than it was five years ago. Conversely, the attitude toward professional computing is poor, and yet the demand for application software is at an all time high. This dichotomy has created an unprecedented opportunity to introduce computer-aided software engineering (CASE) and artificial intelligence tools into the development of application software.

Changes in *business* climate are another source of opportunity. When business is poor, there is a tendency to reduce expenditures for information technology; when business is good, there is a tendency to invest heavily in information technology. Yet when business is poor, an organization has a better perspective on the benefits of information technology, because the focus of the organization is on generating revenue and reducing cost. This is an opportune time to optimize the benefits of technology by investing when the competition is not.

Changes in *science and technology* have provided countless examples of opportunity. Information technology changes, such as the declining cost of computing and direct access storage and the introduction of optical data storage, computer networks, and microcomputers, have presented a wealth of opportunities. For instance, the declining cost of computer processing and direct access storage has made interactive processing the norm. Optical storage provides an opportunity to revolutionize paper-intense industries. Some industries, such as publishing, have already experienced such a revolution.

3.4 Selecting and Implementing

3.4.1 Selecting Opportunities

The opportunity for implementing information technology always exceeds the capacity of an organization to implement it. The following are selection guidelines to help identify the most appropriate opportunities:

▶ Systematically analyze the areas of opportunity.

▶ Talk with staff, peers, and industry representatives.

▶ Start small and build.

▶ Keep the process simple and directed.

▶ Build on the strengths of the organization.

▶ Stay close to the objectives of the organization.

3.4.2 Delegate Day-to-Day Activities

An innovative organization commits 20% or less of the time of the chief technology officer to routine management functions and 80% or more to seeking opportunities to apply technology. The day-to-day service activities of the office of information technology are delegated to the staff, freeing the information technology officer to look for opportunities. The following are examples of organizational guidelines:

▶ Establish an information technology architecture, a clear-cut set of directions and strategies for introducing information technology.

▶ Delegate all routine service functions to the lowest level possible in the organization. Clarify the directions and strategies. Give the staff the authority to make decisions within the confines of the directions, and make the staff accountable for achieving the directions.

▶ Provide direction, not decisions, and require that all problem discussions be accompanied by a recommended solution.

▶ Emphasize automation of routine information technology functions. Unattended data center operations, CASE, and artificial intelligence are opportunities for productivity in the information technology group.

▶ Encourage a do-as-I-do attitude, not a do-as-I-say attitude. Implement all new technology internally whenever possible and demonstrate the rewards to be achieved.

3.4.3 Implementing Opportunities

Implementing opportunities is work, and it requires tenacity. Most organizations do not view the process positively; terms like "blue sky" and "bleeding edge" crop up frequently. The path of least resistance is to focus on problem resolution and to continue using familiar technology even when it has outlived its usefulness. Here are some suggestions for implementing opportunities:

▶ Create a climate in which change, not success or failure, is rewarded. Start with the technology staff and market the concept to other organizations. In her book *The Change Masters*, Rosabeth Moss Kanter looks behind the scenes at some of America's most important companies to describe a climate that fosters change. A profile of that climate is shown in Table 3.1.

Table 3.1 *General Characteristics for Innovation*

Economic climate	*Up*	*Down*
Change issues	Normal	Accelerated
Organizational structure	Matrix	Centralized
Information flow	Free	Restricted
Communication emphasis	Horizontal	Vertical
Culture	Clear	Unclear
Emotional climate	Trust	Mistrust
Rewards	Abundant	Scarce

From Rosabeth Moss Kanter, *The Change Masters* (New York: Simon & Schuster, 1983).

► Create an environment in which it is possible to identify and implement opportunities. The goal is to commit the chief information technology officer to the search for opportunities and 20% of the information technology staff to implementation of the changes.

► Choose opportunities that are in alignment with the fundamental objective of the organization. It is important that senior management be able to relate to the opportunistic approach.

3.5 Conclusions

Information technology always seems to be in crisis. The industry is in another of its periods of unrestricted change. The natural inclination is to resolve this crisis by limiting change. But change in the information technology industry is not a problem; change is an opportunity, an opportunity that needs to be reinforced. The problem is the unrestricted or undirected aspect of the change. However, because the opportunity for change always exceeds the capacity to exploit it, only selective change need be reinforced.

The solution to the crisis is to reengineer information technology. The solution is in the simultaneous acceleration and direction of the introduction of information technology. The return on this solution is enhanced with an opportunistic approach. In this scenario, the information technology executive, typically the most accomplished technology facilitator, tests the internal and external sources for innovation. The information technology executive is committed to a stable, problem-free environment and delegates the day-to-day operations to senior staff and commits as much as 80% of his or her effort to the pursuit of opportunities.

In 1172, construction on the tower of the cathedral of Pisa was interrupted when the architect became aware that the tower was a bit out of plumb; it had in fact sunk six feet into the ground on the south side. When work resumed, no attempt was made to correct the problem. Instead the weight of the upper stories was distributed in such a manner to maintain equilibrium. The architect risked failure to create a structure that has delighted many generations of tourists.

The key to the opportunistic approach to information technology is first to create an environment in which change, not success or failure, is rewarded. The second step is to develop an opportunistic approach to the selection of information technology change. The last step is to extend systematically the life of existing software investments until opportunities are identified.

4

Orchestrating Reengineering

The alternative opportunities for satisfying business information system requirements increased substantially over the last five years. Hardware solutions previously limited to mainframe computers can now be based on client-server technology, workstations, or personal computers. Software solutions can be turnkey, packages, or products developed in house. In-house software can be developed with traditional languages (COBOL, PL/1, or FORTRAN), fourth-generation languages (4GLs), Pascal, C, C++, or application generators.

This does not exhaust the solutions. Solutions can be specifically hardware engineered or firmware based, or they can be any combination of all of the foregoing hardware and software alternatives. The result is a requirement for a guiding framework within business organizations to guide the reengineering of information technology. This framework is commonly called an *information technology architecture.*

Engineering an information technology architecture can be elusive. However, such an architecture is achieved by focusing on the key business and organizational issues that drive information technology and using them as a catalyst to facilitate implementation of an information architecture.

4.1 Influencing Factors

4.1.1 Asset Utilization

The direction of information technology is largely governed by the direction of past information technology decisions. An organization cannot ignore its previous financial investment in mainframe-based technology, small business computers, personal computers, and communication networks and the tens of millions of dollars it has invested in custom and purchased software. Information systems are a large investment. It is not practical to assume that these assets or even a portion of the assets can be easily replaced.

4.1.2 Operation of an Organization

Information systems support the mission of an organization and are rarely the mission. Regardless of the character of an information architecture, organizations tend to evolve into such an architecture over a long time. As this evolution proceeds, information requirements increase, staff changes, management styles change, and organizational philosophies evolve. In support of these dynamics, it frequently makes good business sense to, or it is expedient to, enhance the existing asset base. As a result the existing base of information assets continues to grow even as a new architecture takes form.

4.1.3 Cost of Labor

New computer technology is becoming available at an ever-increasing rate, and the ability to use this technology also is increasing. However, the single most important obstacle to installing information-based technology continues to be the labor-intensive nature of transforming information requirements into machine-usable form. This obstacle is made more complex by the economics of this process; the cost of labor is increasing while the unit cost of computer processing is decreasing. The result is that the direction of information technology is being driven by economics. The trend is toward the following approaches.

Minimization of Programming

Existing software assets are being enhanced and modified to trade off increasingly expensive labor for the decreasing cost of computer power. When software development is necessary, the trend is toward the use of less labor-intensive but more computer resource–intensive programming languages (4GLs), object technology, or application generators (computer-aided software engineering, CASE).

Implementation of User Driven Systems

Flexible information systems are being designed. Organizations with a vested interest in the information are being given an opportunity to access information using high-level languages. Entire systems are being designed by information consumers and central databases are being used as information repositories to support these activities.

Utilization of Purchased Software

Application software packages are being purchased with increasing frequency for applications that are common to an industry. It is recognized that this software may be more computer resource–intensive and may not entail the most current or effective technology.

Implementation of Turnkey Systems

Business solutions that involve a combination of purchased software and hardware packaged to satisfy a specific and narrow business need are becoming more frequent. These systems may or may not fit into existing architectures, but they are difficult to replicate in a cost-effective way with compatible technology.

4.1.4 Common Architecture

Since its inception, computer-based information technology has been striving to achieve a common architecture. Attempts have been made to standardize in a single computer language, communication protocol, hardware architecture, operating system, document interchange protocol, wiring standard, and magnetic storage encoding standard for almost every aspect of information technology.

Each attempt at standardization has resulted in both acceptance and rejection. Each attempt adds a new alternative, and few of the obsolete alternatives are ever eliminated. There is little financial incentive for hardware and software vendors to standardize, but there is considerable financial incentive not to standardize. Even IBM does not have a common architecture across its hardware and software product line. IBM is moving toward standardization, but as it moves in that direction, it continues to expand and build on the nonstandard aspects of its product line to add nonstandard products in response to customer demand. The likelihood that any one architecture will become the standard or even the predominant architecture is slim.

4.1.5 Distribution of Functionality

In the early days of data processing, departments relinquished responsibilities to central information-processing departments. This was the only alternative available for realizing the benefit of the computer. Information processing assumed responsibility for data entry, computer processing, scheduling, report generation, and report distribution. Information technology evolved, and computer literacy is now common. As a result, responsibility for the operation of information systems is being returned to departmental management.

4.2 Architectural Function

The factors that drive the evolution of information technology are business and organizational issues, not technical issues. An organization has a limited capacity to absorb change and still satisfy its mission. It can afford to make a limited financial investment to accomplish that change. To achieve a mission and still implement an information architecture requires a mechanism that guides this change and those moneys in a specific direction. The functionality required to achieve such an information architecture is as follows.

4.2.1 Leverage

Leverage the existing base of information systems, hardware, communications networks, and end-user computing by expanding and building on them.

Functions

Distribute existing information-processing functions to the source of the information, the organizational units that originate or use the information. Eliminate unnecessary information handling. Most organizations can make a tremendous amount of functionality available at a reasonable cost in a timely manner by expanding the use of their existing systems.

Equipment

Leverage the existing base of computer equipment (mainframe, workstation, and personal computer) by downloading and uploading data, using the equipment for terminal traffic, and using it for cooperative processing. The functionality for downloading already is available; it only requires organizational acceptance to actuate it.

Communication Network

Expand the use of local area networks (LANs), wide area networks (WANs), personal computer, client-server technology, and existing mainframe communication networks to distribute functionality, connect unlike equipment, and download data files.

End-User Computing

Increase the effectiveness of the information technology specialist by designing systems that integrate end-user computing skills into the development process. Encourage end users to design their own queries or reports. Integrate computing skills into the position description of end-user departments.

4.2.2 Flexibility

Build flexibility into the system development process by developing an open architecture, using purchased software, procuring turnkey systems, CASE technology, and object technology, and encouraging end-user computing.

Open Architecture

An organization integrates a variety of hardware and software solutions in a harmonious manner. This entails stand-alone processing, cooperative processing, and centralized processing.

Purchased Software

Purchasing software allows an organization to take advantage of the very best commercially available software solutions.

Turnkey Systems

Computer solutions couple hardware and software into a stand-alone technology package that may differ from the technology that is pervasive in the organization but satisfies a specific business need.

CASE Technology

CASE involves use of computer technology to automate the software development process. It improves software quality by automating the development process and improves flexibility by allowing software to be modified and regenerated.

Object Technology

Object technology is an emerging technology that promises to take reuse of program code to a new level. As a result, it is an attractive way to facilitate structured, self-documenting, highly maintainable, and reusable program code.

End-User Computing

End-user computing is integrated into the overall information system architecture through direct access to central data storage facilities or through distribution of information to decentralized computing facilities.

4.2.3 Standards

Develop a good set of standards as a measure to guide implementation of the information technology architecture.

Guideline

An architecture provides standards for voice and data communication, document interchange, hardware procurement, software procurement, and software development. Standards are a mechanism for directing the evolution of an information technology architecture. Alternative solutions are evaluated against the standards, which allow the organization to guide solutions in the direction of the architecture.

Malleability

A crucial element of standards is malleability. Some solutions work better than others, and over time they are replicated and become the dominant solutions. Standards must be malleable enough to absorb this experience factor and change accordingly.

Conformity

Some solutions make good business sense but do not conform to the architecture. Such deviations should be able to cohabit without penalty. However, the standard must clearly state the ramifications of deviation. Awareness of the ramification of a deviation makes these decisions less arbitrary. Some of these deviations will be successful and will be replicated. These are opportunities for breathing new life into an architecture.

Productivity

Standards are an area for productivity gain. They focus in on the favorable aspects of each area and reduce the need to test the entire universe of alternatives when a decision is required.

4.3 Implementation Strategy

Implementation of an information architecture is an iterative process. Business and human factors cause change: technology changes, organizations evolve, and some strategies work well whereas others do not. The architecture has to have a mechanism to direct that change.

4.3.1 Asset Inventory

An information technology architecture is a composition of past information technologic accomplishments and potential new technologic innovations. The logical starting point is to inventory and understand the organization's current base of information technology assets.

► What is the underlying philosophy of the current architecture: centralized, decentralized, cooperative, mixed?

► What is the nature of the hardware environment: single vendor, single vendor with original equipment manufacturers' (OEM) equipment, mixed vendor?

► What is the nature of the hardware operating software: batch or on line, vendor dependent, vendor independent, hardware dependent?

► How is the communication network designed: in support of specific applications, vendor specific, independent of application or vendor?

► What is the nature of the telecommunication software: single monitor, multiple monitors, integral part of the operating software?

► What is the composition of the application software: purchased, turnkey, custom (second-, third-, fourth-generation language, application generator, CASE, object technology)?

► What applications are common to the industry and how many are installed in the organization?

This is a sample of the kinds of questions that can be asked when developing an asset inventory. Areas such as these are the kind that influence future direction. It is beneficial to verbalize the current status of the organization.

4.3.2 Information Requirements

Understanding the information requirements of an organization goes a long way to identifying the pervasive nature of an information technology architecture. The kind of architecture used by a bank, hospital, insurance company, food service company, or educational institution correlates highly with their information needs. The architecture varies according to the size of the organization and its management philosophy.

Solicit information requirements from organizational units. Do not spend a long time on this collection process. Keep the time frame short. Organizations usually have some high-visibility requirements, and it can normally be

assumed that these are the highest priority. Given time, more esoteric requirements will surface. It is difficult, however, to separate these from more important needs. Remember, this is an iterative process, and requirements are
addressed again in another iteration. Be specific in your request. Ask for the
following:

▶ A description of the information requirement

▶ The benefits derived, both tangible and intangible

▶ An estimate of labor required to implement

▶ Evaluate the request as mandatory, strategic, or discretionary

Organizing the results of this process is probably the most difficult part. A
suggestion is to group the requirements according to application, sequence
them by dependencies, and list them in sequence as mandatory, strategic, or
discretionary.

4.3.3 Establish Strategies

The alternative approaches for addressing information requirements cause
them to be logically grouped into specific strategies. To establish an architecture, it is helpful to identify these strategies and to assign the information
requirements to one or another of them. One helpful way to group requirements is on a two-dimensional plane: horizontal and vertical. Visualize the
information systems as an inventory of application systems stacked one on
top of another. The strategies in this conceptualization would be either horizontal or vertical.

Horizontal versus Vertical

A *horizontal strategy* addresses one system at a time on a horizontal plane. An
information system on a horizontal plane, payroll for example, would be
replaced or enhanced in some substantial way (upgraded to an on-line system,
or reinstalled as a client-server application, for example). In this strategy, the
target system is addressed as a unit without regard to interface with other systems. This is the most common form of leading development project.

A *vertical strategy* addresses a single strategic objective, for example, paperwork reduction, electronic report distribution, or distribution of functionality. It works down through the horizontal layers of information systems in a
vertical manner, accomplishing the objective without regard to system. This
approach to system development is not common but can be effective.

Horizontal and vertical do not encompass all strategies. To round out this
scenario there are also request and departmental strategies.

Request versus Departmental

A request-driven strategy addresses individual requirements for change, repair, or enhancement one on one with minimal regard to the direction of the information architecture. This is the strategy that typically consumes a large portion of information development labor and threatens to consume it all.

A *departmental strategy* addresses information requirements outside the two-dimensional plane of the existing base of information systems. The strategy can consist of tactics such as turnkey systems or user-developed applications. The distinguishing characteristic of this strategy is that it is outside the two-dimensional framework of the base of information systems with nominal interface back into the two-dimensional framework. The solutions within this strategy are more likely than any other to deviate from the pervasive architecture. This strategy is becoming increasingly common.

4.3.4 Prioritize Requirements within Strategy

Projects are assigned to one or another of the strategies chosen. They are prioritized within strategy according to one or more of a combination of methods, such as financial return, support for strategic objective, and maintenance of the business. Once the priorities are established, the existing pool of labor can be allocated to the categories.

The demand for technology always exceeds the available labor. This creates an opportunity to test the proposed solutions for satisfying information requirements to determine what alternative approaches make sense. When a portion of the available labor is reassigned to these alternative approaches, or moneys are redirected into the alternative approaches, new directions for the architecture can be tested. If successful, the new directions can be worked into the architectural framework.

A word of caution is in order. Demand for information systems always exceeds available labor, and this is an opportunity for frustration. This condition results in a tendency to seek a heroic solution to the backlog of demand, to pick an appealing technical solution and to bet the entire pool of resources on it. To avoid this temptation, it is beneficial to understand that most new technologic innovations are not successful but that extensions of conventional technology are successful (Figure 4.1). It is important to understand that choices such as use of outsourcing, client-server hardware, proprietary software, and purchased applications are not necessarily superior to other alternatives. Each of these techniques has to be judged on its own merit (Figure 4.2).

Figure 4.1
Common
Misconceptions
about Technology

> **Misconception 1:**   The criterion for determining the implementation of technology should be "best possible" not "good enough."
>
> **Misconception 2:**   "Good enough" is determined by careful rational choice. not be convention—that is, by what consumers have learned to accept or expect.
>
> **Misconception 3:**   Most innovations are successful and should be.
>
> **Misconception 4:**   What you do not know about a new technological advance is probably good; Murphy's Law rarely applies.
>
> **Misconception 5:**   In most instances, radically new technology turns out to be more desirable than advances and extensions of conventional technology.
>
> **Misconception 6:**   The success of a new technology rarely depends on the adequacy of available infrastructure.
>
> **Misconception 7:**   Making technology effective doesn't involve developing routines and standards, achieving greater precision, and working under constraints.

From Lowell Steele, "Managers' Misconceptions about Technology," *Harvard Business Review* 6 (November/December 1983): 133-40.

4.3.5 Information Technology Architecture

On the basis of the information compiled, it is possible to develop and verbalize an information architecture. This architectural statement is the main element of an information technology strategic plan. The outline for such a plan might look like the following:

▶ Information technology architecture

▶ Application system plan

▶ Computer capacity plan

▶ Software and communication plan

▶ Budget forecast

Figure 4.2 *Twelve Data-Processing Myths*

Myth 1: The use of computer based systems for commercial and technical applications is good per se and thus does not require cost/benefit analysis for justification.

Myth 2: Distributed processing using client/server technology is inherently economically superior to central processing using mainframe systems.

Myth 3: Reliability of telephone lines is a significant problem in remote on-line computing.

Myth 4: Turnaround time is a universal and accepted method of measuring performances of computer system.

Myth 5: Locally designed computer systems are enhanced and improved over systems designed for remote processing.

Myth 6: A large scale computer facility that is totally unscheduled is innately bad. Conventional wisdom suggests that a sophisticated computer based scheduling system is required to achieve high performance.

Myth 7: Database management systems are inherently good; therefore, everyone should have one.

Myth 8: It is impractical, if not impossible, to effectively separate system design from programming.

Myth 9: A new system is complete and ready for production when all programs are completed successfully.

Myth 10: Systems documentation is an important part of the system process, but there simply is no time to complete documentation and meet schedules.

Myth 11: Packaged systems are very good for the systems' needs of other companies, but our requirements are so unique that we build our own from scratch.

Myth 12: Modifying the existing system to meet new requirements will be more expensive than starting from scratch.

From J. Robert Riggs, "Twelve Data Processing Myths," *Computerworld*, 6 October 1986.

Strategic plans are iterative in nature, and the strategic plan is tied to the architecture. Strategic planning has become the mechanism for a dynamic information technology architecture.

4.4 Role of the Chief Information Officer

What is the role of the chief information officer (CIO) in this scheme? One method for identifying the role is to compare the performance of the CIO with the activities required to plan, develop the architecture, and construct a building. Sigmund G. Ginsburg used this analogy to evaluate the performance of the chief executive officer in an article in the June, 1988, issue of *The President* titled, "The Five Major Roles of an Outstanding CEO." The same analogy holds true for the CIO.

When applied to the CIO, the construction analogy portrays the CIO in the role of a planner, architect, engineer, construction manager, and a facilities manager. The construction analogy also works well for the common roles of a CIO—software architect and processing business manager. Through this analogy, the performance of the CIO is evaluated and rated, providing the opportunity to isolate opportunities for improvement in the performance of a CIO.

4.4.1 Planner

Information technology is being introduced so rapidly that it is no longer necessary for users to wait for the information service department to satisfy their needs. Hardware costs are so low that any group can install a server and develop its own systems. As a result, systems are springing up all over organizations.

Building independent systems works well in the short term, but it lays the foundation for long-term problems. The systems inevitably have to interface with other "independent" systems, as for data comparison or consolidation of independently generated reports. In this environment, the CIO must establish a master plan that meets organizational needs and avoids the difficult and expensive job of converting these systems to make them compatible.

Information technology planning orchestrates the rapidly changing base of information technology alternatives and ensures that it is in concert with the information architecture and the business plans of the organization. Unmanaged, changes in technology generate solutions that satisfy immediate needs but may be expensive to clean up. In this context, the role of the CIO as a planner takes on increasing importance.

4.4.2 Architect

In the role of architect, the CIO takes the plans of the organization and translates them into a cohesive architecture that utilizes the best technology opportunities. However, the opportunities for satisfying business information systems are increasing at an astonishing rate. Hardware solutions previously limited to mainframe computers can now be applied to departmental computers, personal computers, or client-server technology. Software solutions can be turnkey, packages, or products developed in house. Solutions can be specifically hardware engineered (firmware), or they can be a combination of hardware, firmware, and software.

A CIO can no longer take the path of least resistance. A CIO needs to develop an information technology architecture or a guiding framework within the business organization to direct the evolution of information technology. A CIO needs to select the correct solution, staff the organization with people receptive to these solutions, and market the architecture to a generally apathetic management. Taking advantage of these solutions while maintaining harmony with the business objectives and the culture of the organization is a considerable challenge.

Most organizations view information technology as a cost of doing business. There are examples of the strategic use of information technology, but the examples are few and far between. When business is poor, information technology expenses are reduced, as in any other unit. When business is thriving, there is a tendency to invest heavily in information technology.

There is a simple maxim of information technology that best characterizes the influence of organizational culture on information technology. "No matter how good the information technology, if people do not want it, it will not work." Further, "no matter how poor the information technology, if the people want it, it will work." There are countless examples of brilliant technology that did not work because the marketplace did not accept it. This simple maxim cannot be overlooked in the rush to implement an information technology architecture.

Change is the norm for information technology, and the opportunity for change exceeds the capacity to absorb change. Some change has a higher return than other change. These characteristics imply that the CIO continually has high-return opportunities available to implement information technology, but these opportunities are camouflaged by many other less valuable opportunities. An innovative CIO is one who keeps the architecture alive and vital by seeking out and implementing high-return opportunities for change in information technology.

Organizations are becoming comfortable with information technology and are coming to expect technologic change. By almost any realistic measure, the track record for implementing new information technology is noteworthy achievement, despite immense uncertainty and low odds of success. As new information technology is implemented, the uncertainty and the odds lessen, but the lead times for acceptance and implementation continue to be long. The availability and maturity of technology are key elements of an information technology architecture.

4.4.3 Engineer

The engineering role of a CIO is probably the most visible aspect of the position. In most organizations, the CIO has risen into the ranks of senior management because he or she has demonstrated managerial skills by engineering information technology–based application systems.

The strength of the CIO is typically in the engineering aspect of information technology, and there is a strong inclination for the CIO to continue to play a dominant role in this aspect of information technology even though that role may be limited to only software engineering. The role of the CIO is not engineer but that of chief engineer, whose role is to develop a strong staff of engineers to implement the plans and architectures. This base of engineers includes software, database, technical service, and computer center engineers.

The technical service staff needs to engineer a hardware and software computing environment that supports the architecture while the database staff engineers a data-management environment that supports both the objectives of the data guardians and the application support staff. The software engineers are designing software systems in support of the mission of the organization and the computer user. The software engineers also have the formidable task of automating application development using tools such as object technology, CASE, and rule-based systems. The computing center, which is the operation arm of information technology, is reengineering the way it operates. The computing center is engineering an automated computer center—the unattended computer center program.

It is not enough to have plans and vision; the CIO needs to develop a strong engineering structure to implement the information technology plans and architectures. The measure of a strong CIO is no longer how strong an engineer he or she is, but how strong an engineering organization he or she develops.

4.4.4 Construction Manager

The range of construction projects spans all aspects of the CIO's area of responsibility: software system development, computer center development, database design, computer platform selection, and computer user support. The role of CIO as construction manager typically is associated with the creation of new software systems. As some of the installed technology ages, however, the role of the CIO shifts more and more toward remodeling software systems to make them conform to the changing needs of the business, to better fit the culture of the organization, and to better fit the technologic architecture. Extending the life of a software system asset while improving its flexibility and responsiveness is a significant shift in the role of CIO.

Another change in responsibility is the shift to providing support for end-user construction projects, personal computer-based systems, client-server-based systems, or even mainframe-based systems using fourth-generation languages or application generators. This support role involves managing construction of projects in which the construction staff does not report to the CIO. This is a new management concept for most CIOs.

One of the important obstacles to the expansion of information technology is a lack of confidence on the part of computer center users, organizational management, and even computer center staff that computer centers can meet their needs. Through years of unacceptable quality, these groups of people have been conditioned to believe that the computer center will not be available when it is needed or that response time will not be adequate to get work done. What has developed is a fundamental lack of confidence on the part of key groups of people that information technology in general and computer centers specifically can meet their expectations. The role of the CIO is to automate the computer center and restore confidence.

The role of the CIO in the computer center has traditionally taken a back seat to the construction of software systems. However, the importance of the role of the computer center business manager has increased. Computer centers are experiencing a quality crisis. They are not automating themselves and have become an obstacle to the expansion of information technology. The CIO has to take on a new mission. The objective of this mission is *quality,* and the project is unattended computer center operation.

In the role of construction manager, the CIO is still implementing software systems in support of the mission of the organization. More important, the CIO is automating the computer center and the application development process as well as implementing a computing and data management structure that supports the long-term needs of the organization.

The construction manager role of the CIO consists of far more than simply constructing software systems.

4.4.5 Facilities Manager

The role of facility manager is the day-to-day management role of the CIO. The duties of the facility manager consist of managing the operation of the computing center, ongoing support for software systems, staff management and development, budget management and development, and addressing crises. The CIO is a diplomat and a protocol officer. The position requires that the CIO meet and greet visitors. The CIO must ensure that the information technology group projects a positive image to peers, senior management, and the public.

The role of the facility manager is not mundane. The success of plans, architecture, engineering, and implementation is based on maintaining stability. Instability results in a problem-solving environment, and problem solving has a magnetic effect. It attracts and consumes all the energy of a CIO. The priority of the CIO becomes problem resolution, resolution to the exclusion of achieving the objectives of the organization. This type of facilities management is self-destructive. Because the impact of problem resolution is devastating, the prerequisite for good facility management is an existing stable environment with a minimum of problems.

The role of the CIO–facility manager is to meet the day-to-day duties of the information technology group, to project a positive image, to provide stability, and to seek opportunities to further the implementation of technology in support of organizational objectives.

4.4.6 Evaluating the CIO

CIO is a relatively new position. Most candidates for the position come from the ranks of MIS directors, and the performance of this position in many organizations has been disappointing. In many cases, the candidates have not recognized the need, and worse yet, they have not been given the opportunity to develop information technology plans and architectures. It is not uncommon for an MIS director to receive low marks for these functions.

The result of poor planning is a Catch-22 whereby it is not possible to develop a high-quality engineering staff or implement the required computer center and application development automation projects without a clear plan and architecture. Without automation and the engineering staff, the information technology function is fraught with crisis after crisis, and it is not possible to develop a plan and an architecture. The result of this Catch-22 is that grades for engineering, construction management, and facility management can be equally low.

Selection of a CIO is usually based on decision-making and interpersonal skills, and the MIS director is frequently not given the opportunity to develop these skills. Information technology continues to be handicapped by a 1950's reporting structure that relegates MIS directors to reporting to financial management rather than corporate management and thus eliminates the opportunity to focus on organizational objectives.

Emphasis on the planning and architectural role of the CIO is required. Developing business and technology plans that conform to the corporate culture allows development of an information technology architecture. The CIO who achieves a good grade for planning and architecture can improve his or her grade for engineering, construction management, and facilities management. This creates a win-win environment in which improved day-to-day performance increases the opportunity for improved planning, and improved planning increases the likelihood of improved day-to-day performance.

Because the position of CIO is relatively new, such grades are not necessarily bad. If the MIS director has managerial skill and is given the opportunity to focus on planning and architecture, the quality of grading can increase rapidly. It is therefore important that corporate management grade the CIO or the CIO candidate and use this grading as a basis for introducing development plans and organizational changes. Organizations have not recognized the need for a CIO or an information technology architecture for very long. The best CIOs are the ones who recognize that to create and manage information technology in support of organizational objectives, they need outstanding performances in each of these five construction skills.

4.5 Conclusion

Information technology is akin to a symphony in which hardware, software, and turnkey solutions are like instruments. The architecture is an orchestration of these instruments, and on the basis of the objectives of an organization and the availability of solutions, the composition of that orchestra changes.

Organizations need to build as much flexibility as possible into its system architecture, recognize the value of past successes, and leverage them with the potential of new technology. This is not a simple task, but the harmony derived from orchestrating the rich variety of alternatives available through strategic planning can be rewarding to an organization.

5

Developing Strategies

Strategies are the catalyst for orchestrating information technology change. Strategies ensure that change is in concert with the information architecture of the organization. In this context, information technology change is good. Given these strategies, it is possible for independent groups to purchase or develop systems and minimize the future cleanup activities that result from such independent development. This chapter identifies a method for developing such strategies.

5.1 Strategies

Imagine planning information technology strategies. What likely springs to mind is an image of a chief information officer (CIO) sitting in an office formulating the course of action that technicians will implement. Now imagine the same CIO *crafting* strategy. A very different image is likely to result. What springs to mind is not so much thinking and reasoning, but an interaction with technology. This interaction results in a learning process through which creative strategies evolve. It is this image of crafting information technology that better captures the essence of information technology strategy development.

When asked to define an information technology strategy, almost anyone will define it as a plan for implementing future technology. However, when asked what strategies are actually being pursued, the same people will probably define strategies in terms of past behavior. The reason is that strategies are almost always an extrapolation of past behavior patterns into intended behavior. This is an important concept, because the direction of information technology is largely governed by the direction of past information technology decisions.

Virtually everything that is written about information technology strategy depicts it as a deliberate process. In reality, a strategy can emerge in response to an evolving situation just as easily as it can be developed through a process of deliberate formulation. Conventional views of strategic management portray strategic planning as being one of continuous change. This view is ironic because organizations pursue strategies to set direction, to lay out courses of action and elicit cooperation from their members for a common objective. By almost any definition, a strategy imposes stability on an organization.

In actuality, change in strategy is not continuous but occurs in bursts followed by varying periods of stability. Managing strategies is, therefore, a matter of managing stability, not change. When management imposes strategies, it is imposing stability, not change. To develop truly innovative strategies, a CIO has to be a pattern recognizer, a learner who recognizes the patterns of new technology most beneficial to meeting the objectives of the organization. The strategist uses these patterns to stabilize the rapid introduction of new technology, to focus the energies of the organization on the changes that are most beneficial, have the least overlap, and make the best use of resources.

5.2 Managing Change

The rapid introduction of information technology is not only good but also essential to competition in a world economy. Computers affect almost all aspects of our lives. Analog devices control energy consumption in the buildings where we work and play; they control the processes and machines in our industry. Supercomputers are integral to scientific research. Word processors are essential to news media, offices, and scholarly pursuits. Digital computers are the backbone of businesses. Personal computers have made their way into the smallest businesses, our homes, and schools. Games, toys, watches, telephones, and cash registers use the same technology. There seems to be no end to the application of information technology. The correct objective of an organization is to identify ways of accelerating the introduction of information technology while minimizing the negative impact of change.

Not only is the introduction of technology good, but also any change that furthers the introduction of information technology is good. However, it is important to recognize that some changes have a more positive effect than others, and some changes conflict with or are redundant with others. The most important aspect of change is the limited capacity of most organizations to implement change. There is, therefore, a real need to accelerate but at the same time direct the introduction of information technology.

To understand the necessity to direct change, it is necessary to understand the nature of the change management process. Changes continuously surround us. Changes either work or they don't; they are either good or bad. If good, they are usually given an opportunity to stabilize. After the period of stabilization, the process is ready to start again. If the change is unsuccessful, the process is terminated and reverts back to a ready state.

The danger in this process is on the failure side. When successful, changes are an incentive for additional change. When changes are unsuccessful, there is a tendency to revert and not make any further changes. This is unfortunate, because the insight gained from the unsuccessful change improves the likelihood of success for the next change. Therefore, the correct approach is to promote change while downplaying the impact of unsuccessful change.

The opportunity for change almost always exceeds the resources to affect change; this is especially true in information technology, in which the demand always exceeds the capacity to satisfy it. Some changes, when combined with others, have a negative impact; some changes have greater returns than others, and some fit the objectives of the organization better than others. As a result, the likelihood of successful change is increased when it is compared with the criteria for high return or with organizational objectives. In this scenario, the changes that best fit the direction are chosen. These changes are prioritized, and only those with the highest return are addressed.

The key to this process is to create an environment in which change, not success or failure, is rewarded. Because some changes fit the needs of an organization better than others, it is necessary to establish directions. Changes are compared with those directions, and only the changes that best fit the needs of the organization are selected. Selection is accomplished by means of prioritizing the changes that best fit the needs of the organization, and the changes with the highest return are addressed first.

5.3 Information Technology Drivers

Rapid change in information technology is not a problem. The problem is failure to establish directions and to test these changes for compliance with those directions. In an environment of uncertainty, a common feature of rapid change in information technology, there is a natural tendency for staff to comply with stated direction. The objective should therefore be to promote directed change in information technology rather than to limit the introduction of change. To establish directions, it is helpful to reiterate the three factors that drive the direction of information technology.

5.3.1 Business Factors

Information technology is normally viewed as a cost of doing business. When business is poor, information technology expenses are reduced. When business is thriving, there is a tendency to invest heavily in information technology. The result is that no matter how good the technology is, it has little chance of success if business conditions do not foster its introduction.

5.3.2 Human Factors

No matter how good the information technology, if people do not want it, it will not work. Further, no matter how poor the information technology, if the people want it, it will work. This simple maxim is often overlooked in the rush to implement new information technology. As with business factors, it is an opportunity waiting to be exercised. The objective is for users and staff to view information technology as exciting and job enriching, not as threatening, making them want to embrace it.

5.3.3 Technology Factors

By almost any realistic measure, the record for implementing innovative new information technology is noteworthy achievement. As new information technology is implemented, the uncertainty and the odds lessen but the lead times for acceptance and implementation continue to be long. As a result, practitioners of information technology have learned that the expectations and use of information technology have to correspond with the way technology actually changes.

5.4 Directions

Because information technology is a composite of past information technology decisions and the introduction of new technologic changes, a logical starting point for establishing direction statements is to inventory the organization's current information technology assets. The asset base can then be expanded to include applicable information technology trends.

5.4.1 Asset Base

Some generalized computer architecture issues are applicable to developing an asset inventory. These computer architecture issues influence future direction, and it is beneficial to verbalize them to the organization. As discussed in chapter 4, these include the following:

▶ the underlying philosophy of the current architecture;

▶ the nature of the computer hardware environment;

▶ the nature of the computer hardware operating software;

- ▶ the design of the communications network;

- ▶ the nature of the telecommunication software;

- ▶ the composition of the application software; and

- ▶ the applications common to the industry and how many are installed.

This list is not comprehensive and can be tailored to the organization. Understanding these issues helps organizations to understand their current information technology architecture. Questioning these issues can have a cleansing effect; it can clear up misunderstandings about why things are done. To continue the process, more detail is required. Because information technology support organizations are frequently divided into application software, computer, and technical service groups, it is helpful to organize the asset inventory in this manner.

5.4.2 Application Services

Application services is responsible for the design, development, implementation, and support of computer software. It typically includes ancillary functions such as training, database, security, and support for end-user computing. An asset inventory for application services can include the following:

Statements of high-level objectives

- ▶ Increase on-line processing.

- ▶ Provide access to data for end-user computing.

- ▶ Increase the flexibility of application software systems.

- ▶ Purchase application software.

- ▶ Develop applications with fourth-generation languages (4GLs).

- ▶ Reengineer applications into client-server technology.

Identification of specific technology in use

- ▶ Database software

- ▶ Computer programming languages

- ▶ Security software

- ▶ Text editors

Catalog of all application systems

- ▶ Software, purchased or developed

- ▶ Languages used

▶ Age of software and general condition

▶ Batch or on line

▶ Mainframe, departmental, client-server, or personal computer

Definition of project management techniques

▶ Structured design method

▶ Project definition standards

▶ Project prioritizing and reporting methods

▶ Criteria for cost justification

5.4.3 Computer Services

Computer services is responsible for the operation of the computer center. Usually this includes functions such as computer operation, data entry, equipment installation, computer scheduling, and media handling. An asset inventory for computer services can include the following:

Statements of high-level objectives

▶ Source data capture

▶ Twenty-four-hour on-line availability

▶ Service level agreements

▶ On-line report distribution

▶ Elimination of operator intervention

▶ Nonstop, fault tolerant computing environment

Computer hardware inventory

▶ Computers

▶ Terminals

▶ Communication devices

▶ Tape and disk equipment

▶ Ancillary equipment (water chiller, uninterruptable power supply)

5.4.4 Technical Services

Technical services is responsible for selecting and maintaining the operating, communication, and support software for the computer center and for the installed base of client-server technology. An asset inventory for technical services consists of all the operating, communication, and support software used in the computer center and in any computers networked into the computer center. Statements of object and direction for the technology are not necessary; in most cases, they are an integral part of the high-level architecture that results from the generalized questions asked at the start.

5.4.5 Information Technology Directions

The information technology direction of an organization is governed largely by the accumulation of all past information technology decisions. Few organizations have the opportunity to scrap what they have done in the past, and even fewer would choose to do so given the opportunity. As a result, the directions that are important to one organization are not important to another. From the entire universe of available directions, each organization has a different subset. At a high level, however, there are some pervasive directions for information technology that are independent of organizations.

5.4.6 Computers

Computers are generally classified as centralized, decentralized, or personal on the basis of location in an organization. Computers originally were both expensive and decentralized. As computers became popular, most organizations chose economy of scale—they established a centralized computer center. The cost of computing decreased, and it became cost effective to have decentralized or departmentalized computing equipment. Software, however, became more expensive than hardware, and a large portion of total computing remained central. The cost of computing continued to decrease, and computers found their way to the desk top, the home, and remote locations. It is now cost effective to network these computers into what is defined as client-server architectures.

Now what? It appears that the next step is an architecture that combines the strength of each device. Sometimes referred to as *cooperative processing*, it has as its features the following:

▶ A large central computer (either a mainframe computer or server based on how one defines it) has as its mission the storage of large repositories of information.

▶ Midrange computers and workstations (the logical successor to personal computers) share the central data and act as the workhorses. The satellite computers do distributed processing in cooperation with the server and the mainframe computer, thus the name cooperative processing.

▶ The large and midrange computers become utilities, operating without human intervention. The point of human interface shifts to the workstation—unattended computer operation.

The key elements in this vision of the future are central repositories of data, cooperative processing, and unattended operation.

5.4.7 Software

Database technology has shifted from hierarchical to relational. There is little growth in the area of hierarchical mainframe databases (IMS/DB, CA-IDMS, ADABAS, TOTAL); the growth is in the area of relational databases. Although more computer resource intense, relational databases are more flexible. They provide fewer obstacles to changing data structure and make data retrieval easier. Because the cost of processing has decreased, processing power has been traded for flexibility, and this is a good trade. This makes it easier to access and retrieve information in a client-server computing environment. This makes fourth-generation language independent of the database, enhancing portability and flexibility of the application code.

Application software is one of the main obstacles to expanding information technology. Developing application software remains a labor-intense and error-prone activity. Software is typically crafted. Programmers typically operate with few constraints on their personal idiosyncrasies or on their personal preferences for elegant solutions. The result is software that is not reusable or maintainable.

Solutions to the problem of developing application software are available. Computer-aided software engineering (CASE) tools, rule-based systems, and object technology are available although not widely used. CASE tools automate development from requirements definition through generation of software code. Some CASE tools do reverse engineering, converting existing software back into designs, easing the maintenance workload on existing software. CASE-generated designs can be modified, and new computer programs can be generated when maintenance is required. CASE technology is incomplete, but it can add value to software engineering in its present form.

Rule-based or expert system software, like CASE, is in its infancy. With the onset of client-server technology, rule-based software has become far more usable, but it continues to have restrictions and thus a less immediate value. Object technology is an emerging technology that has demonstrated great promise. It promises to take reuse of program code to a new level. It is an attractive way to facilitate structured, self-documenting, highly maintainable, and reusable program code. The concept of reusable code fits in well with CASE technology.

5.4.8 Communication

Communication is essential to all the foregoing directions. All the scenarios call for sharing data, distributing processing, and so on. Local area networks (LANs) are key to tying personal computers, workstations, or servers together in clusters and tying these clusters into the mainframe computer or larger networks (for example, the communication highway). Wide area networks (WANs) are used to tie mainframe computers or large distributed servers together. Communication traditionally has been the function of the hardware vendor. However, the direction is to tie the computers of different vendors together with common communication protocols.

5.4.9 Open Architecture

The highest-level direction is open architecture. Application software traditionally has been tied to the computer architecture of a vendor (IBM, DEC, and so on). Although programming languages like COBOL and FORTRAN provide some vendor independence, it is limited to the point of being valueless. Operating systems, telecommunication software, database software, and programming languages, especially fourth-generation languages, tend to be tied to a vendor. However, the market is moving toward operating systems that are vendor independent, to fourth-generation languages that are independent of databases, for example. This frees the computer user to choose elegant solutions without costly software conversion.

There is a growing awareness on the part of suppliers that the potential size of the marketplace is so large that everyone would benefit from making software easier to develop. Open architecture is a giant step in that direction.

5.5 Strategy Adoption

At this point, the asset base includes a good synopsis of the organization's information technology base, including hardware, software, methods, and procedures. It also includes a list of the information technology directions that best assist an organization in making the transition from where it is to the pervasive directions of the technology.

Developing an information technology inventory is an iterative process that should be shared with the computer professionals, the computer users, and the audit staff. Explain the objective of the inventory and request the input of these workers. When comfortable that the inventory includes the kind of directions or technology needed to support the organization's objectives and to keep the technology alive and vital, classify the asset base into the following categories:

Strategic: A direction that the organization wants to move toward. An example of a strategic direction is to develop on-line systems or purchase software whenever possible.

Nonstrategic: A direction that the organization wants to move away from. An example of a nonstrategic direction is elimination of obsolete programming languages or elimination of data entry.

Sustenance: A direction that, if it were to change, would have no impact on achieving the objective of the organization. Such directions include a text editor for programmers or utility software in the computer center. These items assist the staff in achieving their objective, but using one versus another would have no long-term impact on achieving the organization's objectives.

The asset base has been transformed into statements of direction and the directions classified into strategies. These strategies are used to resolve the problem of allocating staff and establishing priorities. To allocate staff, start with the sustenance strategy. Allocate whatever staff is required to achieve stability, remembering that the long-term objective is continually to reduce this allocation. Allocate a minimum amount of staffing to eliminate the nonstrategic. Nonstrategic items are overhead; they contribute to the effort required to sustain the mission of the organization. As sustenance is eliminated, staffing is redirected into the strategic. Last, allocate all remaining staffing to accomplishing the strategic.

To establish priorities, use the strategic as a barometer; compare all projects to the strategic. Measure the contribution of each project to the objective of achieving the strategic. The projects with the greatest contribution are given the highest priority.

5.6 Conclusions

Information technology is always in a period of unrestricted change. The natural inclination is to resolve this continuous crisis by limiting change. However, change is not the problem; the problem is the unrestricted aspect of the change. In essence, change is good, and we need to promote it. However, the opportunity for change always tends to exceed the capacity for it.

Strategies, by definition, limit and direct change. The factor that has the most impact on the selection of strategies is past information technology accomplishments. Strategies therefore can be developed by means of compilation of an inventory of past information technology decisions. By expanding the inventory to include technology that achieves the objectives of the organization, an organization keeps the technology alive and vital.

In summary, the entire process consists of developing an inventory of an organization's current information technology and an inventory of the applicable directions for information technology. The combined inventory is stratified into strategic, nonstrategic, and sustenance. The strategies are easy, the difficult part is implementation, as follows:

► Implement the strategic directions

► Eliminate the nonstrategic directions

► Minimize the resources that are allocated to sustenance

The challenge to this approach is to keep the asset base vital. It must reflect the needs of the organization and the pervasive direction of the technology. Vitality allows an organization to redirect information technology toward a comprehensive yet flexible computing architecture.

Part 2

Reengineering Techniques

6

Quality and Information Technology

The single most important obstacle inhibiting the rapid expansion of information technology is the inability to quickly create high-quality, low-cost software that meets the expectations of the computer user and operates flawlessly without human intervention. On the hardware side of information technology, manufacturers have been able to produce successive generations of hardware at less cost with increasingly greater capacity and greater performance. On the software side, however, the computer user has not been able to take full advantage of these advances. Software is still manually developed, specification by specification and line of code after line of code.

There are two ways to develop high-quality software. Quality can be inspected into the software, or quality can be built into the software. In the first case, the software requirements are defined, errors are identified, and the errors are corrected. The software design is developed, errors are detected, and the errors are corrected. The software is coded, errors are detected, and the errors are corrected. The software is tested and again detection and correction are performed. The software is installed and again detection and correction are performed. When presented this way, software development is a scary process. As much as 50 percent of the time can be spent inspecting and correcting errors. It is no wonder software development lags way behind hardware development.

When quality is built into software, the process takes on a different perspective. The software is produced, but the effort is expended on identifying the source of the error. The source of the error is located, and effort is expended on methods to permanently resolve the error-producing condition. This sounds like "apple pie and motherhood," but in most cases, the importance attached to getting the software out on time is so great that no time is spent on the source of error. In effect, software development continues in much the same way as it did twenty or twenty-five years ago. Little has been done to automate the software development process.

Information technology professionals are inspecting quality into their software and are doing a poor job of it. The easiest way to increase productivity and reduce support problems is to break this cycle by building quality into the product. The prize is software that meets specification with less than half the effort.

6.1 Problem Definition

Developing an application software system is detailed, intricate, and labor intensive. The detail, intricacy, and effort required to develop a medium to large program are equivalent to the effort and detail expected of monks in monasteries during the Middle Ages when the Bible and other precious documents were transcribed by hand. The solution to their problem was automation, and the solution to the software problem also is automation.

Software development requires an understanding of business methods and procedures and an understanding of what information technology is available. The implementer must have analytical, reasoning, and interpersonal skills. Implementation also requires a high level of precision. If that is not enough, the task is further complicated by several external factors.

6.1.1 Introduction of New Functions and Procedures

Software systems do not automate existing tasks. Automation generates opportunities to accomplish tasks differently; this requires the design of new procedures. For example, an on-line accounts payable system changes the way that suppliers are paid. It eliminates the need to develop transmittal forms, reduces the labor-intensive process of manually checking the status of payments, and provides organizations with more positive control over cash. It provides management with control information that was previously not obtainable. The software system replaces procedures that were developed and tested over years of operation, but the new automated procedures must be developed quickly and work properly the first time.

6.1.2 Involvement of Many Functional Areas

Complex on-line information delivery systems are almost never developed for a single user. Several functional areas and sometimes several companies are involved, each with its own requirements and perspective on how these requirements can best be satisfied. A large part of the software development process is spent trying to resolve conflicts and negotiate compromises. Getting a group to agree to a new set of procedures is never an easy task, but when it involves sophisticated computer-based software, it is a large obstacle.

6.1.3 Project Size and Complexity

There is a dichotomy between the size and complexity of projects and the way they affect the future of an organization. An organization develops one or maybe two complex systems over a long time span. Such systems alter the way the organization does its business, and frequently the direction of the organization changes during the elapsed development period. On the other hand, existing complex systems are subject to countless small changes that are limited in scope and frequently not in concert with the overall technical direction of the organization. The result is that at any one time a large portion of the software systems are not in synchronization with the technical direction or organizational objectives.

The size and complexity of software projects almost always exceed the estimates of the software developer and the expectation of the end user. Most organizations have already installed the easy applications, and all that remains are the large, complex applications that require new and advanced technology.

6.1.4 Changing Environment

Development of a software system takes time. A complex system can take from one to five years to design and install. During this time, the project is affected by countless changes. Changes in organizational goals, product development cycles, competitive impact, governmental regulations, and the impact of users' being able to see the results of their specifications or gaining insight into the problem can alter the priorities and requirements of the system. Changes in information technology can make the design obsolete. The high demand for information technology professionals makes staff turnover likely.

Building application systems in an environment of shifting requirements, changing economic conditions, changing personnel, and constantly improving information technology almost requires the wisdom of Solomon. For the software developer, it is akin to playing Russian roulette with an automatic weapon.

6.1.5 Lack of Understanding

Information technology is frequently misunderstood. It is complex and subject to a great deal of media hype. Management does not understand the impact of designing new procedures, the complexity of the development process, or the changing environment. Computer users do not understand the role of information technology professionals or how to communicate and work with these people. Information technology professionals frequently concentrate on the technology and do not understand the business. This whole process is exacerbated by the apparent ease with which personal computers and client-server technology seem to satisfy user needs.

6.2 User Satisfaction

For the last twenty years the information technology industry has focused on techniques for improving productivity. The result was the introduction of a plethora of tools, including text editors, libraries, code generators, fourth-generation languages (4GLs), CASE tools, object technology, and rule-based systems. Despite these tools, the complexity of software systems still increases, and user satisfaction continues to be elusive.

Compensating for this lack of user satisfaction, specialized groups were formed, in effect, to inspect quality into the product. These groups include help desks, quality assurance groups, computer center acceptance test groups, development centers, and database administrators. The amount of labor dedicated to management and support functions in most information service groups now represents 40 percent to 60 percent of all software development staff. As a result, the consensus among information technology professionals is that user satisfaction continues to be elusive and software remains as difficult to develop as ever.

The solution to the software development dilemma is to concentrate on user satisfaction through quality rather than concentrating on productivity. The easiest way to improve productivity is to produce error-free software. If software is developed correctly the first time, there is no need for quality assurance functions, the software support effort goes away, and user satisfaction increases.

In a November/December, 1987, *Harvard Business Review* article titled "Competing on the Eight Dimensions of Quality," David A. Garvin discusses the eight dimensions of quality. Understanding the dimensions of quality and how they apply to information technology is critical to improving user satisfaction.

6.2.1 Performance

Performance is the primary operating characteristic of a software system. This covers diverse aspects of software systems such as expected response time for an on-line system, turnaround time for batch-oriented systems, ability to operate the batch and on-line portions of a system simultaneously, amount of computer capacity to operate the software, portability of the software from one platform to another, and availability of databases for ad hoc processing.

Some performance standards are based on subjective standards, and other standards are based on aspects of technology that are measurable and therefore objective in nature. The importance of performance is in understanding computer users' expectations. The ability to meet computer users' expectations for performance is an important aspect of quality. It also is an aspect of software design and development that tends to be completely ignored, a basic contributor to poor software quality. No one receives a commitment from the computer center or the computer user about what their performance expectations are.

6.2.2 Features

Similar in nature and closely related to performance are features. Features are the "bells and whistles" of a software system. They are are added to a software system after the basic requirements of the system are satisfied. Examples of features are ad hoc data query, labor-saving functions for low-volume activities, and the ability to select information for inclusion into other technologies such as word processing or graphics.

To many users of information technology, superior quality is less the ability to meet the day-to-day needs of a software system than it is the ability of the software system to accept new features, features that were not anticipated, or features that are the logical extension of the basic requirements of an application system. Flexibility, ease of use, and other such features in a software system are aspects of quality that tend to grow in importance after the software system is installed and the day-to-day requirements are satisfied.

6.2.3 Reliability

Reliability reflects the probability of the following:

▶ The software system will work correctly when it is required.

▶ Response time will be adequate and the content of the data is correct.

▶ Meeting user expectations will result in user satisfaction.

The most common measure of reliability for the hardware component of software systems is mean time to failure. Reliability typically is a critical aspect of the software component of software systems only during the early days of installation. During this period, the measure of reliability is frequency of failure. Frequent failure is a relative measure that tends to produce a negative aura that can stay with a system long after problems are resolved.

Another measure of reliability is ability of the software to perform during periods of peak demand or after it is subjected to enhancement or modification. Failure at these times does not seem to have the lasting effect it has during the period of initial installation. However, frequent change does seem to be interpreted as a measure of unreliable software, driving computer users to want a replacement solution to the perceived unreliability. Reliability increases in importance to an application system user when it affects the ability of an organization to meet routine business schedules.

6.2.4 Conformance

Conformance is the most commonly recognized dimension of quality. It is the degree to which a software system conforms to the requirements of the users. In manufacturing, conformance typically is defined as the ability of the product to satisfy the requirements of the design; in software, it is conformance to the stated requirements of the computer user.

The subtle difference between stated requirements and design is significant. Requirements for a software system can be satisfied through a design in many different ways. Some designs satisfy the requirements in a less labor-intensive manner, with more options for flexibility, or in a manner more responsive to the demands of computer users than other designs. The perception of conformance is higher for some software systems than others, although each may meet the specified requirements. An important aspect of software conformance is the question, "How does it conform?" It is important that software systems not only conform to the requirements of the user but also conform in an acceptable way.

6.2.5 Durability

As a measure of the life expectancy of a software system, durability has not been a particularly important measure of software quality. The history of software systems is short; few systems have been around for more than five to ten years, and those that have been around have been subject to substantial technologic conversions. The result is that not much importance is attached to software durability.

As the cost of software development increases at a pace far in excess of hardware costs, there is increased emphasis on flexibility and the ability to extend the life of systems. There is a shift from a creationist mentality, whereby requirements are satisfied by creating a new system, to a reengineering mentality, whereby requirements are satisfied by extending the technologic life of software systems. In this environment, durability takes on a new dimension of importance.

6.2.6 Serviceability

As a dimension of quality, serviceability is the ease with which software can be repaired, modified, or enhanced. With manufactured products, consumers are concerned with serviceability only if they perceive a high likelihood that it will require repair. Software systems are perceived differently. Software applications are typically perceived as being both unreliable and subject to change by external and internal requirements. Furthermore, software typically has a long life (10 or more years), and organizations are subject to many changes that result in software maintenance and enhancement. Serviceability is an important dimension of quality for software systems. As emphasis shifts from creation to reengineering in software design, this aspect of quality takes on more importance.

6.2.7 Aesthetics

The last two dimensions of quality, aesthetics and perceived quality, are the more subjective dimensions of software quality. Aesthetics is the appearance of the software system. It means something different to users, management, and technicians. To users, aesthetics is almost always the appearance of display screens or reports, ease of use, readability, or continuity of format from one screen or report to the next. To technicians, a beautiful system is one that is easy to maintain and does not consume excessive resources. In software systems, aesthetics is closely related to serviceability. Because appearance is highly subjective, it is likely to take on or lose importance on the basis of staff changes. Ability to service the software system easily can increase or decrease the importance of aesthetics.

6.2.8 Perceived Quality

The complexity of software systems acts as a barrier to users' having an in-depth understanding of the performance, features, reliability, conformance, durability, and serviceability of software systems. Over time, computer users develop a perception of the software system; unfortunately in many cases, it is a negative perception.

Most discussions about software systems within an organization address the failure of software systems to satisfy one or more of the foregoing dimensions. Almost always the internal discussion is negative. However, as technicians, users, and management alike discuss business with their peers in other organizations, there is a strong tendency for these folks to discuss the positive aspects of their software systems. If the features discussed by another organization are missing, the negative perception of the organization's software system is further reinforced.

Perceived quality is a strong driving factor in software systems. It is not uncommon for organizations to replace a software system because the general perception is that the system no longer meets the needs of the organization when it might easily have been reengineered to satisfy the shortfall. Perceived quality is a diabolical aspect of software system quality. All of the aspects that make software system development difficult also make it easy to develop negative perceptions.

6.3 Improving the Quality of Information Technology

Like most business activities, the effort required to improve information system quality follows the 80/20 rule: 80 percent of the improvement comes from 20 percent of the effort. Therefore, the natural question to ask is, "Where should the effort be concentrated to maximize the results of a quality improvement effort?"

The answer to this question is found in an adaptation of the same practices that apply to manufacturing. Applying W. Edwards Deming's fourteen points for improving quality to software development is a good starting point (Figure 6.1).

1. **Establish a constancy of purpose toward quality software systems.** Define in operational terms to computer software users exactly what you mean by quality software. Specify standards of software quality for development, support, and service as viewed for the next year and five-year period thereafter. Define the computer user whom you are seeking to satisfy. Put resources into hardware and software tools to automate the productivity of software system development staff. Focus on tools that automate the process, and eliminate error creation opportunities.

2. **Adopt the new philosophy.** Software and hardware error has become an accepted part of information technology. Unacceptable are software that does not fit the job, hardware that does not perform as specified, technicians who do not know their jobs, technicians who are resistant to the introduction of new technology, staff who are afraid to suggest new alternatives, and incompetent managers who correct and excuse mistakes instead of correcting the cause. Information technology managers must put resources into this new philosophy with commitment to ongoing training.

Figure 6.1 *The*
Fourteen Points
That Are Deming's
Way Out of the
Crisis

I:	Create constancy of purpose for improvement of product service.
2:	Adopt the new philosophy.
3:	Eliminate dependence on inspection to achieve quality.
4:	End the practice of awarding business on the basis of price tag alone. Instead, minimize total cost by working with a single supplier.
5:	Improve constantly and forever every process for planning, production, and service.
6:	Institute training on the job.
7:	Adopt and institute leadership.
8:	Drive out fear.
9:	Break down barriers between staff areas.
10:	Eliminate slogans, exhortations, and targets for the workforce.
11:	Eliminate numerical quotas for the workforce and numerical quotas for the management.
12:	Remove barriers that rob people of pride of workmanship. Eliminate the annual rating or merit system.
13:	Institute a vigorous program of education and self-improvement for everyone.
14:	Put everybody in the company to work to accomplish the transformation.

From W. Edwards Deming, *Out of Crisis* (Cambridge, Mass.: MIT Center for Advanced Engineering, 1986).

3. **Eliminate dependence on inspection to achieve quality.** Require evidence of quality of software regardless of whether it is purchased or manufactured. Inspection does not produce quality. Inspection is too late and is unreliable. When needed, require immediate and permanent corrective action for all software problems. Institute a rigid

program of feedback from computer users with regard to their satisfaction with software on the eight dimensions of quality. Identify the quality evaluation criteria, and communicate it to computer users, staff, and suppliers.

4. **End the practice of awarding business on the basis of price alone.** Instead, minimize total cost by working with a single supplier or a reduced number of suppliers. Suitable measures of quality require a reduced number of suppliers. The problem is to find a supplier or suppliers that can furnish statistical evidence of quality. Work with suppliers so that they understand the procedures required to achieve the expected level of quality. Take a clear stand that price has no meaning without adequate measure of quality. Without rigorous measures of quality, organizations drift to the lowest bidder, and low quality and high cost are the inevitable result.

5. **Constantly improve the quality of software system development.** Quality improvement is a never-ending process. There is no acceptable level of quality; continue to improve quality forever. When evaluating this improvement, look at competition and potential competition, and determine what needs to be done to widen the gap.

6. **Institute training on the job.** Restructure training to rely heavily on in-service training. Rely heavily on tutors. This process of in-service training by tutors reinforces both the tutor's understanding of the expected level of quality and defines the responsibilities of the trainee in terms of job expectation. Define all jobs in terms of expectation.

7. **Adopt and institute leadership.** Supervisors need time to help people on the job, and they need to find ways to translate the constancy of purpose to the individual employee. Supervisors should find the source of error. They need information that shows when to take action, not merely figures that describe the level of production and the level of errors in the past. Supervisors need to commit time to people who are not meeting expected levels of quality and not those who are low performers. If the members of a group are meeting quality expectations, some will be low performers and some will be high performers. Teach supervisors how to use the results of surveys of computer users.

8. **Drive out fear.** Break down the distinctions between types of staff within the organization—technical and operations, database, and analyst. Discontinue finger pointing. Stop blaming employees for problems

of the system. Management should be held responsible for faults of the system. People need to feel secure to make suggestions. Management must follow through on suggestions. People on the job cannot work effectively if they dare not offer suggestions for simplification and improvement of the way software is developed.

9. **Break down barriers between staff departments.** Start with internal MIS departments: system development, technical services, computer center operations. Learn about the problems in the various departments. One way would be to encourage switches of personnel in related departments.

10. **Eliminate numerical goals, slogans, and posters imploring people to do better.** Instead, display the accomplishments of management to assist employees to improve their performance. People need to understand what management is doing to make these fourteen points happen.

11. **Eliminate numerical quotas for the workforce and numerical goals for management.** Work standards must produce quality, not mere quantity. It is better to take aim at removing errors and defects and to focus on ways to help people to do a better job. It is necessary for people to understand the mission of the organization and how their jobs relate to achieving that mission.

12. **Remove barriers that rob people of pride of workmanship.** Eliminate the annual rating or merit system. Institute a feedback system; people will know when they have done well and are assisted when results do not meet expectation.

13. **Institute a vigorous program of education and self-improvement for everyone.** People must be secure about their jobs in the future and must know that acquisition of new skills facilitates security.

14. **Put everybody in the information technology area to work to accomplish the transformation.** Create a structure in top management that will push the previous thirteen points every day. Information technology management may organize a task force with the authority and obligation to act. This task force will require guidance from an experienced consultant, but the consultant cannot take on obligations that only management can carry out.

These fourteen points for improving quality are not a solution; they are a formula for hard work. The key to improved quality is working harder and working smarter. They are a skeleton that has to be fleshed out with automated tools and techniques, management commitment, and in-service training.

6.4 Conclusion

The single most important obstacle inhibiting rapid expansion of information technology continues to be inability quickly to create high-quality, low-cost software that meets the expectations of computer users and operates flawlessly without human intervention. Software is still developed manually, a slow, laborious task. The obstacles are complex and legitimate. As a result, little has been done to automate the process. Yet the return on an investment in quality is immense—a software product that meets the expectations of the computer user the first time with a reduction of effort up to 50 percent.

The solution requires a belief that quality is achievable and a commitment to make it happen. If information technology professionals do not accept that flawless software can happen, it will never happen. Everyone must understand why quality has to happen. The first step is to address the human side, belief and commitment. It is only through commitment to quality that productivity can be improved. If computer end users, organizational management, and most important, information technology professionals understand why it must happen, they will buy into the process. If necessary, the error should be in favor of overcommunicating.

Look for the source of error and correct it. Automate as many aspects of computer software development as possible. Use computer-aided software engineering (CASE), object technology, rule-based technology, and 4GLs whenever possible. Transfer as much of the software development process to computer users as they can accept. Every automated tool that reduces human intervention in the software development process improves quality, and every action that reduces the need to communicate specifications for software from users to computer professionals improves quality.

Reinvest the dollars that you save from improved quality in the hardware and software required to automate software development. Reinvest the labor saved in the process of improving quality. The entire process of improving quality is easier to sell to all involved when it is self-funding. The entire process is an opportunity for in-service training to develop new techniques and, more important, new attitudes. Financial return in terms of improved revenues or decreased expenses will follow.

The future of information technology is bound to the ability of information technology professionals to produce high-quality, low-cost software that meets the expectation of computer users. There is nothing mysterious about achieving this goal; it requires a perpetual commitment to identifying and correcting the source of error. The result is a continuous and measurable improvement in quality and productivity.

7

Structured Project Management

Reengineering systems demands that system development managers periodically return to the basics. This chapter presents a simplified four-step project management procedure that consists of documenting, categorizing and ranking, structuring, and reporting on projects. It provides a framework for managing small support projects and a method to help system development managers maintain an inventory of valid project requests. It also allows them to verify whether these requests are consistent with the organization's information technology architecture. It provides a framework for reengineering software systems.

Most system development managers view project management as such a basic management technique that they believe they already understand it and do not have to learn it. Yet system development managers need to relearn effective project management techniques many times during their careers. They not only have to relearn project management but also must train their employees in project management techniques.

In the last 30 years, the primary focus of the project work environment has shifted from development projects to maintenance projects. Most organizations have automated their main business functions. It is not uncommon for a system development department to invest 60 percent or more of its productive time on maintenance or enhancement activities.

The nature of the demands on the system development department also has changed. Users who previously required support are now conducting their own queries and developing reports and their own small system using personal computers and client-server technology. Instead of requesting support for these functions, they are requesting data downloads to servers or personal computers, decision support databases, and system enhancements to make data more accessible. It is common for a system development department to field 3,000 to 5,000 requests each year. The demand on the system development department has become request driven.

This chapter describes a simplified project management procedure that satisfies this request-driven environment. It organizes requests and positions the organization to reengineer application systems. This project management procedure consists of four steps, as follows:

▶ Documenting projects

▶ Categorizing and ranking projects

▶ Structuring projects

▶ Communicating project status

Figure 7.1 illustrates the structure of the project management procedure. The goals of this procedure are as follows:

▶ Separate large projects from small support projects

▶ Provide a less labor-intensive structure for managing smaller support projects

▶ Provide a method to test a large volume of requests and to verify that the changes are consistent with the information technology architecture of the organization

▶ Maintain an inventory of valid requests

▶ Provide a structure for large system development projects

7.1 Documenting Projects

Project management starts with a request for service. Documentation of all support requests is essential to project management. It is impossible to direct technology, meet schedules, rank requirements according to priority, and produce a quality product when there are a large number of phantom, undocumented projects in process. For the purpose of this discussion, the request for information services support is called a *service request.* Service requests are typically forms or paper documents but they also can be electronic documents where electronic mail facilities are available. Documentation of a service request consists of three basic steps, which are outlined in the following sections.

7.1.1 Determining What Requires Documentation

Not all support activities require a service request. One rule for system development managers to follow is that activities that require less than one-half hour per day and no more than four hours per week do not have to be documented. Activities that relate to requests for information, rather than action,

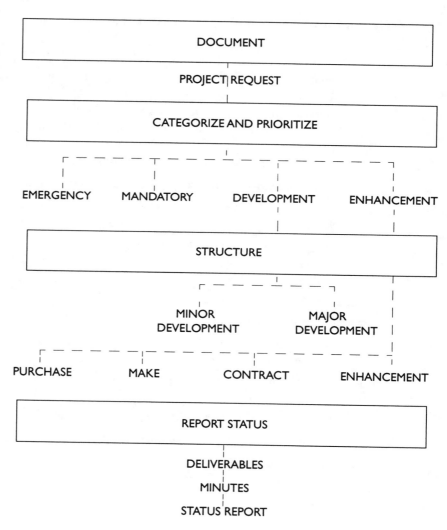

Figure 7.1
Framework of the Project Management Process

DOCUMENT

PROJECT REQUEST

CATEGORIZE AND PRIORITIZE

EMERGENCY   MANDATORY   DEVELOPMENT   ENHANCEMENT

STRUCTURE

MINOR DEVELOPMENT   MAJOR DEVELOPMENT

PURCHASE   MAKE   CONTRACT   ENHANCEMENT

REPORT STATUS

DELIVERABLES

MINUTES

STATUS REPORT

do not require documentation, for example, requests for information on how to solve a particular problem. In a time management system, such activities can be charged to miscellaneous support.

The documentation procedures must not be so rigid that the staff is burdened with documenting insignificant activities. System development managers must limit documentation so the staff can focus on its mission.

7.1.2 Documenting the Service Request

The system development department documents service requests in the simplest way. If possible, users should complete the service request in their own words. It is far more important, however, that the request be documented than that the user do it personally. Although some users resist this kind of bureaucracy, most have become accustomed to written requests for service. If there is resistance, the system development manager should simplify the procedure by putting the form on E-mail, using electronic forms, or taking the initiative and having a system analyst complete the form.

A typical service request contains the following information:

► A unique *project control number.*

► A *project title* that is short, descriptive, and meaningful. The title is a shorthand name that the system development staff uses when discussing the project.

► A *priority designation* of emergency, mandatory, or enhancement. "High" and "low" are not valid designations because users view everything as high priority.

► A realistic *target date* for when the service should be completed. Requests with no target date are low priority. Requests with target dates of "yesterday" indicate that some alternative is already in place; these also are frequently low priority.

► A *detailed description* of the request when available or applicable.

► The *date of origin* of the request.

► The *identity of the requester.*

► The *date the request was received* by the system development department.

7.1.3 Evaluating the Request

A service request is evaluated to determine its validity or benefit to the organization. Some requests can be satisfied through procedural changes. The system development manager establishes a dialogue with the requester and finds out the reason for the request. Frequently, simple procedural changes can simplify or eliminate the need for a software change. In other instances, it is apparent that the solution is different from the request, and a different project develops.

A solution may already be available through existing on-line queries or reports. It is not uncommon for one department to be struggling to compile information that someone else is already receiving. A request should be viewed as an opportunity to evaluate surrounding systems. The request may be the symptom of a larger problem, or an opportunity might exist to gain larger benefits by expanding the scope of the project and reengineering the process.

That a feature can be improved or that a feature is not working correctly may not be a valid reason to start a project. Such requests frequently are time consuming to implement, a way already exists to circumvent the problem, and there is no appreciable benefit.

7.1.4 Acknowledging Receipt and Identifying Disposition

The system development department identifies the disposition of each request within a reasonable time frame. Five working days is an appropriate amount of time. The disposition can be as simple as stating that the request is an emergency and is being addressed, that it will be started on a specific date, or that it is being held pending a priority assignment or further evaluation.

The intent is to communicate. It is crucial to communicate the status and give the user the opportunity to appeal the disposition. It is best to avoid misunderstanding at all cost. Nothing destroys credibility faster than having the user believe the department is working on the request when it is not.

7.2 Categorizing and Ranking Projects

After the appropriate service requests are properly documented, system development managers organize them into a meaningful structure. Projects labeled *Emergency* require immediate attention. *Mandatory* projects are addressed because of changes in the law or the direction of the business. Projects labeled *enhancement* are optional, have no target date, and do not require immediate attention. Those labeled *development* projects require additional analysis before they can be addressed.

Other categories can be proposed. For examples, projects labeled *housekeeping* are those that enhance the ability of the system development staff by enhancing existing technology or introducing new technology. Projects labeled *overhead* account for the hours spent on ancillary activities such as education, sickness, vacations, holidays, and meetings.

Project classifications vary according to the procedures used by an organization. This chapter discusses only emergency, mandatory, enhancement, and development projects because they are the classifications applicable to reengineering. The following sections describe these classifications in detail.

7.2.1 Emergency Requests

Emergency requests necessitate a correction to a system when one of the following error conditions occurs:

▶ Production application software supporting a business function fails completely or produces erroneous results.

▶ A computer failure occurs, and support from information services is required to reestablish computer processing.

▶ An interruption in service occurs because of human error.

Because they represent an interruption in computer service, emergency requests receive the highest priority regardless of project duration or the amount of labor required. To ensure that there are no repeat occurrences, emergency requests are considered complete only when a permanent solution to the problem is installed.

7.2.2 Mandatory Requests

In most cases, a mandatory request is a small enhancement that adjusts for changes in the law, strategic direction, accounting conventions, or other similar conditions. Mandatory support requests are necessary to support the business or to comply with legal requirements. These requests necessitate change to a system by a specific date, and priority for these services is driven by that date.

System development managers need to be cautious of mandatory requests. When the scope exceeds ten days of labor or takes more than one calendar month to complete, mandatory requests have to be scrutinized closely. It is common for most software development groups to have more work queued than they have staff to address it. Requesters therefore attempt to take the engineering staff hostage by attaching discretionary enhancements to mandatory requests, thereby expanding the scope of the mandatory requests. If the scope of the larger requests is valid, they are managed as if they are major or minor developments.

7.2.3 Enhancement Requests

Enhancement requests address small modifications to an existing information system. One rule of thumb for system development managers is to define enhancements as projects that require less than ten days of labor and that can be completed within one calendar month.

System development managers should take an opportunistic posture toward enhancements. An enhancement project is a great opportunity and it makes smart business sense to address as many enhancement projects as possible with a minimum amount of bureaucracy. For example, a project can have high financial return with a minimal labor investment, labor can be available at the time, the timing might be right to implement such a change, or the project might be a favor to an especially supportive individual or department.

Enhancements should be grouped according to the application system being enhanced. This creates an enhancement project that can address each task individually or the entire cluster as a single development project. Enhancement requests can be evaluated, ranked according to priority, and scheduled on a monthly basis by a committee consisting of representatives of the user community.

The number of system enhancement projects typically increases over time. More enhancement requests are received than there is staff available. The speed with which the number of enhancement projects increases is a barometer of the health of the system. If the number of requests is low, it can be assumed that the system is in good health. If the number of requests is high, the system may have to be reengineered.

An effective way for system development managers to determine whether a system has to be reengineered is to perform an operational analysis. With a small investment of time and money, an operational analysis can help an organization solve the problems and extend the life of the system. This is discussed in more depth later in this chapter.

7.2.4 Development Requests

Development projects require large investments in labor and money. An example of such a project is development of an entirely new system to replace an existing system or to extend the life of an existing system. Development projects are divided into two categories—major development and minor development.

Major Development

Before a major development project is undertaken, the users and the system development department jointly conduct a feasibility study. Major development projects require substantial commitments of labor and money and result in the purchase, development, or major enhancement of an information system. Because of this large commitment, the results of such feasibility studies are presented to a steering committee before the projects are scheduled. Major development projects require more than sixty work days and may extend over several years. In addition, the staff produces a major deliverable every six months.

Minor Development

A minor development project frequently consists of an improvement to an existing information system. It is more complex and labor-intensive than an enhancement but less involved than a major development project and does not have the rigid target dates of a mandatory request. A minor development project requires completion of multiple, interdependent phases to reach a goal, whereas an enhancement does not. A minor development project typically is approved and given its priority by a steering committee. A minor development project takes more than ten but less than sixty work days and no more than six calendar months to complete.

7.3 Structuring Projects

7.3.1 Managing Small Projects

System reengineering for emergency, mandatory, and enhancement requests is both an opportunity and a resource drain. It is common for an organization to receive 3,000 to 5,000 requests per year. Emergency, mandatory, and enhancement projects can consume 20 to 60 percent or more of the labor of an information services department. A well-managed emergency project, however, results in a permanent solution to an emergency condition, ensuring that the interruption does not recur. This is an easy way to improve productivity and creditability.

Mandatory and enhancement projects also provide an opportunity to change software systems and make them conform better to the strategic direction of the information services department while satisfying users' immediate needs. Mandatory and enhancement projects present the system development department with an opportunity to introduce change in small, painless increments. These small increments demonstrate the positive effect of new technology and inspire creativity. Over time, the system is reengineered, frequently extending the life of the original investment. However, emergency, mandatory, and enhancement projects usually do not require a great deal of formal structure. None should ever consume a large amount of resources. Therefore, the consequences of an error are never severe.

If the emergency, mandatory, and enhancement service requests are consistently late or the quality of the product is poor, additional structure can be added. As a rule, extensive formal structure can unnecessarily increase the amount of resources required to complete the project while adding little or no value. It is more important to complete as many of these projects as possible while improving quality and increasing the system's strategic usefulness. The one exception to this rule is the mandatory service request. These requests can be large enough to require the same structure as a minor or major development project.

7.3.2 Redirecting System Design

For one of many reasons, a computer-based system may experience a crisis. A system crisis is manifested by an increase in the frequency of requests for change or enhancement and by the accumulation of large numbers of unsatisfied requests. A large backlog of unsatisfied requests may result from the failure of the system to meet the changing needs of the business, a simple lack of priority for the system, inadequate system development staff levels, or a combination of all these factors.

A system crisis often causes users to discard the existing software system and purchase or develop a completely new one. The most common pitfall, however, is for users to assume that there is no alternative to replacing the system. Replacement of a system is rarely the only solution or the best solution for satisfying a system crisis. If the system is replaced, even the specifications of the replacement system are eventually undermined enough by change and enhancement to render the system ineffective, and the cycle is repeated. This can be a never-ending process.

The problem is usually that the architecture of the software system does not have sufficient flexibility to accommodate change and enhancement. The design of the software system assumes a fixed architecture. As the organization and computer technology evolve, the only solution might seem to be replacement of the software system.

To alter this cycle of replacement, the system development manager must define the system change process in terms of reengineering, not replacement. This reengineering perspective is achieved by means of establishing a direction for the system. The system development department must determine what the user wants the system to do in one year, five years, and ten years. The system direction is established by means of evaluation of the operation of the system and identification of the changes required to make the system conform with the organization's strategic direction and the direction of computer technology in general. Examples are the use of on-line processing and supporting the use of client-server technology for end-user computing.

An effective way to redirect the design of a system is to cluster unsatisfied requests for change and enhancement. One way of reaching this goal is to use a project tracking system. System development managers can first cluster requests for change or enhancement on the project tracking system according to application (for example, general ledger, payroll, accounts payable) and then within that group cluster them according to logical processing unit (for example, job, program, subroutine). This makes it possible for system development managers to assess the magnitude and severity of the required changes. By comparing these clusters to the technical and strategic directions of the system, it is usually easy for managers to determine the changes that will further the direction and those that will not.

Most organizations find that 80 percent of the functional capability of a system, even one in crisis, works correctly. The source of the unsatisfied requests for change or enhancement is almost always the remaining 20 percent. The new perspective created by means of clustering small projects makes it easier for system development managers to identify high-return changes or enhancements. By making the high-return areas the department's highest priority, the organization usually can obtain an 80 percent improvement by attacking only 20 percent of the problems. Some cosmetic, low-return changes also can be made.

Clustering allows the system development department to address high-return changes with a very small commitment of staff. It reduces a disproportionate amount of request backlog for the amount of labor invested. In addition, accomplishing cosmetic changes results in an improved relationship with the user who requests the change.

The clustering of mandatory and enhancement requests modifies the development cycle and extends the life of a software system. Through the exertion of a small effort, for example, less than 20 percent of the replacement cost, a software system is altered to correlate with the direction of the organization. Rather than being random, the changes to the system are directed at correction of problems that extend the life of the system through selective maintenance, renovation, or augmentation. Every organization has a choice: It can make random changes to its systems, or it can direct the changes. Clustering is a tool that assists in directing change.

7.3.3 Conducting an Operational Analysis

Although clustering can be used to extend the life of a system, this approach has limits. Clustering addresses only documented requests for changes or enhancement. It does not address benefits derived by introducing new technology such as imaging, telephone voice technology, or client-server computing. One way to extend the effectiveness of clustering is to look for hidden changes, to seek out new technologies, or to identify the reason for a requested change. This process is called *operational analysis*.

An operational analysis is conducted to identify and define the functions of a software system and isolate the requested changes to allow recommendation of a series of changes that customize the system to conform with the system architecture and the direction of the organization. The objectives of an operational analysis are as follows:

▶ Identify and analyze the objectives of the main functions involved in processing data

▶ Identify undocumented improvements that cause unnecessary effort or result in the loss of data integrity

▶ Identify new technology or procedures that improve performance

▶ Formulate remedial actions or suggested improvements

▶ Identify mandatory changes needed to resolve data security or data integrity problems

▶ Calculate financial or other benefits derived from remedial actions

To implement an operational analysis the system development manager has to do the following:

▶ Identify the current status of the system, including the following:

—Source of the data and documents

—People who handle the documents

—Recipients of the output

▶ Review open enhancement service requests and requests for change

▶ Interview personnel who use the system for undocumented changes and improvements

▶ Define how the system works, including the following:

—Paperwork flow

—Processing steps

▶ Segment processing into its logical steps, as follows:

—Data receipt and preparation

—Data input and validation

—Automated processing

      —Management and administrative activities

▶ Document input, including the following:

      —Types of documents

      —Samples of documents

      —Volume per time period

▶ Document output, including the following:

      —Types of reports

      —Samples of reports, for example, manual reports, automated reports, on-line queries

▶ Determine areas for improvement, such as the following:

      —Data receipt and preparation

      —Data input and validation

      —Automated processing

      —Management and administrative activities

▶ Perform a return on investment analysis, including the following:

      —Cost analysis to perform remedial action

      —Benefit analysis

      —Return-on-investment calculations

▶ Rank improvements according to priority and implement the changes in the following order:

      —Mandatory changes, for example, changes that improve the integrity or security of the system

      —Return on investment calculations

In addition to the financial benefits derived from the remedial actions, operational analysis results in qualitative benefits. One benefit concerns knowledge of the system functions. As time elapses and staff members leave, much of the knowledge concerning a system's functions is lost despite documentation. With operational analysis, however, knowledge of the functions of the system is disseminated to a larger audience, which increases the staff's awareness of the functions of the system.

Another qualitative benefit derived from operational analysis is improved communication among various departments. Through participation in operational analysis, the system development staff becomes committed to improving the productivity of the overall system. With working together, the attitude of personnel involved improves, and workers find it easier to work together in the future.

One example of the benefits derived from an operational analysis concerns a food service company that performed an operational analysis on thirteen of its main systems. The analysis showed both qualitative and quantitative benefits. The qualitative benefits were twofold. First, while evaluating the systems, the end-user departments became aware of existing but unused facilities. Use of these facilities increased the effectiveness of the system and the productivity of various departments. Second, small security and integrity problems were identified and resolved, but more important, the company felt confident that its internal financial controls were sound. The quantitative results were much more substantial. For an investment of $90,000, the company was able to realize an annual savings of $250,000 on one system. Conversely, replacement would have cost well in excess of $3 million.

7.3.4 Managing the Large Project

Most major development projects are so complex that they require rigid process control. The traditional approach of establishing requirements and then translating them into designs, code, and operational procedures in phases is a frustratingly slow, labor-intensive, often manual process. Therefore, most organizations should select and use a structured system development method—such as METHOD/1 or Applied Information Development (AID)—or automated approaches to system development—such as computer-aided software engineering (CASE). Both of these areas are beyond the scope of this section.

Minor development projects must be structured but do not have to be encumbered with all the structure required for major development projects. Minor development includes all the key elements of a structured method but is scaled down in proportion to the size of the particular project. These key elements include a purpose statement, a project work plan, a test and acceptance plan, a training plan, a conversion and implementation plan, and any miscellaneous documents.

The purpose statement briefly defines the purpose and scope of the project. The project work plan includes a brief description of each task to be performed in the sequence in which these tasks are to be executed. Each task is uniquely numbered and typically can be accomplished by one person in not less than one day but not more than five days. A minor development project typically includes ten to twenty tasks but can include as few as two and as many as sixty. The work plan should include the following information:

▶ A unique identification number

▶ A one-line task description

▶ The name of the individual performing the task

▶ Estimated hours for the task

The test and acceptance plan is a brief outline explaining how unit testing and integrated testing will be accomplished. It identifies who performs the test and who validates the test. This plan defines the acceptance criteria for the project and the user staff responsible for acceptance. The training plan explains the training required and how user training will be accomplished. The conversion and implementation plan explains any conversion that may be necessary and how the system change should be implemented. Miscellaneous documents are any other information that may be pertinent to the project. These can include work requests, changes to the database, new database formats, and any new screen or report layouts.

In most cases, because of their size, minor development projects are enhancements to existing systems rather than development of new systems. If an overview of the existing system is not available, one should be developed and should accompany all project reviews.

7.4 Reporting Status

The last step in the simplified approach to project management is status reporting. System development managers do not need elaborate written documentation for a project to be successful. In many cases, elaborate written documentation is viewed negatively and is considered too bureaucratic by both management and users. In addition, it is almost always distasteful to information service professionals.

The key to success in reporting project status to others is having the correct documentation at the correct points during the project. Documentation may vary from having little or nothing for emergency, mandatory, and enhancement projects to having deliverables for each phase of the method and minutes from project walk-throughs for major development projects. Documentation includes a status report that consolidates the activities for all types of projects: development, enhancement, mandatory, and emergency.

7.4.1 Deliverables

A project manual is maintained for each major development project. This manual includes the deliverables specified in the method for each phase of the project. The manual is a working document and includes copies of any associated documentation, such as system overview and correspondence. A similar, though much abbreviated, project manual is maintained for minor development projects. This manual is usually a single deliverable rather than a series of deliverables, as is the case for major development projects.

Regardless of the medium (for example, document or repository) the deliverables are evolutionary—they increase in number as the elements of the development project become available. Deliverables for emergency, mandatory, and enhancement projects need not be any more than completion of the service request document and an update of standard system documentation when the project is complete.

7.4.2 Minutes

Almost every structured development method includes a structured walkthrough of the deliverables at the end of each development phase. System development managers discuss the priority and status of emergency, mandatory, and enhancement requests at monthly user committee meetings. If the system development department does not hold such meetings, it is in jeopardy of losing the opportunity these projects present. System development managers discuss the priority and status of minor and major development projects at monthly or quarterly executive steering committee meetings.

Minutes are issued for committee meetings as well as for structured walkthroughs. The minutes identify attendees and agreements based on an agenda issued before the meeting or walk-through. Such minutes are often carefully read by participants and interested parties. Errors and oversights are quickly called to the attention of the system development manager or committee member.

It is often difficult for committee members to make positive recommendations about the structure and priority of a software development project, but it is usually far less difficult for them to identify obvious errors and oversights. System development managers should distribute the minutes to as wide an audience as possible. If nothing else, minutes provide a running commentary on the progress of the project. They are a communication medium, and it is far better to err in favor of overcommunicating than of undercommunicating.

7.4.3 Status Reports

A status report can be issued monthly or quarterly. A status report is a consolidated document that includes the status of all projects, both application software development and support projects such as computer center, database, and technical service projects. This document is concise. It highlights important accomplishments, summarizes all projects, and concludes with a short description of the status of each project. The description of the status of each project includes something like the following: a description of the major development project, the targets for major milestones, and a list of the accomplishments made during the period. A status report identifies problems that can interfere with meeting the target dates and suggests solutions. A status report also includes the project plans for the next period.

Enhancement, mandatory, emergency, and minor development projects are presented in summary form. Only major accomplishments or problem areas are highlighted. It is usually beneficial to supply the following statistics on these projects: the number received since the last status report, the number completed, the number in process, the backlog number, and the number of labor hours expended.

7.4.4 Talking Status Report

Structuring projects as emergency, mandatory, enhancement, and development is an opportunity for parallel development. Multiple project teams can work on different aspects of the same system. However, in this scenario, one group can undo what another has accomplished.

This effect is mitigated, in part, with a talking status report. A structured walk-through of the status report in the presence of all project managers allows each manager to discuss the status of the projects and what the manager intends to address in the coming reporting period. In an open forum, project managers have an opportunity to query the implications of other teams' changes, thereby avoiding some of the pitfalls that occur when different teams work simultaneously on different aspects of the same system. A talking status report ensures that everyone in the information service department understands the current status of projects, and it verifies the integrity of the information.

System development and computer center managers should hold a weekly coordination meeting. The agenda for this meeting is to discuss pending changes or potential conflicts among information service groups. These managers should hold a short meeting each morning to discuss any emergency projects that were initiated during the last 24 hours. This ensures that recurring problems are being addressed and that permanent solutions are being identified and implemented for any emergency projects.

7.4.5 Communication

The purpose of these techniques is to promote communication. Project deliverables communicate the requirements, design, and implementation plans for the information systems. The meeting minutes communicate the collective agreements among the participants in the system development process. The status report communicates the collective status of all system development projects, and the talking status report improves coordination. The greater the communication, the less likely it is that an aspect of a project will be overlooked or that a participant will do something to jeopardize the success of the project.

7.5 Project Management Software

Project management software assists system development managers in managing time, costs, and resources effectively. Many of the products are designed to plan, track, and analyze activities that can range from simple enhancements to multiyear development projects. Project management software originally was used solely for mainframe computers, but today the most effective project management software is designed for microcomputers.

Most software products provide a set of tools to assist developers to plan a project, create and define activities, assign resources, apply resource costs, schedule resources, and perform in-depth analysis of possible project scenarios. The "what-if" type of analysis available with most project software allows developers to answer common questions, such as, "What if we add more resources?" "What is the best way to reduce the elapsed time?" or "What do we save if we complete one month sooner?" Some of the more valuable features of project management software include the following:

► Program evaluation review techniques (PERT) charts or network diagrams to provide a visual representation of the relation between two tasks

► Gantt charts to depict the starting and ending dates of activities

► Automatic scheduling to derive the ending date of a project on the basis of the starting date and the duration of the intermediate tasks

► Cost allocation to control costs such as labor, software, hardware, computing resources stated in each task description

▶ Automatic resource leveling to determine the optimum task schedule

▶ Resource calendars to track holidays, vacations, and other time restrictions

Some common Windows-based microcomputer products include Harvard Project Manager from Software Publishing Corporation, Microsoft Project from Microsoft Corporation, CA-SuperProject from Computer Associates International, Project Outlook from Strategic Software Planning Corporation, and Topdown Project Planner from Ajida Technologies. For the Macintosh computer, there is Micro Planner from Micro Planning International and MacProject II from Claris Corporation. Most of these projects can be used to determine finish date, critical path, and duration. They also provide tools for managing resources, costs, and schedules.

7.6 Conclusion

Project management is a technique that must be revisited many times. This process can become complex because the requirements for project management change as information technology changes. Reengineering applications and porting them into different platforms has created new challenges for project management. It can be simplified, however, with a return to fundamental project control techniques. The four-step process outlined in this chapter helps organizations reach this goal. Minutes, status reports, and communication meetings ensure that the project participants have a common understanding of requirements, problems, and progress.

Project management techniques are not to be used independently. To manage projects successfully, the system development department must have a structured development method and at least one committee to develop priorities and other procedures, for example, a cost-benefit analysis procedure, a feasibility study procedure, and an operational analysis procedure. The most important prerequisite, however, is the desire to put the process in place and a belief that it will yield better information systems.

8

Operational Analysis

After thirty years of computing, system professionals are still installing new computer-based systems. However, a large percentage of these new application systems are only a redesign or reinstallation of an existing system.

Organizations are discovering that many of their systems are obsolete or that the technology base for their systems are obsolete, and they assume that there is no alternative to replacement. If the demand for replacement systems were to disappear, a large percentage of that much-taunted multiple year backlog of new systems would go away. One comprehensive method to reduce the need for replacing systems is operational analysis, briefly discussed in chapter 7.

8.1 Misconceptions

The phenomenon of redesigning and reinstalling systems is based on the following misconceptions about new system development:

1. The criterion for determining the requirements for a new a system should be "best possible system." Every system installed is the result of a long series of compromises between cost and performance.

   These compromises reflect the values of system users and result in a system that is good enough, not best possible.

2. "Good enough" is determined by means of careful, rational choice; that is, with careful thought and evaluation rather than what the requester has learned to accept or expect.

   What actually happens is that widely shared beliefs, even when mistaken, do more to shape the design of a system than does rational choice. At times, what is good enough is actually even better than what is required to achieve the goals of the system.

3. Most new systems are successful and should be.

In reality, the failure rate for a new system, in whole or in part, is high. To be successful, a new system must demonstrate substantial advantages. It must be less expensive to operate, require less clerical effort, or provide more accurate results than the old system. It is difficult for a new system to achieve these kinds of results.

4. A radically new system is more desirable than advances and extensions of existing systems.

Despite all the good press on new systems, most moneys go into extensions of existing systems. Extensions of existing systems are "good enough." They require far less risk, give promise of more timely results, and are more cost effective than development of new systems.

5. The success of new systems rarely depends on acceptance by the proposed users.

Developing a new system with dramatic new attributes does little or no good if the proposed users are not receptive, if the means to implement the new system are not available, or if the users do not understand the system.

8.2 System Evolution and Revolution

The concepts of evolution and revolution are fundamental to reengineering. The term *evolution* describes the prolonged period of growth in a system in which there are no dramatic upheavals in the operation of the system, such as maintenance or enhancement. The term *revolution* describes the periods of turmoil in the life of a system, such as changing hardware vendors, operating systems, or technologies (for example, client-server).

By its very nature, evolution creates its own revolution. At some point in the life cycle of a system, factors external to the system affect the system in a manner that the evolutionary factors cannot accommodate, producing revolution. The periods of evolution are governed by four rules that determine the speed and direction of the system evolution.

8.2.1 Rule 1: A System Is Not Static

Systems are always changing; new systems or subsystems are emerging while others are becoming obsolete. A perfect example of this is the banking and insurance industries, in which government regulations and market demands necessitate massive changes. These external influences cause new subsystems to be created.

8.2.2 Rule 2: The Process of Evolution Is Slow but Continuous

Evolution does not occur at a consistent speed. It is subject to acceleration and deceleration. Sudden major change, however, is almost nonexistent.

8.2.3 Rule 3: Similar Systems Are Related in Concept and Descend from a Common Origin

Also called the rule of common descent, this concept is especially evident in areas such as computer architecture, computer operating systems, database systems, and manufacturing systems. An Indiana-based food-processing company found this third rule to be true when it was evaluating manufacturing systems for a new processing and distribution facility. It discovered that a sophisticated on-line manufacturing system was directly descended from a batch-oriented system developed in the 1960s. Furthermore, a subset of that technology had evolved for use on departmental computers. Research further revealed that some of the system's leading competitors held common origins. This was the result of key system designers' moving from one company to another and designing similar but enhanced versions of the system. This is not uncommon; similar types of relations exist in software developed for other industries as well.

8.2.4 Rule 4: System Evolution Is the Result of Compromise

System evolution is not the result of shrewd design; it is the result of a long series of compromises. This compromise is a two-step process. The first step is the existence and formation of variation in a system to satisfy the specific needs of the user. No two systems are ever installed the same way. This is especially evident with the installation of software packages. Almost every company exercises certain tailoring options during the installation of purchased software.

The second step is improvement through selection. Of the thousands of variations in the application of any system, certain variations demonstrate themselves as having more value than others, for example, the aforementioned flexible architecture in purchased software. These are the characteristics that have the greatest likelihood of surviving. These characteristics are selected and are available to be carried forward as the system evolves.

Smooth evolution is not inevitable; it cannot be assumed that system growth is linear. During the last twenty years, the introduction of new technology has had a marked effect on the life expectancy of a system. Numerous case histories show evidence of substantial turbulence spaced between

smooth periods of evolution. These turbulent times are periods of revolution; they represent a serious upheaval that causes elimination or replacement of a system.

8.3 The Traditional System Cycle

For any one of a multitude of reasons, a system may experience a turbulent
period—a system crisis. In this crisis, the user does the following:

▶ Outgrows its present system

▶ Identifies an opportunity for cost reduction

▶ Requires faster, more accurate, more detailed information

▶ Experiences a change in technology

▶ Determines the system is no longer efficient

▶ Discovers that the product is not supported by a software supplier

As a result, a completely new system is designed. The task is attacked with
the optimistic outlook that the ills of the existing system can be overcome.
The designers believe they are developing a lasting, durable product that will
withstand the test of time, a finished product. Thus this process is defined as
the *finished product system.*

Because there is no such thing as a utopian system, a conceptual finished
product system often takes up multiple person years, ends up late or understated, is implemented in an atmosphere of trauma, goes through multiple
specification changes, and causes turnover of users and management information services (MIS) development personnel.

The most common pitfall, however, is to assume that there is no alternative to replacing the system. Replacing a system is rarely the only solution or
the best solution for satisfying a system crisis. This is clearly shown by the
phases of the finished product system development scenario (Figure 8.1),
which involves the following:

▶ A *requirement definition* phase, in which the requirements to be met by
the system are determined, documented in detail, and approved.

▶ A *design* phase, in which a physical solution to the requirements is
determined. This phase usually proceeds from a general design to exact
specifications for the construction of each system component.

Figure 8.1
Successful Evolution

> For the reengineering process to be successful, certain principles for success have to be recognized and exploited. These principles are as follows:
>
> • It is usually easier to modify and improve something than to create something entirely new.
>
> • Learning is gradual and iterative and is accomplished through example.
>
> • Users cannot accurately specify system requirements until they have used them.
>
> • Identifying improvements to a system allows a greater chance of success than does identifying all attributes for a new system.
>
> • Identification and implementation of high-return improvements reduces the need for new system development, sometimes indefinitely.

▶ A *development* phase, in which the system is constructed, tested, and verified. Because this is the most labor-intensive phase, it can be eliminated or greatly diminished through the use of purchased software or turnkey systems.

▶ An *implementation* phase, in which the transition is made from the current mode of operation, manual or automated, to the new system.

▶ A *maintenance* phase, in which the system is continually enhanced and revised to meet the ever-changing needs of the user. This phase ends after a long series of changes and enhancements. The end comes with a catastrophic failure and is followed by system replacement.

In broad terms, a finished product system is defined as a fixed product that is developed to fixed specifications with a fixed life cycle. It is assumed that the company evolves during the maintenance phase and that the system changes to reflect this evolution. The fixed specifications of the system eventually are subverted sufficiently to make it ineffective. The problem is not that the specifications of the system evolve but that the architecture was designed without sufficient flexibility to allow evolution. A finished product system assumes a fixed architecture; as the company evolves the only solution to the evolution is revolution, replacement with a new system.

8.4 Replacement

Replacement is rarely the only or the best alternative. Revolutionary alternatives include the following:

Replacement: Elimination of system and replacement with a purchased package solution or a finished product solution

Elimination: Discontinuation or gradual phasing out of a system when it loses its business value

During the evolutionary stage, no one ever thinks of replacing the system. During the revolutionary stage, most companies' knee-jerk reaction is to replace the system, when in fact the system can be renovated or augmented. An example is that of an Ohio-based food service company that spent $750,000 to replace a financial system only to realize that the new system was very similar to the old. The old system could have been enhanced and augmented in less time and at considerably less cost.

Evolutionary alternatives, however, include the following preferential solutions:

Maintenance: Changing the system to meet legal, organizational or strategic changes in the direction of a business

Renovation: Changing the base system to add the new functions of the system while correcting technical deficiencies

Augmentation: Changing the system to add new functions or correct existing functions by building new features on top of, or around, the system

Structuring the use of these solutions through operational analysis is the foundation for system reengineering.

8.5 New Perspectives

The first step to altering the replacement perspective is to define the system change process as evolutionary, not revolutionary. This evolutionary perspective can be achieved with reengineering. This consists of evaluating the operation of a system, a process hereafter defined as *operational analysis*. An operational analysis is used to identify and define the functions performed with a system in an operational environment. The objectives of operational analysis are as follows:

▶ Identification and analysis of the objectives of the main information processing functions

▶ Identification of areas for improvement, areas that cause unnecessary effort or result in the loss of data integrity

▶ Formulation of remedial actions

▶ Identification of mandatory changes necessary to resolve data security or data integrity problems

▶ Calculation of financial or other benefits derived from remedial actions

In addition to the quantitative (financial) benefits derived from remedial actions, operational analysis results in the following qualitative benefits:

▶ Knowledge of the functions of a system is disseminated to larger audience and increases the level of awareness of the function of the system. Over time and because of staff turnover, much of the knowledge is lost despite documentation.

▶ Communication among work groups is improved. Through participation in the operational analysis, the involved personnel become committed to improving the productivity of the system overall.

▶ Because of working together, the attitude of the involved personnel improves, and they find it easier to work together in the future.

8.6 Conclusion

When considering qualitative and quantitative factors, it is evident that an operational analysis will have a positive effect on the entire company, rather than an individual department, function, or area, because it measures the overall effectiveness of a system. When all changes that have a positive effect on control and those that give the highest financial return are implemented, the greatest impact can be achieved with a minimum of expense. Typically, 80% of the return can be achieved with only 20% of the effort.

With repeated operational analyses, the perspective of a system can be changed to an evolutionary one—a dynamic view that evolves as the strategies of the company evolve. The result is a modification of the development cycle (Figure 8.2) that extends the life of the system beyond the perceived life span.

Exerting a small incremental expenditure of time and money, approximately 20% of the development-phase cost, allows alteration of the evolution of a system to correlate with the direction of the company. Reengineering

Figure 8.2
*Implementation
Steps for Opera-
tional Analysis*

1. Identify the current status of the system
   - Sources of data and documents
   - People who handled the documents
   - Recipients of the output
2. Review open enhancement service requests and requests for change
3. Interview personnel who use the system for undocumented changes
4. Define how the system works
   - Paperwork flow
   - Processing steps
5. Segmented processing into its logical steps
   - Data receipts and preparation
   - Data input and validation
   - Automated processing
   - Management and administrative activities
6. Document input
   - Types of documents
   - Samples of documents
   - Volume per time period
7. Document output
   - Types of reports
   - Samples of reports (manual reports, automated reports, on-line queries)
8. Determine areas for improvement
   - Data receipt and preparation
   - Data input and validation
   - Automated processing
   - Management and administrative activities
9. Perform a return-on-investment analysis
   - Cost analysis to perform remedial action
   - Benifit analysis
   - Return-on-investment analysis
10. Rank improvement according to priority and implement the changes
    - First mandatory changes—changes that improve the integrity or security of the system
    - Second, return-on-investment calculations

From Howard W. Miller, "When 'New' Is Not Improved," *Computerworld* 15 September 1986, pp. 71-74.

forestalls the need for replacing existing systems with new systems. By using the operational analysis technique of evaluating existing systems before they reach maturity and a crisis develops, an organization can extend the life of a system. This facility can be a key tool for reducing the development backlog of a company. Operational analysis provides not only the opportunity to extend the life of a system but also immediate qualitative return in the form of better utilization and understanding of the system and quantitative return when the changes are carried to fruition.

9

Information Technology Change: A Case Study

As an undergraduate student, I read a book by Charles A. Beard titled, *An Economic Interpretation of the Constitution of the United States.* The author suggested that the incentive for the American revolution and the subsequent U.S. Constitution was founded in economics. Right or wrong, the author's suggestion altered the perception that the founding of the United States was a heroic conflict to secure liberty and justice for all and replaced it with the perception that it could well have had a baser economic motive.

I was not thrilled with the assignment, yet the paradigm proposed had a profound and lasting impact. It changed my perception and caused me to question the underlying motive for not only this event but also for other events. Many years later, the impact of the book lives on. It is a clear demonstration that the paradigm used to represent an event affects how that event is perceived.

Paradigms are conceptual structures or models. When applied to developments in information technology, they provide a structure to analyze and understand new technologic developments. In the same way that Charles Beard used an economic model to alter perception of the Constitution, paradigms can be used to alter commonly held perceptions of technology. The caveat is that for the model to work, the information must fit the paradigm and not conflict with the assumptions on which it is founded. Therein is one of the problems with information technology.

Innovation often requires us to rethink the way we perceive technology. One of the barriers to the effective use of information technology is paradigms that conflict with the information on which they are founded. Technology changes and the models do not change; as a result, the paradigms do not fit the facts.

9.1 An Economic Interpretation

After almost three decades of experience with information technology, many companies with advanced information-processing systems are in a position to analyze their experiences. A widely publicized paradigm for analyzing this experience is Gibson and Nolan's four stages of growth of electronic data processing, later expanded into six stages. The premise for this paradigm is that information technology evolves through a series of stages. These stages are based on the condition of the application portfolio, the evolution of the data-processing organization, the status of technologic planning, and user awareness of information technology.

The suggestion is that there is a positive shift in management acceptance and expenditures as the information technology group evolves through the stages, moving from primitive to mature. The implied cause-and-effect relation is that successful implementation of information technology causes increased management acceptance. Increased management acceptance results in increased expenditures.

The success of the information technology group is therefore determined by the ability of the group to develop a mature profile in the growth stages. This is a technology-driven model. In this model, success is defined as the ability of the information technology group to develop a mature technical profile. The accumulated successes of an organization as it introduces new information technology influence the receptivity of an organization to implement new technology in the future.

Although this paradigm adequately describes the evolution of organizations that have moved through the various generations of computing equipment and application software, it is not the only paradigm possible. Success and even failure are in many instances the result of the prevailing economic conditions of the organization or the confidence that management has in the senior technology officer when the technical solution is presented to the organization.

The likelihood of an organization's accepting an innovative technical solution is largely determined by the ability of the organization to afford that solution. In this paradigm, the cause is business conditions (economic factors) and the effect is the increased management acceptance of technology (human factor) and the utilization of the current information technology that complements the needs of the organization (technology factor). Poor business conditions or software system failure have the opposite effect. The result is an increase or decrease in expenditures that parallels the growth or decline in revenue.

By means of evaluating the economic factors and the corresponding evolution of growth of information technology, it is possible to make important observations to guide the long-range direction for information technology planning. The following case study is such an analysis. The analysis establishes the following:

- ▶ An organizational profile
- ▶ An organizational growth profile
- ▶ An impact-of-growth profile
- ▶ The evolution of information technology
- ▶ The economic interpretation
- ▶ The lesson learned

9.2 The Case Study

9.2.1 Organizational Profile

The organization is a food service company operating seven hundred stores in thirty states. In support of these stores, the organization operates a food-processing subsidiary that constructed a new facility during the study, replacing two obsolete facilities. The food-processing subsidiary also has limited sales to commercial customers and franchised stores. Revenue for the company-operated stores in the closing year of the analysis was close to 500 million dollars. The organization employed approximately 22,000 employees and generally experienced a high turnover rate.

The objectives of the organization were as follows:

1. Increase the equity of its stockholders
2. Provide a high rate of return on equity
3. Provide consistent earnings
4. Maintain a dominant position in the restaurant market

The mission of the organization was to provide quality service at a reasonable price in a pleasant, attractive atmosphere. The stated objectives and mission are of great importance because the activities of the information service department were in direct support of these objectives and mission.

9.2.2 Organizational Growth Profile

The period analyzed was the seventeen years from 1970 through 1986. During this period, growth was measured on the basis of (1) number of store openings and (2) revenue increases and declines.

The period was one of rapid growth. The number of stores system-wide increased from 85 to almost 700 and then declined to about 635. The number of company-owned stores increased from 32 to 450; the number of franchised stores increased from 53 to 185. Over the seventeen years, the number of company-owned stores increased three times faster than the number of franchised stores. Company-owned stores opened at a rate of 14 to 1, whereas franchised stores increased at a rate of about 4 to 1. The growth was in the following cycles:

▶ Slow from 1970 through 1972

▶ Upswing 1973 through 1975

▶ Leveling 1976 through 1978

▶ Gradual upswing in 1979 through 1981

▶ Downswing 1982 through 1986

The importance of these patterns becomes more evident when they are correlated with the evolution of information technology, specifically the development of on-line systems.

During the study period, revenues for company-owned stores increased from $16 million in 1970 to $513 million at the end of 1985 and declined to $490 million at the end of 1986. The pattern of revenue growth was similar to that associated with new store openings up to 1981. As a result of a change in business strategy, the revenues continued to increase from 1981 on, although the number of stores declined. A decision was made to stop opening new stores and to introduce new products and services that would increase return on assets. New store openings were curtailed, unprofitable stores were eliminated, and another restaurant chain was purchased. Emphasis was placed on improving the average revenues generated from a store. The result was negative growth in the number of stores but continued growth of revenues until 1986.

The 1980s became a period of cost containment in which the organization controlled cost while developing methods for attracting and maintaining customers. During this period, the restaurant concept evolved into that of a sitdown restaurant, the menus of the stores changed, and a new restaurant chain was introduced. The quality of the food and service improved, and menus were expanded. Over the seventeen years, not only did the number of stores increase fourteenfold, but also the appearance, service, quality and menus of the stores changed dramatically.

9.2.3 Impact of Growth

The first effect of the change was an increase in volume. As the number of stores increased and the concept changed, the volume processed through the core computer-based systems (payroll, accounts payable, accounts receivable, sales, fixed assets) increased tenfold. To highlight the impact, let's look at the payroll system. Payroll for all 450 of the company-owned stores was processed centrally. Within a specific window, the data was received and processed, and checks were produced. Over the seventeen years, the number of active employees increased tenfold to 22,000. Yet the processing window became smaller. This produced a constant demand to reevaluate methods for handling data and document distribution.

Because the business depended on student and part-time help, the stores experienced as much as a three-to-one annual personnel turnover. It had to continue to maintain history on these employees for such documents as W-2s and for personnel analysis. At the end of calendar year 1986, the company had more than 65,000 employees on its payroll master file although it had only 22,000 active employees. In addition, in 1970, the organization operated in only a few states, whereas in 1986 it operated in 28 states. The number of tax changes and legal restrictions increased proportionately. This volume placed considerable pressure on the useful life of payroll and other volume-oriented systems such as accounts payable, sales, and marketing.

The second area of impact was control. As volumes increased, the first areas to be affected were those that involved the actual transfer of funds. Again, payroll and accounts payable and receivable were areas that required control. The construction of a new food-processing facility also produced the opportunity to generate revenues from sales to franchised stores and other food-service companies. This, coupled with revenues generated from franchised stores, increased receivable moneys. The revenues involved generated a new requirement for tighter control over receivables than ever before. Food cost was an important item. The profit margin on an average restaurant check is only pennies, and food loss and spoilage have a profound effect on this margin. As the system became larger, it became more difficult to train management in proper procedures for control of food loss. Last, as revenues increased, there was an increasing need to manage the transfer of funds from local banks to a central bank. The daily float on the revenues of a half-billion dollar business is huge.

The third area of impact was financial analysis. The food-service market is highly competitive. The market was being affected by inflation, and this, coupled with a sagging economy, produced a situation in which it was no longer possible simply to pass cost increases to the consumer, as the oil companies were doing. As the cost of a meal increased, the number of people eating out decreased. The management of the organization was young and aggressive. It was aware of the benefits of automation. As a result, the demand for analysis data increased in the areas of cost analysis, expense modeling, market analysis, energy consumption, site selection, promotion evaluation, and an unending number of one-time financial analyses.

9.2.4 Evolution of Information Technology

The Early Years

In 1971, the organization installed its first computer. Between 1971 and mid 1974, it installed the standard batch-oriented financial applications: payroll, personnel, accounts payable, accounts receivable, sales, and general ledger. In late 1973, the organization made an important decision. Rather than simply increasing hardware capacity, it converted all of its software systems to a database management system. In mid 1974, the work was contracted, the hardware was upgraded, database management software was installed, and all systems were rewritten with COBOL. The only important development activity during this period was a rewrite of the payroll system at the beginning of 1976.

In mid 1976, the organization was prepared to install its first on-line system. Again, the hardware was upgraded, and teleprocessing software was installed. Concurrent with the hardware installation, an electronic cash register point-of-sales system and polling network were installed. With this system a minicomputer was used to automatically poll the network of cash registers, a rather visionary action for that time period. This polling system greatly enhanced the available sales data and resulted in a deluge of on-line applications.

Realizing that it was collecting an ever-increasing amount of data, the organization decided to put data collection on line and decentralize it, moving it back to the user departments. To effect this objective, a second minicomputer was installed for on-line data entry and editing. This minicomputer was connected to the main computer via a direct communication link.

Throughout 1977 and 1978, the main thrust of development activity was development and installation of on-line systems. In the latter part of 1978, the organization made another hardware upgrade and installed interactive computing tools for users as a predecessor to its information center.

Evolution of On-Line Systems

In the 1980s, the direction of computing changed. The first important activity was the point-of-sales, electronic cash register network. The point-of-sales network made all sales, customer counts, and labor hours from each company-owned store readily available. The problem with the network was that it required human intervention—the stores had to set up the registers. As a result of human or hardware failure, each day five percent of the stores were not polled. For the data to be current, an on-line system was needed for input of the missing data.

A database management system was installed in mid 1974, but the on-line teleprocessing driver was not installed. In mid 1977 the driver was installed, and the first on-line system, an order entry and invoicing, production control system was installed for the food-processing subsidiary. With this experience gained, a sales maintenance and inquiry system was developed and installed. In 1978, this sales system was enhanced to provide numerous inquiry screens and to provide the ability to enter sales, customer count, and labor data. With correct current sales and deposit data available, an on-line system was developed to transfer funds from local banks to the central bank.

In 1978, an on-line inquiry was provided for the ledger, and an on-line database was provided for franchised store data. Payroll and personnel additions and changes were put on line along with inquiry capability for that database. Profit and loss (P + L) inquiry was provided to expedite financial closings. On-line data entry was installed and made operational in the areas of high-volume data entry.

In 1979, an on-line capital expenditure system was developed. The significant activity, however, was installation of APL to provide the user community with interactive programming support. This facility was used to develop a budget modeling system. It was an archaic attempt at end-user modeling, but it was highly successful nevertheless.

In summary, the organization addressed its requirements for on-line systems using three different technologies:

1. Traditional systems that involved a mainframe computer and a hierarchical database manager

2. On-line data entry and editing with a minicomputer

3. On-line, user-oriented programming languages that interfaced with the databases

9.2.5 Economic Interpretation

Let's step back and take another look at the organization's growth curve and annotate it with the information technology implemented. The organization started with a rather conventional approach to application system development. Then in mid 1974, it made an important decision: it converted to a database environment at a period when it was still easy for them to do it.

Between 1974 and 1976 growth was dramatic. In response to that growth, the organization began to install on-line systems in areas that supported its corporate objectives. This growth environment attracted young, aggressive management, who required the ability to interact dynamically with its information database. The company responded with APL and, although APL has limitations in a database environment, the approach is successful, and the organization responds with other more user oriented software.

Approximately one year after each of the major changes in its growth pattern, there was a major shift in the system development philosophy of the organization. The information technology group was doing an excellent job responding to the changes in economic conditions. It is also clear that this is a reactive, not a planned environment. The information technology group is responding to changes in the economic environment and, as the environment becomes larger and more complex, its ability to respond quickly decreases. In the face of changing corporate strategies and increasing volumes, information technology has become a supertanker that is a very efficient fuel carrier, but, because of its immense size it takes a very long time to change direction.

9.2.6 Lesson Learned

In response to this situation, the organization chose to implement three correction strategies: planning, flexibility and responsiveness.

Planning

The organization recognized the need to develop and implement a technical direction and strategic long-range plan. In concert with this long-range plan, its information technology area reviewed all its systems and outstanding requests and documented existing shortfalls. It assessed the effect that meeting corporate objectives had on software systems on a year-by-year basis. It established a technical direction that would allow it to meet those strategic objectives, and it developed hardware, software, and personnel plans to support the software development plan. It began to respond to strategic direction rather than wait and react to its implementation.

Flexibility

The organization implemented a database management system to improve flexibility. The business became increasingly more complex, and it could not afford substantial reworking of its software systems every time business conditions changed. It moved to fourth-generation languages (4GLs) to promote ease of maintenance and enhancement. It designed software systems that would evolve as the company changed, rather than going through the trauma of system reworking. It implemented source data entry to reduce the handling of data and to move to on-line processing. It installed store-based computing systems with personal computers to improve the performance of the stores at the grass roots level.

Responsiveness

The organization implemented techniques to make its system development more responsive and its stored information more available for decision making. It incorporated a 4GL as part of the system development life cycle and provided computer users with analysis software such as APL, APL-based spreadsheets, and a 4GL to access data. It gave the computer user access to databases. It enhanced the productivity of its development staff through interactive development software and a data dictionary.

9.3 Conclusion

Human development is punctuated by stages of development: childhood, adolescence, adulthood, midlife, and old age. Humans progress through these stages of development and have experiences that are common to others of similar age, sex, and socioeconomic background. The stages are the basis for commonality, but their uniqueness is the product of many influences, such as genetic birthright, socioeconomic background, education, country of origin, sex, and all the other influences that have an impact on human development.

In a similar manner, the evolution of information technology in an organization is punctuated by stages of development. Unlike human development, the evolution of information technology is an open-ended system. It goes on as long as the organization continues to function. Therefore it can have an infinite number of stages. In this paradigm, it is not the stages that are important; it is the influences that cause the evolution through these stages that is important.

As the human element of the organization changes, as new technology becomes available, and as the economic fortunes of the organization change, the direction of information technology shifts. Each of these factors—human, technologic, and economic—is important, and at any time in development, one or the other can be dominant. However, the factor that is most frequently dominant is the economic factor. The organization in the case study is an example of the dominance of economic factors over information technology.

The analysis period was one of great change for the organization in the case study. The organization reached and was able to maintain a superior level of technical competence. At a period in its growth when its volumes increased, it responded with on-line systems for both its mainframe computer and minicomputers. The impetus for this evolution was clearly economic. The business was growing and changing, and the organization successfully used new technology to mitigate the problems associated with this growth and change. Equally clear is the fact that the availability of new technology and the acceptance of that technology played a large part in the success.

The use of technology was not without flaw. Throughout the analysis period, the use of information technology was reactive. As the business became more complex, the lead time for introducing new technology became exaggerated. This is reverse economy of scale: the larger the business became, the more difficult it became to make small changes in its systems. These errors were recognized, and a strategy was developed not only to avoid these errors but also to improve quality and service in the business units while satisfying stockholders' desire to achieve consistent earnings and maintain a dominant position in the market.

Although the organization took advantage of new technology (database, on-line systems, electronic cash registers, and personal computer–based in-store systems) and it had a receptive management, the driving force for almost all technologic change was economic. Different economic development would have led to different technology.

10

Creating an Evolutionary System: A Case Study

The concepts of creation and evolution are fundamental to reengineering a system life cycle. As we have discussed, the term *evolution* describes the prolonged periods of growth during which a software system is subject to maintenance and enhancement but there are no serious upheavals in the operation of a software system.

The term *creation* describes the periods of turmoil that result in new software systems, such as replacing an accounting system developed in house with a purchased software package, changing a hardware vendor, or changing an operating system. By its very nature, evolution results in creation. At some point in the life cycle of a software system, factors external to the system affect the system in a manner that evolutionary factors cannot accommodate, leading to extinction.

The CEO principle (creation → evolution → opportunity) suggests that there is a natural change in emphasis over time that results in a change in priority and resource allocation. This change in emphasis is the reason that a new software system is installed; creation shifts to modification and enhancement and ends with selective enhancement and modification. An organization can plan to use this natural evolution to its advantage.

The earliest strategy of information technology was to create new software systems. In the early years of commercial computing, the software void was filled with what are today the bread and butter applications of business computing: payroll, accounts payable, accounts receivable, general ledger, manufacturing, inventory, banking, and insurance software systems.

As information technology matured, change took place. There was a shift in emphasis from creating technology-based software systems to maintaining these same systems. In some cases, this maintenance took the form of conversion to more current hardware and software technologies such as database, forth generation languages (4GLs), on-line processing, end-user computing, and client-server processing. In other cases, the maintenance consisted of enhancements to systems to accommodate the introduction of new business units, to accommodate changes in business strategy, or to meet mandated changes in the law. The systems were evolving from a primitive technology to a more advanced technology. Not only did the technology evolve, but also application software systems evolved from simple to complex, from stand-alone application to an integrated body of information systems.

After technology reaches a critical mass, the nature of this change takes on an opportunistic character. The number of opportunities for introducing new technology increases at an exponential rate. Each new application of information technology creates two or more additional new opportunities to use the technology. These opportunities create two or more additional opportunities, until the opportunities exceed the available resources to implement, assimilate, or finance the technology. At this point, organizations move into opportunism. Because almost everything conforms to the 80/20 rule, that 80 percent of the return on these software systems is achieved with 20 percent of the investment, it is fair to assume that only 20 percent of opportunities result in 80 percent of the return. Organizations then move from simple change to selected change, and they look for high-return opportunities. Selected change is the definition of reengineering.

10.1 Reengineering

10.1.1 Creating Opportunity

The operational analysis and reengineering techniques described in earlier chapters are directed at returning creditability to the much maligned process of software maintenance. However, maintenance is not the only way software systems can selectively change: software systems can evolve through creation. Software creation and reengineering are not contradictory in terms nor are they mutually exclusive. It is both possible and desirable to create a system that can be reengineered easily at a later date. The prerequisites for creating a changing system are as follows.

An information technology architecture

Organizations can no longer simply evolve through a proprietary technology. The increasing number of innovative solutions to information requirements cannot be ignored. Information technology is akin to a symphony in which hardware, software, and turnkey solutions are like instruments. The architecture is an orchestration of these instruments. On the basis of the objectives of an organization and the availability of solutions, the composition of that orchestra will change.

Organizations need to build as much flexibility as possible into their system architectures. They must recognize the value of past successes and leverage them with the potential of new technology. This is not a simple task, but the harmony derived from orchestrating such a variety of alternatives can be highly rewarding to an organization.

A System Direction

It is relatively easy to conceptualize setting a direction for the reengineering of an existing software system. In reengineered systems the maintenance and enhancement of existing systems are redirected. With operational analysis, requested maintenance and enhancement are identified, improvements are specified, and a direction is established for the software system. Implementation is achieved through a long series of small projects, sometimes called *chunks*. As changes are requested, they are tested against this direction for conformance. The organization develops a high comfort level that changes are moving the software systems in the desired direction.

Establishing a direction for a new software system is a different matter. There is no history for the design. As a result, the direction requires experience, intuition, and fuzzy logic to determine a direction. Timing also plays an important role in this process. Identifying the portions of the software system that need to be completed first and establishing a sequence of events go a long way to clarifying direction. If a new database is required, identifying the data elements and designing maintenance and reporting procedures help to identify future features. Experience with similar applications or insight into the experience of others is beneficial in establishing direction.

Assume that the direction also is changing. As portions of the new system are designed, other portions become clear. Learning is gradual, and users cannot accurately specify system requirements until they see them. Assume that it is necessary to change earlier designs as directions change. No one is clairvoyant, and allowing room for software system improvement ensures a greater chance of success than trying to identify every feature of a software system. It is usually easier to improve or modify an existing software system than it is to specify all of its features with no prior knowledge.

A Chunking Method

Segment projects into small pieces or chunks that can be developed and evaluated quickly by computer users. Get the product out quickly, and try it out on computer users. The small chunks become prototypes that give computer users a chance to fly before they buy and to make changes before large investments are made. Use of small chunks allows software products to be tested and implemented quickly before barriers are developed. Chunking incorporates all the principles for successful evolution: it is easy to modify, learning is gradual, users see the results of requirements, improvements are encouraged, and high-return functions are isolated.

A good rule is that a chunk should result in a project of six months or less with a usable product delivered in that time frame. After the chunk is complete, future improvements are included in another chunk. There is no limit to the number of chunks; in theory successful evolution could go on forever.

Continuous development does not imply that development of a software system must receive constant labor commitments. There can be periods when the software system becomes dormant, and no improvements are made. During these periods, the changes in other software systems may have a higher priority.

10.2 Case Studies

Two case studies are presented to clarify the differences between reengineering and conventional system development. The first case study discusses the design of a system in which timing constraints made it impossible for the organization to specify all of the requirements before development began. The second case study discusses the design of a software system for a relatively new function—a group takes on a new mission, and it is not clear what is required to complete the mission. Both cases are need-based examples of reengineering design. The design has to be realized in an evolving way, but there is no reason that this need-based technique cannot become the technique of choice.

10.2.1 Example One: Flexible Benefits

A food service company decides to implement a flexible benefits system. The system is an opportunity to improve employee benefits and reduce the cost of benefits to the organization by millions of dollars. The decision is made in October, and implementation is planned for the beginning of the calendar year. The design requires reengineering of the payroll system to accommodate new deductions, a record keeping system for benefits, an interface with the software system of the benefits carrier, an interface into the payable system, and a control and reporting system for the accounting and benefits departments. The requirements of the system exceed the capacity of the information service group to achieve them in the allotted time.

The alternatives are (1) tell management that the group cannot implement a significant business strategy because the computer systems cannot be designed in time or (2) develop a method that supports the implementation strategy. The information service group chose a reengineering strategy.

Architecture

The computing platform consisted of an IBM mainframe computing center that supported a network of remote terminals located in four remote sites by means of a database system and operated on 23-hours-a-day on-line availability. Approximately 60 percent of the computing was on line, and virtually all operational systems were designed with the database system. An on-line query language was available for direct access to database information. The organization also had a history of mainframe-based personal computing. The stated direction of the organization included designing software systems to provide easy access for end users, ad hoc queries, and incorporation of outside services whenever practical.

Direction

The direction for the system was set with a series of brainstorming sessions. These sessions were a group effort, populated by representatives from the benefits group, payroll, general accounting, treasury, and information service. Other participants, such as outside benefits consultants and the benefits carriers, sat in on the process as necessary. The implementation task force determined that the first order of business was to address directional issues for the design and implementation of the flexible benefits system.

Information service emphasized that the directional issues were key and that only a few products were required at each of a number of milestones: the end of the calendar year, the end of the first month, the end of the first quarter, the end of the first year, and some ad hoc reporting as required. On the basis of the timing considerations, the following directional issues were established:

► Establishment of the menus of benefits offered

► Assignment of record keeping to a service bureau

► Disbursement of payment by the record keeper

- ▶ Modification of payroll to support deductions
- ▶ Development of a database for ad hoc reporting
- ▶ Development of only a minimum of internal reporting

It was decided to take an approach that would minimize the internal changes required to the existing systems. It also was decided to use a service bureau that had experience administering such systems for record keeping and to provide a flexible database of human resource and benefit data that could be easily queried by end users. The team realized, and emphasized to management, that there would be problems with the approach but that implementation on time was critical. As long as data integrity was not compromised, these problems would be corrected as the project moved along.

Chunking

The second order of business was to break the project down into a series of chunks to provide deliverables at the critical target dates. At the beginning the team recognized that early milestones are the most important. Later targets have more time available, and the consequences of missing a later target are less catastrophic. The project was segmented on the target dates for the main deliverables: end of year, end of first month, end of first quarter, and end of first year. Because the first target dates were the most time constrained, a conscious effort was made to defer as many features as possible into later segments. The segments were as follows:

Year-end startup: Payroll deduction changes and enrollment procedures

End of first month: Human resources database, accounting and financial extract, and balancing procedures

End of first quarter: Training for ad hoc reporting and end-of-quarter balancing

End of first year: Year-end reporting, reenrollment procedures, tying up loose ends

The project was designed and implemented over about a year and a half. However, the first segments were put into production within months. Had conventional design techniques been used, not even the design would have been complete in the time allotted to the first segment. On the negative side, there was considerable redesign; about 20 percent of the system was reworked because of iterative improvements or problems. This is probably less than that normally experienced with conventional design.

There was a perception problem with the approach. It was assumed that the reengineering was the result of failure to design correctly. This could not be farther from the truth. The reengineering was the result of a conscious effort to get the most important aspects of the software system up and working and to use experience as the basis for developing the balance. This results in the design of fewer features that are infrequently or never used and a software system that mirrors the needs of the organization. The postimplementation rework was comparable to conventional system development methods, but implementation was quicker and required less labor. Considerably less long-term reworking is required than for reworking of conventional system development, and the satisfaction level is much higher.

10.2.2 Example Two: Alumni Development

The alumni development office of a large, private university developed a sophisticated alumni database in support of its mission. The office provided the support for programs such as direct mail and telephone solicitation programs, alumni relations, and records maintenance. In support of its mission, the office decided to implement a flexible alumni database. The system design required development of a retrieval-oriented database in support of highly personalized programs that would evolve over time. The mission of the office was opportunistic; programs would change as opportunities presented themselves and experience dictated. The software system clearly had no predecessor.

The answer was to develop a system that supported the paper-driven manual environment while providing the opportunity to refine the process, reduce paperwork, improve personalization and reliability, and increase responsiveness. The development office and information service group chose a retrieval-oriented, evolutionary implementation strategy.

Architecture

The computing platform was an IBM mainframe computing center that supported a network of eight hundred terminals. The computer center used a database system and operated on 10-hour-a-day on-line availability. Approximately 20 percent of the computing was on line, and all production systems, with the exception of payroll, were designed to use the database system. An on-line query language was available for direct access to database information. More than three hundred users were trained to use the query language, processing in excess of one hundred queries a day.

The stated computing direction of the university included designing software systems to provide easy access for end-user ad hoc queries and providing source control of the functionality of centralized software systems. Its goal was to leverage a large installed base of computers, not only distributing functionality but also distributing computer processing across the university's two thousand microcomputers and two hundred midrange computers.

Direction

The direction for the system was set through a partnership with the alumni development office. Information service emphasized that the directional issues were key and that the design for the alumni database should be retrieval oriented. On the basis of the mission of the alumni office, the following directional issues were established:

▶ A retrieval-oriented design for the alumni database

▶ Development of a facility for ad hoc reporting

▶ Allowance for an advanced data retrieval system

▶ Development of only a minimum of internal reporting

▶ A design that allows updating for source data entry

▶ Segregation of information into separate files (biographic data, gift data, research data, and text)

▶ Maintenance of summary data for quick retrieval

▶ Consideration to interfacing with a telemarketing computer

The approach limited the initial scope of the software development project to developing a sophisticated database directly maintainable by the development office and to providing support for the manual procedures of the group. At the same time, it provided opportunities to streamline the process through advanced data retrieval facilities and a front-end telemarketing computer. The team did not attempt to design in detail the entire software system but instead established an architecture that could expand as the alumni development office gained experience with the tool.

Chunking

The second order of business was to break the project down into a series of chunks to provide deliverables in reasonable time increments. At the beginning it was recognized that the driving factor was to deliver a system that would meet the day-to-day mission of the development office. The early phases were labor intensive on both sides of the partnership, but experience and shrewd planning helped identify the areas of high return, and streamlining occurred. The project was segmented into the following logical work units:

Alumni database: A database system that consists of biographic and gift-giving history. A research master, prospect master, a text master, and other smaller supporting databases were to be added later. The system provided on-line updates to speed processing, supported immediate retrieval by means of a 4GL, and routinely was used to produce pledge cards for prospects for telephone solicitation.

End-user data retrieval: An end-user retrieval tool to allow the alumni office to retrieve the most common kinds of information with a minimum of technical knowledge.

Advanced data retrieval system: An advanced, menu-driven, rule-based retrieval tool to select complex information and produce specialized outputs such as labels, reports, on-line screens, complex letters, and files without programming knowledge. The forethought to provide facilities for outputting files was especially valuable for the next chunk—telemarketing.

Telemarketing: Implementation of a telemarketing system by means of a UNIX-based computer and about thirty-five caller workstations to perform campaign management. The system provided on-line call guides, information files, record updates, and requeuing in addition to automatic phone dialing. The system interfaced with the mainframe database, allowing fresh data to be selected and downloaded to the computer daily. It allowed uploading of corrected biographic data and contribution information. The system improved the effectiveness of phone solicitation and reduced the labor needed for administrative support.

The project was designed and implemented over about a five-year period, but the first segments are put into production within the first year. Features were added as subsystems as users' skill with the system increased. Telemarketing was added when the users' expertise and budget to support the extension were favorable. From the points of view of effectiveness and productivity, the system continually exceeded expectations and continually improved productivity.

What is presented here is a simplification of the process. In actuality, each chunk may have had more than one intermediate deliverable or intermediate chunk. Had conventional software engineering techniques been used, the project would not have had an opportunity to benefit from the experience factor, and the quality of the result would not have been achieved. The beauty of the evolutionary design was demonstrated in the minimum of redesign that was required to accommodate each new chunk. True, some functionality lost its value as the next chunk was installed, but these functions paid for themselves during their operational period.

10.3 Conclusion

Operational analysis and other reengineering techniques are designed to return veracity and creditability to the much-maligned process of software maintenance. Maintenance, however, is not the only way software systems can change: software systems can successfully change during their creation. Software creation and reengineering are not contradictions in terms, nor are they mutually exclusive. In fact, it is both possible and desirable to create a changing system. The prerequisites for creating a changing system are as follows:

▶ Develop an information technology architecture

▶ Establish a software system direction

▶ Install a chunking software development method

The two different case studies differentiate a reengineered software system from conventional software development. The first study describes the design of a system in which timing constraints made it impossible for the organization to specify all the requirements before the development process began. The second case study describes the design of a software system for a relatively new function—a group takes on a new mission in which it is clear that an opportunistic approach is required to complete that mission. In this case, designing a flexible system that draws on the experience of the computer users results in a sophisticated design that cannot be achieved otherwise.

Both case studies are examples of need-based reengineered design, but there is no reason that this need-based technique cannot be the technique of choice.

11

Year 2000

Most of today's computer programs are coded with only a two-digit year (dd/mm/yy). It is assumed that the year is prefaced with the digit 19. Such programs, therefore, provide no way to differentiate the century as either 1900 or 2000. Use of a two-digit year saves storage and data entry time. Use of a six-digit date format (dd/mm/yy) uses 25 percent less storage than an eight-digit format (dd/mm/yyyy). Leon A. Kappelman, assistant professor of the business computer information service department at the University of North Texas, Denton, Texas estimated that as a result of this economy, the average organization saved one million dollars per billion bytes of storage over the thirty-year period from 1963 through 1992. Kappelman also estimated that these savings can be doubled for date-intensive financial information. Over a thirty-year period tens of thousands of computer installations accumulate massive savings.

Although the practice of using a six-digit date is common and has resulted in massive savings, it leads to incorrect results when the computer performs arithmetic operations, comparisons, or data field sorting with dates after 1999. For example, if a phone call were to be made just after midnight on December 31, 1999, to wish a family member a happy new year, a not uncommon occurrence, the ten-minute call could result in a phone charge for a ninety-nine year call. The compounded interest on a ten-dollar credit card balance in December of 1999 at 18 percent would be in excess of $50 million at the end of January 2000.

The solution to the problem is simple: analyze all active data files to determine whether the year is represented in two digits and then find all applications that use the data. The file format is changed from two digits to four, and every application that uses the data is changed correspondingly. An alternative is to analyze program libraries to identify programs that use a two-digit year, make changes to the software, map the data file accessed with those programs, and change the date format for the year to four digits in the data file. The problem is that finding the programs that use the data and implementing the changes is time consuming. It is not uncommon for organizations not to have source code for software or to have obsolete code in their libraries. What normally is required is a general house cleaning.

The year 2000 process is a paradox of both crisis and opportunity. On the crisis side, the Gartner Group has estimated the year 2000 conversion will cost the computer industry 400 to 600 billion dollars to resolve or about $1.00 per line of code that has to be changed. In addition, there is the cost of business interruption that results from the potential to disrupt all computer processing—automatic teller machines to personal computers. On the opportunity side, this is the first time the computer industry has had to evaluate every line of code, every report, and every on-line screen in both its operating and application software on every platform—personal computer, workstation, midrange, and mainframe computer.

In reviewing their software, computer organizations have an opportunity to analyze software in context and not only resolve the year 2000 code but also reengineer applications, dispose of obsolete code, or install replacement technology at a small incremental cost. Regardless of the approach, organizations will pay the price for the year 2000 conversion. A small incremental investment, however, can result a massive return on investment.

In addressing the year 2000 problem, it appears unlikely that organizations will reengineer applications to other platforms, such as Windows NT or UNIX, or choose to reinstall purchased applications to circumvent the problem. Legacy systems are the most likely winner in this arena. Organizations are likely to consolidate their processing, moving from Wang, Unisys, and mainframe computers and consolidating on more popular devices, such as the IBM AS/400 or Digital VAX computers. Faced with the magnitude of the year 2000 conversion and suffering from procrastination, organizations are likely to take the path of least resistance.

11.1 Reengineering

For a small percentage of organizations, the year 2000 change is an opportunity to reevaluate core applications and reengineer them to conform with the direction of technology and organizational strategies. Most organizations make thousands of changes, enhancements, and corrections to software systems every year. If they conform to application system architecture, the changes further the intent of that architecture, and it is possible to direct the evolution of the applications. Organizations have an opportunity either to direct these changes or to let them happen randomly. The first alternative extends the life of applications; the latter results eventually in an eclectic system. By default, most organizations allow the latter to happen.

At some point in the life of an application system, factors external to the application subject them to change. The year 2000 process is that kind of factor. Applications are not static; they are always changing. New systems or subsystems are emerging while others are becoming obsolete. This process typically is slow and continuous, but it is subject to acceleration and deceleration. Because of the economies involved, sudden profound change is rare. System evolution is not the result of shrewd design; it is the result of a long series of compromises. For example, an organization incorporates the year 2000 changes but does not port the application to a different computer platform.

Smooth change is not inevitable; it cannot be assumed that system growth is linear. During the last thirty years the introduction of new technology has markedly affected the life expectancy of an application system. As a result, these periods of dramatic change are spaced between smooth periods of evolution. These turbulent times are periods of revolution; they represent a serious upheaval—elimination or replacement of a system.

For any one of a multitude of reasons, a system may experience a turbulent period, a system crisis. As a result, a completely new system is designed. The year 2000 process is just such a crisis. The most common pitfall, however, is to assume that there is no alternative to replacing the system. Application systems are normally considered to be commodities, a fixed product, developed to fixed specifications with a fixed life cycle. It is assumed that the organization evolves during the maintenance phase and that the system changes to reflect this evolution. Specifications of the system eventually are subverted sufficiently to make the system ineffective. The problem is not that the specifications of the system evolve but that the architecture was designed without sufficient flexibility to allow evolution. This mind-set assumes a fixed architecture; as the company evolves the only solution is to replace it with a new system.

Replacement is rarely the *only* or the *best* alternative. The following portfolio of reengineering alternatives can extend the life of a system:

Maintenance: Changing the system to meet legal, organizational, or strategic changes in the direction of a business

Renovation: Changing the base system to add the new functions of the system while correcting technical deficiencies

Augmentation: Changing the system to add new functions or correct existing functions by building new features on top of, or around, the system

The first step in reengineering is to assume that system change is evolutionary. This evolutionary perspective can be achieved by means of evaluating the operation of the system, a process referred to earlier as operational analysis. Operational analysis is conducted to identify and define the functions performed by a system in an operational environment. The objectives are as follows:

▶ Identification and analysis of the objectives of the principal functions involved in processing information

▶ Identification of areas of improvement, areas that cause unnecessary effort or result in the loss of data integrity

▶ Formulation of remedial actions giving priority to mandatory changes, which are necessary to resolve data security or data integrity problems

▶ Calculation of financial or other benefits derived from remedial actions

In addition to the quantitative (financial) benefits, operational analysis results in the following qualitative benefits:

▶ Knowledge of the functions of the system is disseminated to a larger audience. This increases the level of awareness of the function of the system. Over time and because of staff turnover, much of the knowledge is lost despite documentation.

▶ Operational analysis improves communication among various work groups. Through participation in the operational analysis, the involved personnel become committed to improving the productivity of the overall system.

▶ The attitude of the involved personnel improves, and they find it easier to work together in the future.

When considering the qualitative and quantitative factors, it is evident that operational analysis positively affects the entire organization rather than an individual department, function, or area, because it measures the overall effectiveness of an application. By means of implementing all the changes that positively affect control and those that give the highest financial return, the greatest impact is achieved with a minimum of expense. Eighty percent of the return typically is achieved with only 20 percent of the effort.

By repeating operational analyses, even when the organization is not faced with something as apocalyptic as a year 2000 conversion, an applications direction is an evolutionary one. A dynamic view evolves as the strategies of the company evolve. The result is modification of the development cycle, which extends the life of the system beyond the perceived life span.

Exertion of a small incremental expenditure of time and money, approximately 20 percent of the development phase cost, allows the evolution of an application to be altered to correlate with the direction of the company. Instead of guaranteed replacement, the life of the system can be extended through selective maintenance, renovation, or augmentation, or if necessary it can be replaced or outsourced.

11.2 Year 2000 Compliance

11.2.1 Impact Analysis

To realize the opportunity contained in the year 2000 conversion, organizations must first review their overall business objectives and technology strategy. This is an opportunity for organizations to validate that their information technology architecture is synchronized with their business objectives. If they are not synchronized, it is an opportunity to realign information technology strategies. There may be ways to save money by eliminating an application that is not strategic and by implementing a new application that is or by outsourcing an application to a service provider. The organization is already spending money on the year 2000 conversion, so what it is looking for is an opportunity to receive financial return by making a small incremental investment.

The next step is to assess computing platforms, operating software strategies, purchased and in-house developed software, and existing tools and software. The organization is identifying areas of improvement, areas that cause unnecessary human intervention, or areas that result in loss of data integrity or jeopardize data security. Technologic analysis targets missing or obsolete code, elimination of which reduces the scope of the year 2000 project and improves subsequent application maintenance procedures.

All active data files are analyzed to find instances in which the year is represented in two digits; all applications that use the date field are identified. The alternative is to analyze program libraries to identify programs that use a two-digit date and correspondingly change the data files. The problem is that finding the programs that use the date and implementing the changes is a considerable effort. It is not uncommon for organizations not to have source code for active software. Implementation of an operational analysis includes the following steps, which were identified in detail in Figure 8.2.

1. Identify documents

2. Analyze MIS service requests

3. Interview client personnel for undocumented changes or cost-saving opportunities

4. Analyze processing steps and paperwork flow for opportunities to eliminate manual handling with electronic exchange

5. Segment processing

6. Document information input

7. Document all outputs

8. Determine areas for improvement

9. Perform a return-on-investment analysis

10. Rank changes

—First by mandatory enhancements—changes that improve the integrity or security of the system and can be implemented in parallel with year 2000 changes

—Second by return on investment calculation—changes that synchronize the information technology architecture with business objectives. These may save money by eliminating applications that are not strategic and by implementing a new application that generates improved profits or reduces expenses.

11.2.2 Action Plans, Schedules, and Conversion

An organization is ready to develop plans and strategies to implement the year 2000 changes in each application. The mandatory changes are usually addressed first. These applications are judged vulnerable. There is a fault that makes them a security risk, data integrity risk, or legal risk; they do not conform to legal or regulatory standards. These changes usually constitute reengineering of the application system; therefore the changes are made in house, if possible, by staff familiar with the applications. This expedites the fault reduction and quickly satisfies the year 2000 conversion.

The second group of applications are those that are redeployed. An application may be reengineered to take advantage of new technology, or it can be discontinued because it is outmoded or redundant. Replacement also can entail substituting an application with a purchased turnkey application or outsourcing it to a service provider.

The final group of applications are the straight year 2000 conversions. They are the residual applications that necessitate only that a two-digit year be converted to a four-digit year. This is the area in which automation tools are most productive. It is likely that most (as many as 80 percent) of the programs will fall into this category.

After the correction strategies are established for each application system, they have to be implemented according to a rigid schedule. Regardless of the chosen tactic (reengineering, replacement, or conversion), project management techniques, testing procedures, and change management are mandatory. Reengineering is an acceptable option for mission-critical applications for which the organization has in-house staff and the resources to enhance legacy applications. Turnkey implementation of proprietary applications that bring technologic architectures into synchronization with business strategies is a successful strategy when organizations have sufficient funds to use outside resources.

Implementation of the residual conversion, the largest part of the year 2000 conversion, is the area in which automation tools are most effective. Automation tools typically address the conversion from either a code or a date perspective. The conversion typically starts with the computer code; each two-digit year is identified and converted to a four-digit year. The ADPAC SystemVision Year 2000 is an example of this type of code conversion tool. An alternative approach is date conversion whereby a call statement is inserted at the appropriate place in the code. The call statement accesses an external routine in the date conversion software. Date conversion software includes packages such as Calendar Routines from TransCentury Data or DateServer 2000 from Computer Software Corporation.

11.2.3 Automated Software

A large part of the solution is automated tools. Automated tools range from products that attempt to automate the entire year 2000 conversion (none actually automates the complete process, it is too complex)—that is, analysis, planning, management, conversion, testing, and implementation—to automation tools that are limited to performing specialized portions of the process. Tools that fall into the first category include CA Discover 2000 from Computer Associates International, Factory 2000 from Intersolv, SystemVision 2000 from Platinum Technology, and Vision: Solution 2000 from Sterling Software (Table 11.1). Specialized tools that fall into the latter category include the following:

▶ Abend-Aid, adapted for year 2000 analysis and testing by Compuware

▶ A year 2000 inventory tool for in-house applications (SoftAudit/2000) and an inventory tool for purchased applications (SoftAudit/One) from Isogon Corporation

▶ Giles, a directory of cross-application relations for isolating year 2000 changes, from Global Software

▶ UniKit, a product that lets organizations model and test CICS applications on a UNIX system, from Fisher Technologies

11.3 Conclusion

Over the last three decades, organizations that have any investment in legacy systems have gone through numerous conversions. Early computer users cut their teeth changing second-generation applications to third-generation applications. Later they converted IBM DOS or DOS/VSE applications to OS/MVS. Conversions were required to implement MVS/SP and MVS/VSE. My staff expended substantial effort to change code as a result of upgrades from one version of COBOL to the next. When I consolidated organizations into a common computer center, JCL was converted and standardized. One organization made a substantial investment in converting to IMS DB/DC, and later those applications had to be converted to batch message processing (BMP) for full on-line and batch processing. In another instance an organization merged and changed names, forcing a conversion and standardization of report titles and screen titles.

The foregoing list could go on and on. The moral is that there is nothing unique or unusual about the year 2000 conversion other than that the entire industry is doing it at the same time. Anyone who has been through this has learned how to make these changes. Most of the time, they were done behind the scenes with little or no support from management. This time a tremendous amount of press about the year 2000 change has generated a greater awareness of the problem and made organizations more willing to fund the change. The vast market for the change has resulted in a substantial amount of software and support service.

Organizations have the opportunity to leverage this opportunity. By using operational analysis to evaluate application systems, organizations can identify opportunities to extend the life of an application system and identify mission-critical opportunities for changing technology while implementing the year 2000 changes needed to keep the organization running.

Operational analysis provides the opportunity to extend the life of a system. It also provides immediate qualitative returns in the form of better use and understanding of the systems and quantitative returns when the changes are carried to fruition.

Table 11.1 *Year 2000 Software Providers*

Company and Address	Product	Company and Address	Product
ADPAC Corp. 425 Market St., 4th Floor San Francisco, CA 94105 415-777-5400 415-546-7130 FAX	SystemVision 2000	Cognicase 425 Viger Quest, Suite 303 Montreal, Quebec H2Z 1X2 Canada 800-322-3386 514-866-6161 514-866-6260 FAX	Cogni-2000
Alydaar Software 2101 West Rexford Rd., Suite 250 Charlotte, NC 28211 704-544-0092	SmartCode	Computer Associates International One Computer Associates Plaza Islandia, NY 11788 800-225-5224 516-342-5224	CA Discover 2000
Assent Logic 180 Rose Orchard Way, Suite 200 San Jose, CA 95134 408-943-0630	RD100 Software Tools	Computer Horizons 45 Old Bloomfield Ave. Mountain Lakes, NJ 07046-1495 800-321-2421 201-402-7400 212-980-4676	Signature 2000
Cap Gemini America 111 Wood Ave. South Iselin, NJ 08830 908-906-0400	Transmillenium Services	Computer Software Corporation 24864 Detroit Rd. Cleveland OH 44145 800-908-2000 216-333-8888 216-333-8288 fax	DateServer 2000
CD Group, Inc. 555 Triangle Pkwy., Suite 100 Norcross, GA 30092 800-203-9190	Transition/2000	Compuware 31440 Northwestern Hwy. Farmington Hills, MI 48334 800-535-8707 810-737-7300 810-737-2718 fax	Abend-Aid Xpeditor/IMS Xpeditor/CICS Xpeditor/PLUS Xpeditor/TSO Xpeditor/Xchange

Table 11.1 *Continued*

Company and Address	Product	Company and Address	Product
Data Dimensions, Inc. 2000 Skyline Tower 10900 NE 4th St. Bellevue, WA 98004 800-499-1979	Ardes 2k	Ironsoft, Inc. 4323 Winnequah Rd. Monona, WI 53716 800-236-0141 608-695-1896 608-221-8018 fax	Analyzer 2000
Edge Information Group 2250 East Devon Ave. Des Plaines, IL 60018-4510 708-297-2020 513-948-8906	Edge Portfolio Analyzer	Isogon Corporation 330 Seventh Ave. New York, New York 10001 800-568-8828 212-376-3200 212-376-3280 fax	Softaudit/2000 Softaudit/One Tic Toc
Evolutionary Technologies International 4301 Westbank, Building B, Suite 100 Austin, TX 78746 512-327-6994	ETI*Extract	Izar Associates, Inc. 4 Emery Ave. Randolph, NJ 07869 201-442-0577 201-442-0633 fax	Fieldex 2000
Global Software, Inc. P.O. Box 2813 15 Depot St. Duxbury, MA 02331-2813 781-934-0949 781-934-2001 fax GILES@globsoft.com	Giles	Mainware, Inc. 7176 Pioneer Creek Rd. Maple Plain, MN 55359 612-932-9154 612-932-9155	Hourglass 2000
IBS Conversions 2625 Butterfield Rd., Suite 102 E Oakbrook 60521 630-990-1999	Solutions 2000	McCabe & Associates 5501 Twin Knolls Rd., Suite 111 Columbia MD 21045 800-638-6316	Visual 2000 Environment
Intersolv, Inc. 9420 Key West Ave. Rockville, MD 20850 800-582-1600 301-838-5000	Factory 2000	Micro Focus 2465 East Bayshore Rd. Palo Alto, CA 94303 800-318-4259 415-856-4161 415-856-6134 fax	Challenge 2000

Table 11.1 *Continued*

Company and Address	Product	Company and Address	Product
Oracle Systems Corporation 500 Oracle Pkwy. Redwood City, CA 95065 415-506-7000 415-506-7200	Developer 2000 Designer 2000	Silvon Software 900 Oakmont Lane, Suite 400 Westmont IL 60559 800-874-5866 630-655-3377	INTO 2000
Platinum Technology, Inc. 1815 South Meyer Rd., Suite 10 Villa Park, IL 60181-5225 708-620-5000 800-442-6861	SystemVision 2000	Software Eclectics, Inc. 10955 Jones Bridge Rd., Suite 131 Alpharetta, GA 30202-7343 800-457-3113 770-667-9117 770-667-9417 fax	SE/ONE
Quintic Systems, Inc. 3166 Des Plaines Ave., Suite 36 Des Plaines, Illinois 60018 800-699-1169 708-699-1169 708-699-1214 fax	Century Source Conversion	Software Migrations Limited Mountjoy Research Center, Unit 1C Stockton Rd. Durham, DH 1 3SW United Kingdom 44+(0)191 386 0420 44+(0)191 386 1243 fax	Fermat 2000
Reasoning Systems 3260 Hillview Ave. Palo Alto, CA 94304 415-494-6201 415-494-8053 fax	Software Refinery Refine/COBOL	Sterling Software Applications Management Division 5900 Canoga Ave. Woodland Hills, CA 91365-4237 800-587-1002 818-716-1616	Vision: Solution 2000
SEEC, Inc. 5001 Baum Blvd. Pittsburgh, PA 15213 412-682-4991 412-682-4958 fax	COBOL Analyst	Techforce BV Saturnusstraat 60 P.O. Box 3108 2132 HB Hoofddorp The Netherlands +31.23.56.22929 +31.23.56.27052 fax sales@techforce.nl	Cosmos Y2000 Workbench

Table 11.1 *Continued*

Company and Address	Product	Company and Address	Product
TransCentury Data Systems 111 Pine St., Suite 715 San Francisco, CA 94111 415-255-7082 415-255-4584 fax	Calendar Routines	Viasoft 3033 North 44th St. Phoenix, AZ 85018 800-525-7775 602-952-0050 602-840-4068 fax	Enterprise 2000
Trecom Business Systems 333 Thornall St. Edison NJ 08837 908-549-4100	Solution 2000		

Part 3

Reengineering Tools

12

Reengineering Computing

Converting to client-server technology is distracting many computer centers from·other opportunities for service improvement and expense reduction. These opportunities include software reengineering, object technology, computer-aided software engineering (CASE) technology, rule-based system technology, and computer center automation. Client-server technology is considered state of the art, and mainframe and departmental computers have become passé. Yet it is difficult, at this point in its evolution, for client-server technology to accommodate the sheer bulk of more than thirty years of computing. Much of this computing is still paper based and batch oriented. Client-server technology does not adequately address the following:

Management tools: In a *Computerworld* interview, A. D. Little contended that there are few management tools for performance, capacity, scheduling and rerun control, change control, disaster recovery, tape management, storage management, and the management reporting requirements of modern computing.

Security: Centralized mainframe computer centers still struggle with security, and client-server technology exacerbates this struggle by opening new vistas of opportunity for security violations.

Software development: It is suggested that developing software by means of client-server technology is less expensive than development by means of traditional methods. This has yet to be demonstrated, and it is almost certainly untrue. Regardless, management is not likely to write a blank check based on vague promises. The initial cost of conversion is high. Training, consultant fees, and rewriting COBOL code into another language are expensive. Finally, the life expectancy of client-server hardware is short, and the real cost of replacement is yet to be determined.

Connectivity: Employees in different functional areas need to share information. Yet it is common for the interoperability of different computing platforms to make communication complex and problems nearly impossible to isolate. Organizations want to reduce complexity, not create it. They continue to rely on mainframe-based control, standards, and security for mission-critical applications. They are too slow to move away from it.

Batch processing: From 40 to 60 percent of all computer processing is batch oriented. Most organizations have not assimilated the concept of electronic information, for example electronic reporting, electronic data interchange/ electronic funds transfer (EDI/EFT), electronic signatures, electronic vaults, and electronic mail into their operating procedures. Organizations continue to input paper-based documents into computers and output billions of pages of print. Client-server technology is not batch oriented. It is not likely to ever be batch oriented, nor do we want it to be.

Some things will change immediately. Many applications can take advantage of the new technology. However, mainframe and departmental computing is not going to be immediately mothballed in favor of client-server technology. In the meantime, reengineering of legacy systems as an alternative to client-server technology continues to be one of the best business strategies.

Mainframe and departmental hardware and software providers are not going to roll over and play dead. They will compete with client-server technology by improving the price performance of mainframe hardware and by reducing the cost of software. It is already happening. Reengineering a computer center and its legacy systems while strategically introducing client-server technology could result in both optimum service improvement and expense reduction.

12.1 Reengineering Legacy Systems

If information service is to continue to play an active role in the effort to better control cost, then application system reengineering should be included as part of its overall computing architecture. This section describes an approach for maintaining and repositioning legacy systems to make them more cost effective and competitive. This approach can achieve substantial benefits by refurbishing newer systems that go through several modifications or use loose standards.

To make more information available in less time, information service departments implemented a variety of proprietary technologies, developed new systems, and added capabilities to existing ones. The amount of system integration, development, and maintenance activity required to accomplish this left them with little time to properly care for the base of aging legacy systems.

Legacy systems are often in a state of disrepair, suffering from the use of outmoded technologies and years of changes at the hands of different information service personnel. For many companies, these systems age with few, if any, improvements to the program structure, complexity, or hardware and software technologies. New systems frequently are easier to use, more flexible to modify, and operate more efficiently than legacy systems. Unfortunately, no staffing is applied to bring legacy systems up to standard.

The tide is turning. Emphasis is being placed on expense reduction and improved financial performance. Information service budgets are being cut, business processes and computer systems are being reengineered, application systems are moving away from centralized computer centers and rehosted in operating divisions using departmental computers, and computing is being outsourced or downsized to client-server technology.

When the expense of maintaining legacy systems is evaluated, it is apparent that management must seriously consider system reengineering as an integral component of cost containment and business process reengineering. This section addresses an approach to maintain and reposition legacy systems to align them with system goals that are cost effective and competitive.

12.1.1 System and Business Process Reengineering

The increasing popularity of business process reengineering has placed greater pressure on information service to keep pace with similar system reengineering projects. A study done by G2 Research, Incorporated, projected that the total market for business process reengineering would grow from $5.3 billion in 1992 to $12.5 billion in 1997. The computer system reengineering market was expected to grow from $17.6 billion to $39.8 billion in the same period. Companies maintain and reposition legacy systems to make them more cost effective, competitive, and easy to use, freeing resources to support activities associated with business process reengineering.

The normal profile for legacy systems is as follows:

► They are usually more than seven years old.

► They may or may not be mission critical.

► They entail outmoded or varied proprietary technologies.

► They have poorly structured program code.

► They have ineffective reporting systems.

► They make inefficient use of application development and user resources.

To further complicate these systems, the original design and development teams have changed, leaving the current support team without a complete understanding of the detailed operation of the system. In other words, legacy systems are usually the systems that everyone fears and no one wants to support.

12.1.2 The Reengineering Process

Reengineering encapsulates an entire system, regardless of size or complexity. Reengineering also provides the information service department with the ability to evaluate its functional and technical attributes and recondition the system to improve cost and maintainability. The process comprises five key phases: preliminary inventory analysis, encapsulation, application analysis, production standardization, and design recovery. Each phase is defined briefly as follows:

Preliminary inventory analysis: The scope of the reengineering effort is determined, such as the systems to include, and the priorities of the systems to be reengineered are established.

Encapsulation: An inventory of the components of a system is generated.

Application analysis: Applications are evaluated according to three aspects, as follows:

—Functional fulfillment

—Technical quality

—Fit with the information service strategic plan

Production standardization: Many past mistakes are eliminated and an understanding of the functional and technical aspects of the system is provided.

Design recovery: Detailed system documentation is provided, and the application software to be reversed and forward engineered is positioned.

The results of the reengineering effort, together with other forces that influence the strategic direction of a system, are used to determine the reengineering strategy for a system. Reengineering improves the performance and maintainability of a system and incorporates internal and external business forces.

12.1.3 Preliminary Inventory Analysis

Before reengineering begins, a preliminary analysis of the existing systems is performed to determine the overall scope of the reengineering effort. This analysis is an abbreviated version of the encapsulation and application analysis phases.

During preliminary inventory analysis, the inventory of applications is quantified and analyzed to determine which systems should be included or excluded from the project. It is not necessary to develop a detailed inventory of the system components. Information service should, however, determine the approximate number of executable jobs, procedures, and programs for each system.

While conducting the analysis, information services has the opportunity to evaluate the quality of each system and to estimate the amount of time required to complete the four remaining phases. From this analysis, a detailed project work plan is developed for the remaining phases.

12.1.4 Encapsulation

Encapsulation is essential to reengineering because it ensures that the system components (for example, job control, program source, load modules, copybooks) are identified. An accurate component inventory must be developed before the analysis is begun. Although it is possible to include components in the inventory after the analysis has begun, the inventory may be expensive to reproduce.

After the inventory is completed, it may be necessary to verify that the modules executed in production are the same as those identified in the inventory. Ways to verify the quality and integrity of the inventory include reviewing source edit statistics, equating source modules to load modules, and system testing.

The extent of the effort required to develop an accurate inventory is inversely related to the quality of the controls provided within the information service change-management procedures. For example, a change management procedure that incorporates excellent controls requires less inventory and verification effort than one with few controls.

Encapsulation is conducted to identify all possible system components and shakes out those that are not a part of the system. Although several software tools are available to assist defining the component inventory, using a combination of both manual and automated analyses provides the most accurate inventory in the least amount of time. This usually is accomplished by means of manual digging through the system to identify libraries that contain misplaced system components and by using the automated tools to piece together the remaining components.

Encapsulation establishes a definitive inventory of all system components. The inventory alone may reduce information service expenses associated with analyzing the production and departmental libraries and any other activities that may be required to locate the components that satisfy a user's special request. The accuracy of the system analysis required by a new development or maintenance activity may be improved because all system components have been identified and are easily located.

12.1.5 Application Analysis

Although reengineering presents the opportunity for information service to improve the performance, maintainability, and cost of a legacy system, it shortsightedly does not include a more strategic review of these systems. This initial review should be conducted to evaluate systems according to three primary attributes, as follows:

► Ability to support the functional requirements of the users of the system

► System design and use of technology

► Conformance with the information service architecture and strategy

Evaluation of these three criteria provides insight about the value that the system provides to the business. A system that adequately supports the business needs of the user but operates with outmoded technology is more valuable than one that provides little or no functional support to an organization but operates with all of the latest technology. To complete the analysis, the functional and technical attributes of the system are mapped to the information service strategic systems plan to determine the reengineering strategy for the system. The system target chart in Figure 12.1 is an example of this system mapping.

The forces that influence the reengineering strategy must be considered because they may directly affect the order in which revitalization activities are performed. For example, if the business strategy is to outsource information service operations, management should focus the information service effort on activities that maximize use of resources. This focus achieves lower operational costs for production systems. Specific areas of focus include utilization of central processing units, utilization of disks and tapes, on-line performance, database efficiency, system backup and restoration procedures, and documentation. The sector in which a system is placed in Figure 12.1 provides a basis for formulating a system reengineering strategy.

Targeting the Reengineering Strategy

The system target chart (see Figure 12.1) is a single representation of two separate charts that are blended to communicate reengineering alternatives for

Figure 12.1
*System Target
Chart*

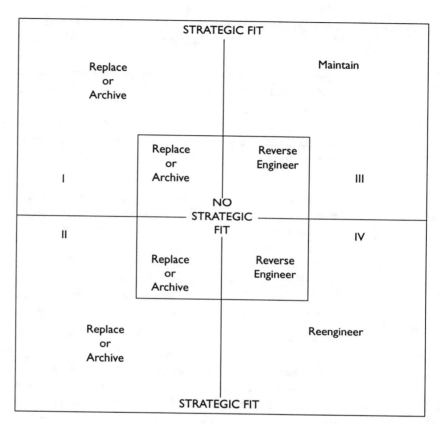

one or more systems. One chart evaluates the technical and functional attributes of the system, and the second chart evaluates the core competencies of the system to determine strategic importance. Positioning a system within a sector provides a basis for formulating the best-fit reengineering strategy.

Each system is rated on the basis of the information gathered during the preliminary inventory analysis and encapsulation phases of reengineering. In general, systems that fall into quadrants I or II provide little functional support to an organization and therefore are considered less valuable than systems that fall into quadrants III or IV.

System Target Analysis

The chart shows four quadrants (I to IV) and eight sectors (two sectors per quadrant). Sector positioning is based on the strategic fit of the system. Systems whose core competencies support the information service strategy are placed outside the inner square (the bull's-eye). Those that do not support the information service strategy are placed inside the square, regardless of the functional or technical rating of the system.

Quadrant I: Quadrant I of the system target chart (see Figure 12.1) represents systems that provide little functional support to the business and use outmoded technologies or are poorly designed and constructed. Systems in this sector that provide functional support but are technically obsolete need replacement. Systems in this sector that are functionally obsolete (for example, no longer support a business function) can be archived or deleted.

The following example illustrates this point. One organization maintained a system that relied on manual processes to collect revenue data in the form of paper receipts. It took fifteen to twenty business days for a data entry service bureau to enter the receipts into the system. Users complained that the system forced them iteratively to print reports, compute adjustments on a microcomputer before entry to the system, and reprint the reports to determine the net effect of the adjustment. Analyzing and modifying reports took a great deal of time, and in many cases, the users had to resort to building a new spreadsheet or database system to produce their own reports.

Systems in a similar state of disrepair are fairly common. Quadrant I systems usually consume considerable information service resources and increase user frustration. In the example, considerable time was required to produce the manual receipts and compare the computerized reports with the manual receipts. This system was replaced with a new automated data collection system that used a relational database on the mainframe computer. A new conversational interface was written to assist users with the on-line processes, and all remaining programs were reengineered to improve maintainability.

Quadrant II: Quadrant II of the target chart represents systems that provide little functional support to the business, but use current technologies or are well designed and constructed. Technology, no matter how advanced, has little value unless it supports a business requirement. Generally speaking, systems that provide functional support to a business should be replaced; those that do not can be archived or deleted. However, for those systems that do not fulfill functional requirements, the best alternative may be to salvage and redeploy technology components to new or other existing systems.

Quadrant III: Systems that fall into quadrant III or quadrant IV support the business functions performed by the organization. They provide the greatest flexibility with regard to alternative system strategies because they provide more business support than quadrant I and quadrant II systems. Although both quadrant III and quadrant IV systems support the functional requirements of the business, only quadrant III systems use current technologies, are well-designed and constructed, and use information services resources efficiently.

Quadrant III represents systems that provide the best functional and technical support to the business. These systems are usually the most cost-effective users of information service resources. Supporting the strategic system plan, quadrant III systems are best positioned for the future and should continue to be maintained as usual. Systems that fall within the bull's-eye are positioned to be reverse engineered to take advantage of other technologies, such as client-server hardware, database software, and communication technology.

A simplified example of a quadrant III system is an on-line purchasing system that satisfies the user's functional requirements, is well designed and coded, is easy to maintain, and uses information service resources efficiently. If the system were based on a CA-IDMS database using CICS for communication that corresponded to the strategic system plan, it would be positioned outside the quadrant III bull's-eye and therefore would be maintained as is. If, however, the strategic system plan called for a sweeping conversion to an Oracle database using UNIX, the system would be placed within the bull's-eye, and the system would be reverse engineered to convert the system to the new database architecture.

Quadrant IV: Quadrant IV systems satisfy the business functional requirements but do not score well on design, code construction, or use of technology. The prognosis for systems in this sector is still positive, however. If a quadrant IV system fits the strategic system plan (its position is outside the bull's-eye), the technologic components of the system support the strategy but the system design or construction is difficult to maintain.

Systems that fall into this category are usually reengineered. In the context of the target chart only, computer system reengineering differs from reverse engineering in that reengineering operates on a system at the source-code level, whereas reverse engineering operates on a system at a higher technical level, hardware platform, database architecture, or communication monitors. Reengineering implies improving the maintainability of a system by eliminating unused code, incorporating object programming techniques, and using reverse engineering software products.

These program-level changes may be made by automated or manual means. The use of automated tools speeds the modification process. When using these tools, however, the information service must review and test the regenerated source code to verify that system functionality is not altered. This method is the preferred approach for large source programs because manually converting large programs is extremely time consuming and requires the same level of verification as the automated tools.

Quadrant IV systems that do not fit the strategic system plan require more than code-level modifications. These systems usually require conversion to a new database or other technical architecture. In this case, systems are usually reverse engineered to reposition the system for the new architecture.

12.1.6 Production Standardization

The goal of production standardization is to revitalize the existing system after years of changes performed by different information service personnel using different programming techniques and styles. Revitalization transforms a legacy system into one that performs better, is easier and more cost effective to maintain and operate, and uses resources more efficiently. Nearly every information service organization has at least one system that can benefit from this revitalization process.

Reengineering allows information service to approach the system from two directions simultaneously: functional and technical. A functional knowledge of the system is required to identify and document the business attributes that are supported by the system. The technical aspect of this two-pronged approach provides information service with detailed knowledge of the processing within the system and the information necessary to improve the maintainability and performance of the system. Reengineering of legacy systems cannot be performed in a vacuum, especially production standardization.

To obtain an accurate functional understanding of a system, information service should meet with system users to determine the functions performed by the organization, the information required by the organization, and the information the organization currently receives from information service. The objectives are to determine the value users place on the system and the positive and negative functional and technical attributes of the system.

Information services simultaneously can initiate the activities that focus on analyzing and improving the technical aspects of the system. A preliminary analysis of several systems in the inventory can be performed to determine the areas that may benefit most from the use of automated tools. A word of caution before purchasing the newest tools: It is essential to ensure that the tools perform the functions needed to perform the analysis. For example, some tools can restructure program source code to improve system maintainability, document the structure of the system, and document input and output.

For one insurance company, this reengineering approach and the use of a purchased software package reduced the monthly financial closing time from 25 days to 5 days. For another company, converting tape data sets to disk and improvements in the disaster recovery process for one batch job improved processing time by nearly 3 hours.

When the reengineering effort is completed, information service has a system that is more cost effective to maintain and operate and is better positioned to react to internal and external business forces, such as outsourcing, downsizing, business process reengineering, or changes in government regulations. Production standardization provides benefits to information services and the business regardless of the priorities imposed by internal or external forces.

12.1.7 Design Recovery

The final phase of a reengineering effort is design recovery. Design recovery captures certain elements of the current system design, incorporates these elements into a CASE tool, and provides information service with the ability to accurately document the functional and technical aspects of the system. This repository of up-to-date system documentation does the following:

▶ Improves system analysis and maintenance time and cost

▶ Improves the learning curve for new information service personnel

▶ Provides a basis for engineering these systems more competitively in a CASE environment

The process of extracting and loading mainframe system design elements (for example, program names and their relation to other programs, data files and records, and data record attributes) to a personal computer or mainframe-based CASE tool is not always straightforward. Automated analysis and documentation tools designed to pass this information to other products (for example, CASE or data dictionary) are available. However, this is not necessarily a standard feature of these products. The element extraction process is simplified if this feature is available. Otherwise, an extraction program may be written to perform the extraction function.

The extraction process currently applies to data elements only. The processing or logic aspect of a system cannot yet be extracted and passed to the CASE tool. Some vendors are trying to develop this logic link between the system and the CASE tool, but such products are not expected to be commercially available in the near future.

The documentation produced from this phase provides insight into the functional purpose of the system, the main components of the system, the technology used to provide system functionality, the organizations that use the system, and the interfaces to other systems. This documentation can be used to support forward engineering, downsizing, outsourcing, and other information service reengineering strategies.

12.2 Conclusion

If information service is to continue to play an active role in the effort to control expenses, computing has to be integrated into the fabric of organizations. Organizations need to reengineer their business processes to better utilize the investment they have made in computing. This does not exclude the use of outsourcing, rehosting, or client-server technology. It should, however, include reengineering of legacy systems as part of the overall computing architecture.

Although this chapter targets legacy systems, information service also can achieve substantial benefits from reengineering newer systems that were developed with loose standards or were designed to replace manual systems without integrating computing into the fabric of the organization.

System reengineering presents information service professionals with an effective approach to maintenance because it reduces the operating costs of systems, improves system maintainability, and positions computing systems to support the information service architecture. It supports activities associated with business process reengineering, outsourcing, and converting to client-server technology. Computer center automation and reengineering of legacy systems avoid the expense of replacing a system with a purchased package that is in a similar state of disrepair or installing a new technology base when it is not required.

13

Client-Server Technology

Client-server architectures, together with modern methods for improving software, are changing the alternatives available for designing computer systems. Information service managers know that saving money is a corporate imperative and that converting to client-server technology is an idea that has a good shot at reducing expenses. Unfortunately, the managers often do not have enough information to come up with sound, implementable architectures to be used during reengineering.

Part of this problem is that the industry uses term *downsizing* rather than the term *converting*. The term *downsizing* is used so loosely that almost any vendor can claim that its product should be part of a downsizing solution. The purpose of this chapter is to clear up that confusion so that information service managers can correctly identify opportunities for reengineering application systems to client-server technology on the basis of fact, not rhetoric.

Microprocessors are the building blocks not only of individual personal computing but also of larger, more powerful client-server systems. These systems can be large personal computers with multiple microprocessors, which are generally used as servers. A more interesting and flexible approach is to use personal computers as building blocks of a larger system. An approach to doing this is to reengineer from a time-shared mainframe approach to a client-server solution. In this environment, both the clients and the servers are fully independent computers capable of performing certain processing tasks. This independence and processing power differentiate the client-server environment from other kinds of multi-user systems.

For example, most time-shared systems have all processing performed with a central large computer. If mainframe-attached desktop terminals are replaced with personal computers, users may be confused into believing that this is client-server computing. In reality, all that has happened, in most cases, is that the personal computer has been turned into an expensive terminal. It is critical to keep this distinction in mind when considering computing options.

13.1 Strategic Direction

Client-server technology is touted as the solution to virtually every problem faced by information service managers. Common sense, however, tells professionals that this is not true. This leaves information service managers in a quandary. Because it seems as if everyone in the business world is talking about changing architecture to client-server systems, those who do not take a good, long look at this alternative to host computing risk being considered out of step with the times.

Nevertheless, an information service manager who rushes to adopt this technology without doing a thorough assessment finds that its value to the organization is limited or that the approach is inappropriate for a particular application. The manager also may find that the organization simply was not ready to make the move to client-server computing.

The key is to assess accurately whether changing architecture is the right approach for the organization. It well may be, if the following criteria are met:

▶ The organization has large development backlogs, and users report an inability to participate in the development process.

▶ Computing costs are over budget.

▶ The data and analysis belong to dozens of groups of users, many of whom are eager to have better tools and more control.

▶ Although data may have to be stored centrally, frequently updated copies are distributed to users more easily and economically than by giving them direct access to the data on a single shared computer.

On the other hand, an organization is a much less suitable candidate for changing architecture to client-server technology if it falls into one of the following categories:

▶ The organization has a large computing problem that has to be run as a single database. In this case, an organization might want to consider the new parallel computing solutions that are coming along in the client-server market.

▶ The organization has serious security problems.

▶ The organization recently implemented one or more large mission-critical mainframe-based applications.

▶ The organization is not ready to put personal computers on all users' desks.

Keep in mind that a firm may not be ready for downsizing to client-server technology, but client-server technology may be useful for a new application or upsizing the desktop environment. A mix-and-match approach is fine. It may be a good way to gain eventual permission to evolve into changing the architecture in an organization that otherwise finds it a threatening concept. There are many roads to the future, and there are many shortfalls in the technology today that will not be there tomorrow.

13.2 Evolving Technology

The personal computer allows more people than ever before to share in the benefits of computing at continually lower costs. For example, the terms *upsizing, rightsizing,* and *downsizing* are currently used casually to cover conversion to a variety of technologies and processes. To help clarify this situation, the following definitions are provided. Organizations can help dispel confusion by insisting on precise use of these terms by suppliers, consultants, and analysts.

13.2.1 Upsizing

Upsizing occurs when personal computers and networks that may already be connected in noncomplex systems (such as printer sharing) are upgraded with servers, more robust network operating systems, and system-level applications. This process takes place naturally as users reach the limits of their current system, identify new technologies to solve their business problems, and grow toward larger, more complex solutions. Some organizations do this with little or no planning, and their systems reflect that lack of forethought. Other organizations are well aware of the change that is occurring and have mechanisms in place to guide that change such as architectures and reengineering.

13.2.2 Rightsizing

Rightsizing occurs when an organization selects the correct architectural solution for its computing needs. This frequently happens when an organization is solving a problem with a new system rather than fine-tuning or expanding an existing system. It is easier to move to a new architecture when the organization is writing on a clean slate.

13.2.3 Downsizing

Downsizing happens when a computing solution involves moving down in computing size and cost but not necessarily in power, for example, from a time-shared approach on a mainframe computer or minicomputer to a client-server solution. Because downsizing involves substantial changes, it is the most difficult of the three growth patterns to manage. This is especially true because downsizing may involve eliminating jobs, retraining employees, changing vendors, and rewriting mission-critical software applications. To be worth this much pain, the rewards should be great.

13.3 Client-Server Strategy

The next generation of information processing systems encompasses many attributes and configurations; all are characterized by the following properties:

▶ To maximize throughput and improve the economics of delivery, computing power is distributed among mainframe computers, departmental computers such as UNIX minicomputers, or proprietary computers such the Digital Equipment Corporation VAX or Hewlett-Packard 3000 and servers, and personal computers.

▶ Systems depend on many different services and new technologies in addition to the traditional DB2-style databases. These new elements include object request brokers, transaction processors, relational and object-oriented databases, and graphical user interfaces such as the X Window System.

▶ Users are directly involved in the specification, design, and building of client applications. At the same time, information service maintains control over corporate information resources.

▶ Clients can be intelligent, and as much processing as possible is off-loaded to them.

▶ Maintenance costs are lowered and reusability is increased through the use of object-oriented technology.

▶ Clients can move to a variety of different types of machines, for example, personal computers, X-terminals, and UNIX workstations.

▶ Many systems from different vendors operate harmoniously on a variety of platforms.

These properties of software systems augment the following traditional requirements and expectations of information service professionals:

▶ Information service must retain control of enterprise-wide information systems.

▶ The systems must provide fast and secure transactions based on enterprise data and must support multiple users.

- The systems must integrate smoothly with the software systems already in place.

- The systems must provide a uniform development environment that supports multiple developers.

- The systems must provide clean and effective integration with computer-aided software engineering (CASE) tools and methods.

The IntelliCorp KAPPA client-server architecture is an example of an architecture that addresses such requirements. It provides information service with client-server tools to integrate into an installed base of mainframe computers, personal computers, and UNIX servers and workstations based on IntelliCorp object-oriented development tools on both personal computer and UNIX platforms.

13.4 The Client-Server Model

The client-server model starts with a personal computer and a development system. The model consists of three parts, as follows:

- The client architecture comprises a development environment and a deployment facet. The client development environment provides end-user interface development, logic, desktop integration, and server subscription tools. This environment yields deployable clients to provide local intelligence and data and access to local data servers. It also provides a module for communicating with servers of various types.

- Servers are typically responsible for the primary logic operations, access to enterprise data, enterprise modeling, and reasoning components of applications. The server becomes the focal point for group programming and software development, both for building clients and for new services. The server mediates multi-user and multi-developer support of the system and integration with version management software, transaction processing tools, CASE tools, and so forth. The server also provides a number of tools for publishing the services it provides to the network, including communication protocols and an object request broker.

- The communication and network module provides a transport-independent protocol for communication between clients and servers. It also provides uniform access to a heterogeneous mix of other hosts and servers on the network for servers and clients.

13.5 Scenarios

One possible configuration of the client-server architecture is the three-tier architecture, as follows:

▶ Clients running on personal computers or workstations

▶ Servers running on UNIX workstations, minicomputers, or other computer servers

▶ Other servers running on mainframe computers or minicomputers

13.5.1 Client Processing Scenario

The typical processing cycle of a client is the following:

1. Present a screen to the user and wait for input.

2. Analyze user requests and decide which actions to take. This analysis is performed on the client.

3. Retrieve data, if required, from local desktop data.

4. Request other required data and computing services from servers.

5. Wait for and collect responses from servers.

6. Analyze responses from servers and draw conclusions (client-side processing).

7. Respond to the user by updating the screen.

In steps 2 and 6 of the cycle, the client performs various kinds of analysis and processing. This is an important feature of clients. They contain local processing power. In step 3 the client uses its own data access capabilities to retrieve data stored locally. In steps 4 and 5 the client uses servers provided on the network. Opening and maintaining the required communication links with these servers is made possible by the communication module.

13.5.2 Server Processing Scenario

A typical processing cycle for a server is as follows:

1. The server is initiated and registers its existence and its services with the network manager, or the network manager receives a request from a client for a particular service and initiates and registers the appropriate server.

2. The server waits for connections from one or more clients through the network manager.

3. The server receives client requests, procedure calls, or object request broker services.

4. The server unpacks and analyzes the request and performs the operation, accesses a relational database management system (RDBMS), invokes other services from other servers, and performs compute-intensive logic. It then packages the response and communicates it back to the requesting client.

5. As the server loads and unloads modules or applications, it informs the network manager of the changes in services that it provides.

6. At any point after satisfying a service request from a client, the server can start over at step 2 or terminate with appropriate de-registering of services at the network manager.

Servers are managed asynchronously by the network manager (step 1). In step 4, servers are able to act as clients to other servers, provide services themselves, or do both.

13.6 Client Architecture

A client application is a program with which users interact that allows them to use services provided by one or more servers. A client manages the end-user interface, input verification, and desktop integration components of the application. It may also perform local logic processing and access data on local databases. An important goal of the client architecture is to provide a common set of end-user interface construction tools that allows clients to be portable across all platforms.

13.6.1 Client Development Environment

The client development environment provides an easy-to-use graphical interface for programming, including object and application browsers, programming language editors, and debugging tools. The development environment also provides end-user interface development tools, desktop integration or data access tools, and a browser interface to the network manager's server subscription capabilities. The interface with the network manager allows client developers and users to specify which services they require and to learn which services are available on the network.

13.6.2 End-User Interface Construction

The client architecture provides the following capabilities for constructing client end-user interfaces. These end-user capabilities are portable to all platforms. A *common end-user interface* toolkit contains general window capabilities, including drawing and forms, menus, and tables. A *graphical end-user interface* (EUI) definition and layout tool allows the developer to create and lay out EUI components interactively. With this tool, the user creates components by picking icons from a template. These components may then be sized and positioned with use of a mouse. The properties are set with specialized dialogue boxes or tables. The definition and layout tool allows the developer to use graphics to select, create, position, size, and generally define properties of any EUI component. This tool greatly simplifies the task of creating an EUI and allows easy and rapid manipulation, modification, and management of the EUI components.

13.7 Server Architecture

The server architecture is composed of a number of server engines. These communicate through a protocol mediated by the network manager with client applications. These applications may be written with the client architecture, as described earlier, or they may be proprietary applications.

All server functionality is available to the server's client. The server side of an application is typically responsible for the primary logic operations, access to enterprise data, enterprise modeling, and the reasoning components of the application. All of this is in response to requests from clients. During system development, it is also the focal point for group programming and multi-user support. It also integrates with elements such as version management software, transaction processing tools, and CASE tools, both for developing new services and for developing clients.

The server provides the basic functionalities required by applications, including the following:

▶ Object management and persistence

▶ Mapping and access to RDBMS

▶ Pattern matching object languages (Structure Query Language [SQL] for objects)

▶ Rule-based systems

▶ Application management facilities, code development, multi-user access, and access to version management

▶ Object covers for legacy systems, such as CASE encyclopedias and transaction monitors

13.7.1 Server Invocation

In general a server is initiated as a process on a network. Initiation is explicit by means of direct start-up or implicit by means of a client's request for services that the server provides. The server registers itself and its services with the network manager.

13.8 Communication Architecture

Client-server communication architecture is designed to provide two managers—a communication manager and an enterprise network manager. The communication manager provides communication between clients and servers, including intelligent routing of client requests to appropriate servers so the client need not specify which server is to handle a particular request. The communication manager also provides communication between systems, both clients and servers and other systems such as CICS, databases, object request brokers, or other servers. System and communication protocol may be any of a number of standard process-communication protocols.

The network manager knows about all clients and servers on the network, and initiates and terminates them as needed, routing communication between them, and serving as a registry for inquiries regarding available services.

13.9 When Client-Server Is Not Right

Client-server technology is not the correct answer to every question. It does not save as much over use of mainframe computers as organizations may think, nor is it necessarily the best fit for enterprise connectivity.

This hardly seems possible, given the fervor with which vendors are selling downsizing as a way to cut expenses. For some organizations, however, mainframes are the economical way to handle information. If an organization has a large number of terminals and low computer power requirements, staying with a mainframe computer makes sense. For example, an airline reservation system with thousands of agents and relatively modest computing requirements works well in a mainframe environment, as does a customer service center that uses computer power to answer billing questions.

Conversely, client-server technology wins when computing power requirements are high and the number of terminals or workstations is small. This is the case with computer-aided design and manufacturing operations that employ a small number of engineers who have huge computing requirements.

It all boils down to numbers—hardware and million instructions per second (MIPS) numbers. Specifically, a dumb terminal costs less than one third as much as a workstation, $300 versus $1,500, whereas the MIPS cost of a mainframe computer is about one hundred times more than that of a workstation, $50,000 versus $500. Keep in mind that the MIPS of a mainframe computer tend to be more productive than those of a server because mainframe processors are typically in use 24 hours a day, whereas companies confine server use to business hours.

If a decision based on these costs is too close to call, storage requirements and maintenance and support costs can be tie breakers. The rule is that client-server computing has the storage edge. At $2,000 per gigabyte it is about half the cost of mainframe direct-access storage devices. Mainframe computing, however, tends to do better in the support cost area.

Even with its lower cost per gigabyte, storage in the client-server world is not always the best bet, because the technology is not yet sophisticated enough to exploit this cost advantage. Although mainframe disk management systems let companies implement databases that reside on tens or even hundreds of disk drives, server technology requires that the entire database reside on a single disk drive. Essentially, the data is there but cannot be easily used.

In terms of support, client-server computing is going to cost information service about 20 to 30 percent more than mainframe computing. Client-server costs tend to be higher than those of mainframe computing for the following reasons:

1. Because client-server pushes computing to end users, many companies find they need more troubleshooters and graphical user interface experts to provide on-site assistance at disparate locations. Support costs often are hidden because end users actually do the support, to the detriment of their primary jobs. Companies that spend approximately $3,000 per user for client-server hardware and software spend five times that for intangibles such as peer and help-desk support. In contrast, mainframe end-user support is minimal, consisting typically of a help desk or dumb terminal replacement or upgrade.

2. Client-server software is layered and has a variety of interfaces. Organizations have to make provisions for a number of communication and connectivity packages. Network and communication links cry out for management. Hardware and software products need technical and staff support. Although annual lease costs of mainframe software can be steep, depending on the size of the platform and upgrade fees, they are not necessarily higher than the cost of client-server software.

Client-server software accumulates support costs that diminish its monetary advantage over large systems.

3. Client-server computing is a new area, so few professionals are experienced in managing and supporting client-server operations. Training costs to bring people up to speed are immense.

Because mainframe technology is mature, it is easier to hire people experienced in handling that environment. And staff members are aided by the variety of management tools for mainframe computers. There are products to handle areas such as system automation, performance monitoring, capacity planning, scheduling and rerun control, print management, library management, tape management, disk management, and security. In the client-server world, such tools are nonexistent or too young to be effective.

13.9.1 Enterprise Connectivity

Costs are not the only reason why information service managers stay with large systems. They also rely on the central control, standards, and security measures of a mainframe computer for mission-critical applications. For example, the IBM Systems Network Architecture (SNA) with its features for central oversight and control has been one way in which large information service shops provide uninterrupted information flow. Employees in different functional areas can share information without hassles.

Client-server computing sometimes can clog the information pipe because of the number of computing elements it requires. One recent demonstration of interoperability among four different computing platforms required fifty communication software packages.

Organizations want to reduce complexity, not create it. Besides staying with mainframe computing, they try the following approaches if client-server methods do not work:

▶ Use of departmental computers that store data primarily used in each department. If another department has occasional demand for data, its computers initiate the request via a data link to the departmental computer that contains the target data.

▶ Placing data on a series of specialized database servers connected by local area networks (LANs).

Chief information officers are looking for ways to balance the picture, which usually is tilted in favor of client-server technology. They do not want to avoid client-server just to avoid using a good technology for all the wrong reasons.

13.9.2 Alternative to Client-Server Computing

The story is familiar. The weak economy has put a company under extreme cost-cutting pressure. Management approaches the information system department because it has heard something called client-server computing would decrease costs by a large percentage right away. This is the situation facing the information service department at an electric utility that serves one of the largest urban areas in the United States. The target application is a customer information system used to prepare bills for 3.4 million customers and handle customer billing and service inquiries.

When it came down to it, information services found that client-server technology would not do much in terms of cutting costs. The company would take a hit replacing its 1,300 terminals with workstations that were twice as expensive. The mainframe was in its element. The organization had a large number of terminals and low processing needs. The database used CICS and consumed 11 percent of the mainframe's 83 MIPS (Figure 13.1).

Figure 13.1
Calculations

An electric utility wants to calculate hardware costs for operating a customer information system that produces 3.4 million electric bills per month, 5 million notices per year, and 2 million customer work orders per year. The system requires 9.1 MIPS (million instructions per second) and 40G bytes of DASD (direct access storage device). It uses the following equation:

(Cost of MIPS) + (Cost of DASD) + (Cost of terminals) = Total

Working under the assumption that dumb terminals cost one-third less than workstations, mainframe MIPS cost about 100 times more than workstation MIPS, and mainframe storage costs twice as much as client-server storage, the organization figures its mainframe hardware cost would be the following:

($50,000 × 9.1) + ($4,000 × 40) + ($500 × $1,300) = $1,265,000

Its cost in client-server technology would be the following:

($500 × 3 × 9.1) + ($2,000 × 40) + ($1,500 × 1,300) = $2,043,650

The adjustment in the cost of MIPS ($500 × 3 × 9.1) reflects the fact that mainframe computers are typically in use three times longer than workstations, 24 hours a day,

The information service decision to stay with the mainframe computer is not carved in stone. The service pledged to revisit client-server computing when business needs dictate changes to the functionality of the customer information system applications.

13.9.3 Preserving Investments with Gradual Downsizing

The nightmare for the information service group at a university started with a few end users working on Apple Computer, Inc., Macintosh computers. Before information service knew it, end users were moving off the mainframe computer and into workgroups of Macintosh computers at their own expense. Departments were building their own systems, storing redundant copies of mainframe data, and generating paper reports that had to be rekeyed into the mainframe.

Users were doing this for easy data access, screens they could navigate, and quick return on printed reports. At first, the administrative computing group was going to dump the 76 MIPS IBM 3090 mainframe computer and migrate applications to client-server platforms. Unfortunately, that move would have required a massive amount of resources, including new hardware and software platforms, considerable application rewrites and staff training, recruiting, and outplacement. It would have meant disruption of operations (including compromise of data security, backup, and disaster recovery) and caused system incompatibility. Of most concern was the lack of capacity planning and performance monitoring plaguing the client-server world.

By introducing selective and phased-in migration to client-server platforms, information service gave users what they wanted without destroying the infrastructure of the information service organization. In this way, information service preserved the mainframe investment and avoided maintenance and operational risks involved in a wholesale changeover. It also readied itself for downsizing in the future. The school is in the midst of a pilot project to improve end-user reporting and provide better end-user tools, including graphical user interfaces.

13.10 Conclusion

A client-server architecture provides a number of advantages for organizational computing. In particular, using a uniform object-oriented architecture for both the client and the server provides a large amount of leverage for all aspects of the application development process from analysis, through design and implementation, to maintenance and reusability.

The following list summarizes some of the advantages of the client-server architecture:

▶ Processing power on both client and server sides

▶ Object representation on both client and server sides

▶ Logic and transaction processing on both client and server sides as needed

▶ Uniform object-based engines on both client and server sides

▶ Application management facilities as an integral part of development facilities

▶ Peer-to-peer communication between clients and servers enabling true distributed processing

▶ Ability to interface with UNIX-based transaction processing monitors

▶ Tools for creating and managing distributed applications

▶ Dynamic and extensible EUI with dynamic objects behind it

▶ Data access on client

▶ Powerful development tools on both client and server sides

▶ Object system models for business processes and software

▶ Integration of heterogeneous systems

▶ Integration and enhancement of legacy code

14

Object Technology

Software development is expensive. The dream of software developers has always been to get results in less time for lower cost. The search for tools to accomplish this objective has produced database management systems, query systems, screen development tools, fourth-generation languages (4GLs), graphic programming aids, and code generators. The ultimate dream, however, is to find ways to avoid programming altogether. The best way to not program is to reuse existing code.

The most effective tools already in use are effective because they reuse code. For example, using database management systems, programmers need not develop their own access routines as they did in the past. The developers of object-oriented programming languages and tools promise to take the reuse of code to new levels. There are, however, ongoing debates about the benefits and potential problems associated with object-oriented programming.

Business is demanding a completely new level of integration between new computer technologies and installed systems, the legacy of past computing successes. As a result, information services departments are being driven to remake themselves into smaller, leaner organizations that provide open information service and support for a multitude of small distributed systems. Mainframe computers are giving way to personal computers, servers, and workstations that are networked together. These new distributed systems provide the central processing unit power necessary to process and analyze data from the many sources demanded by organizations searching for a competitive edge.

Rather than providing reports, information technology professionals are asked to support faster business practices by engineering new systems that integrate many different types of company information in real time. The days of evaluating programmers on the basis of lines of code rather than delivery of usable functions are disappearing. Moreover, integration and the reengineering of existing systems must be accomplished without downgrading current service.

This chapter is an exploration of the current use of object technology and its utility in solving business problems in a wide range of companies. Some companies are using object technology as a new approach to building systems; others are reengineering new and old systems into business decision making.

The movement toward wide-scale adoption of object technology in support of a more integrated approach to computing is well underway. Although final results are not available, an unambiguous picture is emerging. Properly staffed, planned, and implemented object technology–based projects are demonstrating results superior to those of traditionally planned and implemented systems in terms of flexibility, user satisfaction, and cost.

14.1 Defining Object Technology

Object technology has been around since its invention in 1969 by Dr. Kristin Nygaard of Norway. At the time, Dr. Nygaard was trying to model a Norwegian fjord and the movement of the ships passing through it. The combination of ship movements, tides, waves, and the irregular coastline made the problem extremely difficult until Nygaard hit on the idea of first modeling each component as a single, autonomous element and then modeling the relations or interactions among the elements. In this way, he could address the dynamic nature of the problem in a way that allowed for a flexible and economical approach to the amount of code needed.

Before the introduction of object technology, and continuing through today, computer programs separated procedures, what you want to do, from data, what the procedures need to operate on. This was the most efficient approach because a programmer could reuse the data by applying many different programs.

Object technology retains the efficiency of reuse but reverses the former process by combining the data and procedures into a single entity called an *object*. Once created, an object can continue to exist, making it easier to find, change, and reuse in other applications. An object is any piece of software that can reasonably support the concept of a name. A more formal definition addresses the need for procedures, sometimes called *methods*, to be resident with some form of data.

14.1.1 Large or Small

Software objects may be either large or small. A grain of sand and Earth are two objects quite different in size and complexity, yet they are both objects. The correct size, or granularity, of objects for the task at hand is important in the design or implementation of object-based systems. It is helpful to think of systems as being composed of objects that have behaviors, support interactions, and relationships rather than as procedures that operate on data. This makes it possible to model real-world objects to duplicate their behavior and characteristics.

14.1.2 Attributes and Methods

Objects also have attributes and methods. This means that they have within themselves a certain number of characteristics, including, for example, color and hardness. They are also capable of actions, such as floating or sinking in the case of boats. Once an object is created, it exists in relation to other objects. Objects are arranged hierarchically in classes according to their dominant characteristics. The class *boat* includes sailboats, rowboats, canoes, and other types of boats. Each type may have subclasses, for example, powered, sailed, or rowed.

14.1.3 Inheritance

Two other widely discussed aspects of object technology are inheritance and polymorphism. Inheritance can be thought of as a technical ditto-plus function. For example, object sailboat is exactly like object boat with the addition of being powered by a sail; all other attributes are the same. A programmer can simply note one object as inheriting all the characteristics of another plus some special feature without having to duplicate all the code in each object. Inheritance is a benefit for programmers because it reduces the amount of code that goes toward duplicating what went before. This reduces errors and may result in faster operation.

14.1.4 Polymorphism

Polymorphism allows an instruction to be given to an object in the form of a generalized rather than a specific, detailed command. If the command given is "move," the object knows that movement is one of its behaviors and how specifically it may move. The simple "move" command is translated differently by the captain of a sailboat, a rower in a racing shell, and the pilot of a tugboat. Although their specific actions, which are internal to their objects, are different, the results are the same—their boats move.

14.1.5 Reuse

Reuse is another important concept. Unfortunately, computer programming, unlike most human endeavors since the mid 1700s, has remained relatively unaffected by the concept of standardized, interchangeable parts. Programmers continue to be rated on the lines of code they generate each day, not the number of programs completed or flexibility for future modification. A key part of the attraction of object technology is that once an object is created, tested, and found useful, it can be cloned and used repeatedly. This has the potential to save software developers untold time, because it saves them from reinventing the wheel.

Reuse also allows substantial reduction in mistakes. Construction of an application from tested, reused parts lessens the possibility of error in the parts and relegates testing to the design and assembly of the correct objects. To attain meaningful levels of reuse, however, a strict design and architectural approach to building and assembling objects must be established. After all, on Henry Ford's assembly line, an exact specification for each part of the tin lizzie was produced, and then each part was given tolerances and shown in its connection to all the other parts that together constituted the Model T. Just as producing parts was not good enough for Henry Ford in the 1920s, it is also not enough now for software assemblies based on object technology. The key is understanding that the scope of the problem extends into the design and architecture of systems and not just the production of objects.

14.2 Benefits

One concern is that objects require continuous maintenance and enhancement to keep up with the changing needs of the business. However, software has always required maintenance. Another concern is that the analysis task required to identify and define appropriate objects is formidable. Advocates of object-oriented programming respond that the best software development efforts result from spending more time in the definition and specification phases; in addition, developers can reuse objects for long-term savings.

Proponents of object-oriented programming point out that the need to define classes and subclasses of objects, the objects themselves, and the attributes, messages, methods, and interrelationships of objects, forces a better model of the system to be developed. Many objects developed in object-oriented programming code are not reused; however, the real benefit is that object-oriented programming code is usually more understandable and well organized than traditional coding methods. The process that forces analysts to define the object hierarchies makes them more familiar with the business that uses the application.

When these problems and objections are analyzed, many of them can be discounted; however, some remain. Viewed in isolation, object-oriented programming is simply an attractive way to facilitate structured, self-documenting, highly maintainable, and reusable code. It fosters reengineering and extends the life of applications. In the context of enterprise-wide application building, however, object-oriented programming presents unique challenges the solutions of which require additional tools and management methods.

14.3 Object-Oriented Programming

As object-oriented techniques gradually find a place in programming departments, there will be attempts to expand the use of this technology from single applications to broad suites of applications and from the sharing of objects among a limited group of application developers to use by application developers and users throughout the organization. To accomplish this expansion of use, object-oriented programming will have to be used within a development framework that is composed of computer-aided software engineering (CASE) tools implemented in a distributed, cooperative processing environment.

A likely scenario of the way that organizations will want to use object-oriented programming is as follows:

▶ Objects will be used by decentralized development groups to create applications that are logically related to one another and that impose common definitions (for example, standards) by various levels of the organization.

▶ Users will use objects to develop limited extensions of basic applications or build local applications, in much the same way spreadsheets and query systems are currently used. Users may access corporate databases in this environment through objects that encapsulate authorized user views of information.

▶ Object-oriented programming will become integrated with CASE platforms not only through the inclusion of object-capable languages but also through repositories of objects that contain both the objects themselves and the definitions of the objects and their permitted use. Improved CASE tools that can be used to manage and control versions and releases of objects as well as programs are needed.

This scenario envisions optimum use and benefit from object-oriented programming through extensive reuse of proved code within a framework that allows authorized access to objects. The current status of object-oriented programming makes this scenario difficult to implement. The effective use of object-oriented programming depends on the ability to solve problems related to two main areas of concern: management of the object inventory and preservation of information security in an object-oriented development environment.

14.4 Managing the Object Inventory

Objects in the inventory must reside in a repository that involves an object-oriented database management system. Objects are identified according to classes and subclasses. This identification provides a means of inventory management. For example, retrieving an object within a class called Accounts Payable would help to narrow the domain being searched for the object. A further narrowing is done by finding a subclass called Vendor's Invoice, and so forth. Polymorphism allows the same object name to be used in different contexts, so the object Unit Price could be used within the context of the Vendor's Invoice subclass and the Purchase Order subclass. Some relational database management systems also allow polymorphism.

Several problems arise as a result of this organizational method. To take advantage of the reusability of objects, the user must be able to find the object with as little effort as possible. Within the classification scheme for a relatively straightforward application, this does not appear to present a substantial problem.

Most organizations undertake the development of applications on an incremental basis. That is, they do not attempt to develop all applications at once. Furthermore, retroactive analysis and description of the data and process flows of the entire organization have failed repeatedly. By the time all the analysis is completed, the users have lost patience with the information technology department.

It is feasible to limit objects to an application domain. However, limiting objects to use within the narrow domain of a single application may substantially reduce opportunities for reuse. This means that developers will have to predict, to the extent possible, the potential use of an object to ensure its maximum utility.

14.4.1 Cross-Application Issues

It is possible to establish a class of objects that may be called cross-application objects. Such objects are the same regardless of the context within which they were designed to be used. For example, the treatment of data related to a specific account in the corporate chart of accounts may always be the same. The word *account* appears in many contexts and uses throughout a business. Therefore, another approach to this problem is that some objects may be assigned an attribute of cross-application usability.

As more object-oriented applications are created, the typical repository is not able to serve the needs of users for retrieving objects. Analysts and programmers who are required to move from one application to another to perform their work may find the proliferation of objects to be overwhelming. Information services has to develop taxonomies of names and definitions to allow effective retrieval.

Developing and maintaining a taxonomy is a massive effort. For example, a large nuclear engineering company realized that the nuclear power plants it had designed were to be decommissioned and dismantled in 50 years. The personnel responsible for dismantling a plant needed to know all about the plant's 50 years of maintenance to avoid potential contamination of the environment and injury to themselves. The company discovered that various names were used for identical parts, materials, and processes in the average plant. Because the plants were built throughout the world, these objects had names in many different languages. If personnel could not name an object, they could not find the engineering drawings or documents that described the object. Furthermore, if they searched for only the most likely names, they would overlook information that was stored under a different name.

A taxonomy project was initiated to adopt and use standard terminology for all components of the plant and all information related to those components. Within two years, a massive volume was assembled; however, several problems surfaced. It was impossible to know when the taxonomy would be complete. New terms had to be created to avoid duplication. The taxonomy manual was so large that engineers and other employees refused to use it. This example illustrates one dimension of the problem of naming and defining objects. In a world of increasingly distributed processing and decentralized use of computing, information technology departments must also consider that analysts and programmers are not under centralized control in all instances and that other personnel, such as engineers, clerical staff, and knowledge workers, use objects to create their own programs.

14.4.2 Retrieval Methods

The ability of users to develop their own programs and applications is one of the greatest benefits that can be obtained from object-oriented programming—it cannot be ignored. Nor can the demands of an increasingly computer-literate clientele be refused. This means that methods for retrieving objects must be available to all users for a relatively small amount of effort. If not, objects will not be reused.

With users as a recognized component of the management problem, another concern emerges. Objects not only must cross application domains but also must exist at various levels of the organization. For example, an object may be defined as applicable throughout the corporation in a given context. Such an object may be called a *corporate object* either because it is in a class of corporate objects or because it has a standard attribute as a corporate object. Another object may be applicable only within a specific strategic business unit and may be called, for example, an Assembly Company object. At the next level, an object may be called a Manufacturing Division object. Objects can be described in this manner down to the level of the desktop or the computer-controlled machine tool.

Two types of tools may come to partial rescue in solving this problem. Text search and retrieval systems may provide the ability to allow users to search for objects within various contexts. The result, however, can be retrieval of many possible objects from a repository, compelling the user to evaluate them before a selection is possible. An approach is needed that allows users to obtain a limited number of possible objects to solve a problem and yet does not force the organization to develop a taxonomy or limit the use of terms. Self-indexing of files for nonhierarchical search may prove helpful, but this may mean using the object-oriented relational database management system (RDBMS) in a manner not compatible with its inherent structure.

Regardless of the method used, there is a need to establish and maintain conformance to documentation standards for objects so that searches for objects return meaningful results. One possible solution is to use a rule-based (expert) system in conjunction with a text search and retrieval system. Rule-based systems can accomplish classification and are capable of supporting natural language interfaces. Ideally, the user describes to the system the nature of the object needed, and the system finds the most appropriate object. The user then describes the application at a high level, and the system finds and assembles all appropriate objects that fit the system context.

14.4.3 Object Maintenance

When objects are used throughout a large organization, it must be assumed that they reside in repositories on a variety of machines in many locations. Each of these repositories must be maintained in synchronization with the master repository of approved objects for the corporation and its divisions. Distributed environments imply additional problems that must be solved before object-oriented techniques can work successfully.

For example, if objects are automatically replaced with new versions, there must be a mechanism for scheduling the recompilation or relinking of programs that use the affected objects. If objects are used in an interpretive mode, replacement automatically affects their use in existing procedures, perhaps to the detriment of the application. Methods used to maintain distributed database concurrence and to control the distribution of personal computer programs throughout a network may be adapted to solve part of this problem. Another approach may adapt the messaging capabilities of objects to send notification of a potential change to any sub-object within the hierarchy of the object being replaced.

Another problem is that identical objects may have to be developed in different languages to meet the needs of users of different computers. Even if objects are developed in the same language, the options are to use either a restricted subset of the language compatible with all potential environments or a language that allows compiler flags to be placed on code and alternative versions of the code embedded in the object. Neither choice is attractive. The first may require other classes of objects to differentiate identical objects used on different machines, although polymorphism can help in this respect. As a result, testing for new or replacement objects becomes more complex.

Organizations need to assign someone the job of deciding which objects should be distributed to which of the distributed repositories. Standard corporate objects may have wide distribution, whereas others may require more limited distribution. Object and object-class management becomes an important administrative job. This is a problem because the purpose is to reduce, not increase, administrative support.

14.5 Conclusion

Increasing expectations for functionality, flexibility, ease of use, integration, multi-vendor systems, and networking have driven software projects to become larger. This results in long development times and expensive maintenance.

There also is the challenge of making a program work in isolation and in an integrated environment with another program, most likely developed by another company.

Modern business demands more information. This necessitates that raw data be accumulated, analyzed, turned into information, and then communicated to someone who can use it in real time. When increased project size is added to this need for more information, the situation quickly spins out of control. Most mid- to large-sized organizations have hundreds of different computer systems running thousands of programs and supporting millions of business decisions every day.

Another problem with object technology is the integration of information and systems from different sources or vendors across different hardware, software, and network configurations. The proliferation of personal computers and the emergence of the information highway highlight this problem. How will all these computers be connected together, and will any of their communications be intelligible across such widely dispersed networks? Larger, more complex software systems, geographically distributed computing, and a consistently growing demand for additional functionality have created a complex computing world.

Complexity and the multitude of different systems that must be integrated have created the need for a complete change in the way we conceive, design, build, and maintain computer systems. This new environment and the ever-increasing power of hardware are the principal reasons the software industry is moving toward object technology. Systems built on object-oriented techniques lend themselves to distribution, integration, and faster, error-free application development. They allow systems to evolve—to be reengineered as business, human, and technologic factors change.

15

CASE Technology

Software applications require flexibility, yet the process for developing these applications is so complex that it requires rigid process control. The process of establishing requirements and translating them into designs, computer code, and operational procedures is a frustratingly slow and laborious manual process. The process is subject to rigid process control, and this rigidity is manifest in the design of the software application. The designers are frequently hesitant and sometimes even resistant to reengineering the design even when they are convinced that it will improve the application. They say, "It will take too long, we will not meet our target" or "It is too difficult to make that change, the design does not easily accommodate it."

Software development also is error prone. Specifications are almost always incomplete. Requesters do not understand their needs until they actually see something. The opportunity for translation error is astronomical.

Another factor is that information technology is alien to most business executives. It is difficult for them to conceptualize how they can best apply technology to business. Conversely, information technology is so complex that most computer professionals become proficient at the expense of achieving insight into business processes. The result is an environment in which business executives understand their requirements only when they see the end result. Computer professionals are not likely to add a business perspective. Under these conditions, there is a high likelihood that a system design will have to be reengineered to the design of both parties. The business environment is not stagnant, further increasing the need to reengineer previously developed software.

The laborious and error-prone aspects of software development make software rigid and difficult to change. An ever-increasing proportion of software development labor is expended on maintaining previously developed software because of the limited scope of understanding of businessmen and computer professionals. The solution to this dilemma is a highly flexible software development environment—computer-aided software engineering (CASE). Over the past two decades, numerous solutions have been proposed to correct the rigidity of the software development process. Computer languages evolved from machine-level code to fourth-generation languages (4GLs). Purchased software was introduced, as were turnkey systems that involve inexpensive personal computers and client-server technology.

All of these developments relieved computer professionals of the less complex aspects of their profession. In all cases, information technology professionals applied the latest state-of-the-art tools to perpetuate the technology. The solutions were applied to specific bottlenecks, but in no case were they applied to the total development process. This situation changed with the introduction of CASE.

15.1 CASE Technology

15.1.1 Definition

CASE has only become recognizable to system and data-processing professionals in the last five years, although its roots extend well back into the 1970s, and its history is evident in many of the products marketed as CASE tools. CASE by definition is a technology that applies an automated engineering-like discipline for the specification of computer software system design, software development, testing and maintenance, and project management.

A common analogy is one that compares CASE for developing software systems to computer-assisted design (CAD) and computer-assisted manufacturing (CAM). The introduction of CAD and CAM revolutionized the manufacturing design process. They have helped accelerate the design process, improve designs, and reduce error and manufacturing expense. CASE holds the same promises for the information technology industry.

15.1.2 Objective

The objective of CASE is to maintain software design in an automated form. It is to specify requirements and expand them into software and database design specifications that are transformed into software that is ready for testing and implementation. The process provides a flexible environment that facilitates change and enhancement by removing the manual transcription that occurs in each phase of the traditional system development life cycle. CASE shifts the emphasis of software development from coding and testing to analysis and design. CASE introduces automated design verification, code generation, and documentation. CASE is used to automate system maintenance and makes prototyping a valid design technique.

15.1.3 Environment

CASE provides an automated software development environment. It differs from all earlier system development environments in the richness of its automation tools. The complete CASE system includes the following:

- ► Support for the common development life cycles with built-in audit capabilities that ensure compliance
- ► An information repository for storing the elements of the software engineering process, including specifications, designs, graphics, and pseudo code
- ► A graphics interface for drawing structured diagrams, data flow diagrams, and data structures
- ► A highly integrated set of tools to automate every phase of the development life cycle
- ► Automated code and dictionary generation from design specifications
- ► Prototyping of new designs and reverse engineering (converting existing software back into design specifications for modification and software regeneration)

15.1.4 Benefits

The benefits of CASE technology are an increase in quality, flexibility, availability, maintenance, prototyping, and productivity. The following is a detailed look at each of these benefits.

Quality: CASE improves quality by providing an automated audit of software design by automating the transformation of output from each development phase into input for the next phase, which ensures a complete and usable design by means of prototyping techniques.

Flexibility: CASE improves flexibility by simplifying software changes and by making the software portable across computer languages, databases, and hardware. Central to CASE technology is the repository of design specifications. This repository allows CASE practitioners to alter design specifications to incorporate changes. The software can be regenerated from this repository. The repository facilitates portability and makes it possible to change the software generators and regenerate software portable across databases and hardware.

Availability: CASE accelerates the availability of software by automating software development. The repository of design specifications is an archive of design techniques that are available for modification and reuse. As the archive is developed, it reduces the need to recreate the design for each application. New applications can be reengineered from prior similar applications.

Simplified Maintenance: CASE simplifies maintenance in two ways. Applications can be regenerated from the design repository as specification changes are identified. CASE also provides an opportunity for reverse engineering. Reverse engineering takes existing software and generates design specifications that are stored in the design repository in a reusable form for future modification.

Practical Prototyping: CASE makes prototyping practical. Software developers have long been aware that it is difficult for end users to visualize the impact of systems until they see the end result. The labor-intensive nature of software development makes prototyping impractical. With the introduction of CASE technology, this technique becomes more practical.

Productivity: CASE improves productivity by providing a repository for reusable system design elements, by automating aspects of the development cycle that were manual (such as coding and documentation), and by automating software maintenance.

15.2 CASE Categories

CASE tools are generally divided into two categories: toolkits or workbenches. The differentiation is based on whether the tool supports a phase of the development life cycle (toolkit) or provides automated support for the full development life cycle (workbench).

15.2.1 Toolkits

A toolkit is a set of tools that support one or more of the software development functions: planning, analysis, programming, maintenance, and project management. Toolkits may be generic or they may support one or more design methods. The functions of toolkits are integrated, but the interface between kits is not. As a result, toolkits can be used alone or in conjunction with one another. Toolkits provide the option of mixing and matching the best products from different vendors and thereby the ability to implement CASE technology in a piecemeal manner. The disadvantages of this fragmented approach are that there is no single repository for the automated design and that the toolkits do not integrate well. Manual interfaces between toolkits decrease quality and productivity.

Planning Toolkit

Information technology planning toolkits automate the process of identifying, categorizing, and prioritizing the areas in which information technology can contribute to the objectives of an organization. Such toolkits provide facilities for documenting and analyzing organizational information requirements. They also provide facilities for decomposing these requirements into data elements and then for structuring the data elements into databases and system requirements.

Analysis Toolkit

Analysis toolkits automate the process of defining system requirements and converting them into corresponding conceptual and functional system designs. Such toolkits typically include facilities such as diagramming tools, prototyping facilities, an audit or checking facility to guarantee completeness, a repository to store data flow diagrams, data entity relations, screens, and reports, and a link to a data dictionary or other repositories. The outputs from an analysis toolkit are functional requirements, data structures, database or dataset designs, and screen and report definitions.

Programming Toolkit

Programming toolkits automate the process of converting a system design into a fully tested and executable program code. Such toolkits include facilities for generating, maintaining, and checking pseudo code. Because the confidence of most users and the quality of machine-generated code are not high, the most frequently produced code is COBOL or SQL. Such languages are manually modifiable and give the user a comfortable feeling. Most programming toolkits also include one or more of the following:

▶ Test data or job control language (JCL) generator

▶ File creation and manipulation tools

▶ Performance monitors

▶ Abend diagnostic tools

Maintenance Toolkit

Maintenance toolkits automate the correction or enhancement process. Both processes are concerned with the reengineering of existing software systems to meet current specifications. A maintenance toolkit includes facilities such as the following:

- ▶ A maintenance facility to manage and document all changes
- ▶ An effort, elapsed time, and potential vulnerability estimating facility
- ▶ A testing facility for generating test data and analyzing output and a code analyzer for analyzing program logic

A maintenance toolkit includes tools for installing code into an operational status to ensure a smooth transition from test to operational status.

Project Management Toolkit

A project management toolkit provides automated software development project management tools. It provides facilities such as the following:

- ▶ Project definition
- ▶ Time and action plans
- ▶ Task assignment system estimating tools
- ▶ Change and version control
- ▶ Project status reporting

It also can include stand-alone tools such as word processing, spreadsheets, and interface into electronic mail.

15.2.2 Workbenches

A workbench is an integrated software development environment that supports either the full range of the software development life cycle or a large portion of the front-end or back-end of the software development life cycle. Like a toolkit, a workbench can be used in direct support of one or more structured design methods, or it can be generic. The most important advantage of a workbench is the automated output of deliverables from one system development phase into the next phase.

Front-End Workbench

A front-end workbench supports the system specification portion of the software development life cycle from requirements through detailed design. A front-end workbench includes tools to automate the requirement specification, conceptual design, and system design.

In some cases, a front-end workbench may include the generation of pseudo code as input to a code generator. The results of this automated process are stored in an automated repository, which is a system specification database available to all system development staff. The system specifications can be used as raw material for generating new systems or for regenerating an existing system.

A front-end workbench includes facilities such as the following:

▶ Data, system flow, and logic diagramming tools to facilitate the development of logical system and data flow structures

▶ An automated repository to store and manage system and program specifications that makes the specifications maintainable and reusable

▶ The ability to create or use external databases and dictionaries

▶ Screen and report painting tools for visual representation of output medium

▶ An interface into a code generator, the most common of which creates either SQL or COBOL code

Back-End Workbench

A back-end workbench supports the code generation portion of the software development life cycle from system design through code generation and testing. A back-end workbench includes tools to automate the generation of pseudo and programming code, of testing and debugging facilities, and of documentation facilities. The output from a back-end workbench is fully tested, documented, and executable programming code stored in libraries. The code is available for the development staff to maintain in a conventional manner if required. A back-end workbench supports the input of program specifications for program code generation.

A back-end workbench includes facilities such as the following:

▶ A facility for the input, change, storage, and control of program specifications

▶ Prototyping data modeling and data dictionary facilities

▶ Screen and report painting tools for visual representation and code generation of output medium

▶ The ability to create or use external databases and dictionaries

▶ A programming code generator and documentation facility, the most common of which creates either SQL or COBOL code

▶ Testing and debugging tools

Integrated Workbench

An integrated workbench supports the complete system generation process from requirement specification through program code generation and testing. The workbench combines the tools included in both front-end and back-end workbenches. No single vendor provides an integrated workbench that adequately encompasses all the features of the development process. However, some vendors working with others have developed interfaces that result in reasonably complete integrated workbenches.

15.3 Selecting CASE Technology

More than forty products are available that can be classified as CASE technology (Table 15.1). There is no free lunch with CASE technology. The combination of new and old products, the range of products from toolkit to workbench, and the sheer number of entries in the market makes selection of CASE technology difficult. For some, the easiest solution to this dilemma is to do nothing. An early investment gives others a competitive edge.

Table 15.1 *CASE Products*

Product	*Vendor Address*	*Phone*
Planning Toolkits		
Project Workbench	Applied Business Technology, 361 Broadway, New York, NY 10013	212-219-8945
Analysis Toolkits		
Design/1 33 West Monroe Chicago, IL 60603	Arthur Anderson	312-580-0033
The Developer 1080 Beaver Hall Hill, Suite 1400 Montreal, Quebec H2Z 1S8 Canada	Anyst Technologies, Inc.	514-840-1155
AutoDraw 4884 Constitution Ave., Suite 1E Baton Rouge, LA 70808	Chen & Associates, Inc.	504-928-5765
CA-IDMS/Architect One Computer Associates Plaza Islandia, NY 11788-7000	Computer Associates	516-342-6000
ManagerVIEW 131 Hartwell Avenue Lexington, MA 02173-3126	Manager Software Products, Inc.	617-863-5800

Table 15.2 *Continued*

Product	Vendor Address	Phone
CASE-Station, CASE Bench 8005 SW Boeckman Rd. Wilsonville, OR 97070	Mentor Graphics	800-592-2210
VIA/Insight 3033 North 44th St., Suite 101 Phoenix, AZ 85018	Viasoft, Inc.	602-952-0050
Data Analysis Toolkits		
DDS-Link, ER-Designer, Normalizer, SchemaGen 4884 Constitution Ave., Suite 1E Baton Rouge, LA 70808	Chen & Associates, Inc.	504-928-5765
Designmanager 131 Hartwell Avenue Lexington, MA 02173-3126	Manager Software Products, Inc.	617-863-5800
SQL*Design Dictionary 500 Oracle Pkwy. Redwood Shores, CA 94065 Programming Toolkits Application Systems	Oracle Corporation	800-345-DBMS
Development Environment 146 Main St. Maynard, MA 01754	Digital Equipment Corporation	508-493-5111
P-TOOL 846 University Avenue Norwood, MA 02062	Phoenix Technologies, Ltd.	781-551-4000
Configuration Builder, 735 SW 150th Avenue Beaverton, OR 97006	Intersolv, Inc.	503-645-1150
Maintenance Toolkits		
ADPAC CASE Tools 425 Market St., Suite 400 San Francisco, CA 94105	Adpac Corporation	415-777-5400
Front-End Workbenches		
Foundation 33 West Monroe Chicago, IL 60603	Arthur Anderson	312-580-0033
Information Engineering Workbench, Logic Gem 3340 Peachtree Rd. NE, Suite 2900 Atlanta, GA 30026	Sterling Software	404-231-8575

Table 15.2   *Continued*

Product	Vendor Address	Phone
Epos 14 East 38th St., 14th Floor New York, NY 10016	SPS	212-686-3790
Information Engineering Facility 6620 Chase Oaks Blvd. Plano, TX 75020	Texas Instruments	214-575-2000
Back-End Workbenches		
Corvet 111 Wood Ave. South Iselin, NJ 08830	Analysts International Corp.	201-535-9844
Install/1 33 West Monroe Chicago, IL 60603	Arthur Anderson	312-580-0033
Gamma 3340 Peachtree Rd., NE, Suite 2900 Atlanta, GA 30026	Sterling Software, Inc.	404-231-8575
Sourcemanager 131 Hartwell Avenue Lexington, MA 02173-3126	Manager Software Products, Inc.	617-863-5800
COBOL/2 Workbench 500 East Swedesford Rd. Wayne, PA 19087	MicroFocus, Inc.	800-872-6285
Netron/CAP 99 St., Regis Cresent North Downsview, Ontario M3J 1Y9 Canada	Netron, Inc.	416-636-8333
Integrated Workbenches		
AX CASE 3000 Hanover St. Palo Alto, CA 94302	Hewlett Packard Company	800-752-0900
Inforem-Page 40 Uxbridge Rd. London W52BS United Kingdom O1O	Inforem LTD	44-1-5670595
Controlmanager, Datamanager, Dictionarymanager, Methodmanager 131 Hartwell Avenue Lexington, MA 02173-3126	Manager Software Products, Inc.	617-863-5800
Natural/Construct, Natural/Predict 11190 Sunrise Valley Pkwy. Reston, VA 22091	Software AG of NA	800-843-9534

15.3.1 Clarify Objectives

Which benefits will be derived from the CASE tools—design, code generation, maintenance, or project management? Most commercial organizations
purchase a large portion of their software, but when software is developed, it
is developed with a 4GL. It is not likely under these circumstances that a
back-end workbench or a programming toolkit will have the highest return.
Use of a front-end workbench, an analysis toolkit, or even a project management toolkit makes more sense. Regardless, it is essential that you clarify your
objectives from the start.

15.3.2 Narrow Options

Choose a CASE product category and analyze the tools within that category. Choose a tool that complements the organization's methods. If a
method is not available, stop the selection process and begin the process of
selecting a method. When beginning the CASE product selection, consider
the following:

Hardware requirements: The options are mainframe, client-server, or personal computer–based toolkits or workbenches.

Tools already in place: An existing database management system
(DBMS), data dictionary, or 4GL increases the need for selecting a
complementary CASE product.

Types of systems to be developed and supported: What are the organization's software development strategies? The requirements for installing on-line minicomputer systems are different from those for on-line
mainframe systems. Requirements for purchased software are different
from those for software developed in house.

Interviews with current users of product: Would the current user choose
the change?

Product demonstration and hands-on experience: Do not overlook the
opportunity to see the product in action.

Available product support and training: Are support and training available? Will the vendor be in business next year or five years from now?
Does the vendor have a good reputation?

The organization's future direction and that of the vendor: Most
CASE products are incomplete and in a state of transition. Is the
stated direction of the vendor in concert with the direction of your
organization?

Make the selection using objective criteria. Choose according to how well the toolkit or workbench does the following:

- ▶ Supports the installed method

- ▶ Integrates with other tools, DBMS, data dictionary, 4GL

- ▶ Integrates with other tools

- ▶ Supports diagramming

- ▶ Supports code generation

- ▶ Performs checking and analysis

15.4 Implementing CASE Technology

15.4.1 Method Selection

Installation of a development method is a prerequisite to CASE technology. CASE technology provides an automated engineering-like discipline for specification of computer system design, software development, testing and maintenance, and project management. CASE automates the development process, the latter being the selected and defined method.

Management must be committed to the development method. The staff and users must be trained, and some level of experience is required. It is difficult, if not impossible, to embrace the concepts of a method and CASE technology simultaneously. There is an old system development adage that states if something cannot be done manually, it cannot be automated. This adage applies to methodology and CASE. Simultaneous installation of both a development method and CASE technology reduces the likelihood of success of either.

15.4.2 CASE Selection

Select the CASE tools that support the method. Depending on the organization, these can be support for single or multiple methods. Multiple division organizations or organizations that are likely to merge with others should seek flexibility through the use of tools that support multiple methods or that are independent of method. Such organizations may find it advantageous not to impose standards that force an organization into a conversion. Smaller organizations can probably ignore this aspect of the selection process.

15.4.3 CASE Pilot

When choosing a workbench, the best route is to select a real but noncritical project to start using the CASE tools. Train the best and most receptive staff on use of the CASE tools. If faced with a decision between the best and the most receptive, choose the most receptive. After training is complete, devise a plan that identifies the expected results and the measurement criteria. Implement the project and evaluate the results on the basis of the evaluation requirements. Do not expect high productivity, because a large portion of the productivity gains from CASE technology come from the reusable aspect of the CASE design elements.

If a toolkit is chosen, you may choose to implement it immediately throughout a department. The procedural impact of installing an analysis toolkit, for example, is not nearly as traumatic as installing a front-end workbench. It is possible to implement quickly and realize immediately the benefits of the toolkit. After the pilot is complete, formalize the CASE procedures, and make CASE the standard for all development projects.

15.4.4 Cautions

Three aspects of CASE require some words of caution. First, CASE is an emerging technology. Although more than forty CASE tools are listed in Table 15.1 and even more are available, none meets all of the requirements of the ideal CASE model. Recognize this shortfall at the start, and select tools that maximize the benefits in your environment. Look for vendors and strategies that show potential for providing long-term solutions to the inadequacies.

Second, many CASE tools are tied to specific structured design methods, databases (IMS, CA-IDMS, ADABAS), programming languages (COBOL, SQL), and hardware vendors. The marketplace is being driven by what is marketable, not necessarily what is best. Software vendors make a large financial commitment to developing their product. To achieve a financial return, they target the largest markets or the most abundant technology. Select products that are flexible and products that support multiple design methods, databases, programming languages, and hardware components. The nature of business is such that mergers and acquisitions are common. Technology is changing. There may be a desire to support a relational database with SQL on hardware from different vendors. Maintain flexibility wherever possible.

CASE productivity gains come from two areas: reusability and maintenance. CASE productivity comes from developing an extensive library of design specifications that can be cut and pasted to form new applications. The benefits of reusable designs are not immediate. It takes time to develop these inventories; benefits are deferred. They are reaped during the reengineering process. The second area of productivity comes from making software reliable at the start and maintainable as time goes on. This reduces the spiraling expense of software maintenance. Again, the benefits are deferred and are reaped only for software that is designed with CASE or if an initial investment is made in reverse engineering.

15.5 Conclusions

If there is one main fault with the information technology industry, it would be the constant search for heroic solutions. The profession has embraced the use of such diverse technology as third-generation languages (COBOL, PL/1), 4GL, structured methods, code generators, object technology, database technology, personal computing, and client-server technology in the hope that all problems can be solved. For now, the solution is computer-aided software engineering, or CASE technology.

CASE is real, and it is usable. Between forty and one hundred products on the market qualify as CASE tools. Some sets or subsets of these tools benefit most software development environments. However, CASE is not a panacea. Only when CASE is orchestrated with other techniques and technologies, such as sound business planning techniques, object technology, rule-based systems, and client-server technology, does CASE achieve its highest return.

CASE is new and incomplete. Many inconsistencies and annoyances often can be fixed in the next release of the product. Many CASE vendors are coming out with new releases two or more times a year. When selecting a CASE product, take these factors into consideration. If such a volatile environment is not acceptable, you may not want to get into CASE at this time.

CASE addresses the issue of quality. Studies have indicated that less than 25 percent of all software projects are completed on time and within budget and that less than 25 percent of all projects meet the expectations of the requester. Therefore, less than 6 percent of all projects satisfy the needs of the requester in the time frame in which they were requested. CASE addresses this problem. It automates the software engineering process and reengineering, improving quality. By reusing automated design elements and through reverse engineering, CASE enhances productivity and provides a high-quality system.

CASE Education Opportunities

Digital Consulting

Six Windsor St.

Andover, MA 01810

617-470-3880

Computer-Aided Software Engineering Symposium

CASE Symposium for Aerospace, Defense and Engineering

CASE Benchmarks: A Seminar Comparing 7 Leading CASE Tools

Software Engineering and CASE Technology

Application Prototyping: Implementing the New System Development Technology

16

Rule-Based System Technology

Artificial intelligence is a broad concept that encompasses a number of very different disciplines, including cognitive psychology, decision theory, operations research, machine learning, robotics, natural language processing, and rule-based systems. Rule-based systems involve creation of computer software that emulates the way people solve problems. Business professionals are most likely to come in contact with rule-based systems in the application of object and CASE technology; therefore, for purposes of this chapter, artificial intelligence is equated to rule-based systems.

Experts solve difficult problems, explain the solution, learn from the problem-solving process, explain the relevance of the solution, and maybe most important, are capable of realizing when they do not know something. A rule-based system, like a human, gives advice by requesting information specific to the problem under consideration and by drawing on its store of knowledge.

The incentive behind rule-based systems is contained in the attributes of knowledge. Knowledge is perishable, and its longevity is tied to the expert. Expert knowledge is scarce and difficult to accumulate, pass on, and use. Expert knowledge often is vague, inconsistent, and widely dispersed over many widely distributed experts. In response to these attributes of knowledge, rule-based systems are used to preserve, clone, and apply knowledge. Rule-based systems are used to pass on knowledge to another generation of experts or users and to encourage its growth and expansion. They are used to make the knowledge more precise and systematic and to collect it into a knowledge base.

Rule-based systems, therefore, provide the benefit of making knowledge more readily available. A rule-based system is impartial in decision making, and it allows total recall. It provides the opportunity to share knowledge over a large user base, and it expedites routine decisions. Finally, rule-based systems conserve valuable experience in an organization and can act as a tutor to pass experience to trainees.

The history of rule-based systems is as old as information technology. Early computer practitioners had high expectations for artificial intelligence. These early knowledge engineers attempted to replicate the problem-solving capabilities of human experts, but the expectations did not materialize as quickly as anticipated. The process of human thinking is far more complex, less structured, and more elusive than knowledge engineers assumed. Furthermore, the intensity of computer processing exceeded the capabilities of available computers.

Early rule-based systems required immense amounts of human labor and immense amounts of computing with special-purpose computers that were not readily available. From a business perspective, rule-based systems were impractical; both the human involvement and the computing resources were more expensive than practical. However, investment in rule-based system technology has risen considerably over the last few years. In light of these investments, it is obvious that the attitude of business is much more receptive toward rule-based systems.

16.1 Uses of Rule-Based Systems

16.1.1 Application of Rule-Based Systems

There are a number of different ways to look at rule-based systems. Rule-based systems can be categorized according to target market (medicine, industry, geologic exploration, insurance, or military) or according to hardware environment (personal computer, server, mainframe computer, or artificial intelligence workstation). A more common way to categorize rule-based systems is according to target user market: nonexpert, technician, or expert. The purpose is to do the following:

Advise nonexperts: These rule-based systems supply expert knowledge directly to nonexperts. They provide advice on taxes or tax preparation, supply financial planning expertise, perform investment analysis, and provide advice in areas such as medicine, gardening, and hobbies.

Improve performance of technicians: These rule-based systems improve the performance of technicians through activities such as identifying the need for preventive maintenance, configuring equipment, performing diagnostics, and assisting with the operation of complex equipment.

Aid or outperform experts: These rule-based systems aid or even outperform the experts. The systems aid experts through activities such as seismic analysis, medical diagnosis, oil prospecting, financial analysis, and tax planning. Other systems outperform the experts in areas such as process control, real-time financial trading, and playing chess.

16.1.2 Examples of Rule-Based Systems

The following are rule-based systems that have been developed and are in use at large corporations or are commercially available for general use:

Auditor: Assists a corporation in analyzing the allowance for bad debts and account receivables

Authorizer's Assistant: Performs credit authorization searches at American Express and makes recommendations to the authorizing agent

Cash Value: Assists in capital project planning, advises on net present value (NPV), cash flow, payback, and risk analysis.

Consultant: A rule-based system that helps IBM field-service representatives prepare price bids

Corp-Tax: Assists accountants with Section 302(b) redemptions

Dendral: Elucidates chemical structures from mass-spectral data

Drilling Advisor: Helps diagnose, solve, and avoid problems with oil-drilling rigs

EDP Auditor: Aids auditors in assessing advanced electronic data-processing systems

Expertax: Helps accountants at Coopers & Lybrand to review ways their clients can accrue taxes and assists in providing tax-planning advice

Financial Advisor: Gives advice on projects, products, mergers and acquisitions as if conversing with a senior financial consultant

Guidon: Performs medical teaching

Hasp: Understands complex, noisy, analog signals for activities such as submarine detection and identification

Macsyma: Performs mathematical manipulations such as integration, differentiation, and simulation equations

Mcyin: Provides medical diagnosis and therapy recommendations

Mudman: Analyzes the drilling fluids or "muds" that are pumped down a shaft to facilitate drilling

PDS: A Westinghouse rule-based system designed to monitor steam turbines and to make maintenance recommendations

Plan Power: Considers a financial situation and matches needs with the most appropriate financial products and services

Platinum Label: A general accounting rule-based system that includes seven expert packages: accounts receivable, accounts payable, general ledger, sales order, inventory, sales analysis, and guide database kit

Prospector: A mineral prospector that identifies sites for ore deposits

R1: Designs complex computer configurations

Sacon: Advises on use of complex software products

Tax Advisor: Provides tax advice to help clients arrange financial affairs to minimize income and death benefit taxes

Taxman: Evaluates the consequences of proposed business reorganizations

Ticom: A system for modeling and evaluating internal financial controls

Xcon: A rule-based configuration tool, designed by Digital Equipment Corporation, used to check sales orders and design the layout of each order analyzed

16.2 The Knowledge Engineer

The array of rule-based system application opportunities is diverse, and the opportunities are almost limitless. However, isolating these opportunities requires an awareness on the part of the organization that such applications are possible, that the results are valuable, and that there will be a commitment to use the results. The technology is new to business, and it requires long-range investment in knowledge engineers and rule-based system software tools.

Knowledge engineers are themselves experts. They specialize in isolating information from experts and understanding the strengths and weaknesses of their chosen rule-based system tools. A knowledge engineer typically identifies an application suitable for solution with a rule-based system, isolates information from an expert, develops a prototype of the rule-based system, and in close cooperation with the expert, develops a working rule-based system. These systems are then integrated into existing automated systems and are turned over to the expert and the system user for subsequent support.

The conventional software engineer also works with experts. However, the relation between the knowledge engineer and the expert is much more intense. Conventional software engineers are concerned with information or business flow. They work with an expert to isolate this business information flow and afterward design software systems to automate this flow. The knowledge engineer, however, is concerned with the thought process of the expert. The interaction between the expert and the knowledge engineer continues from information isolation through development of the working system. Experts frequently take over subsequent support of the rule-based system.

On the basis of the size of the project at hand, more than one knowledge engineer may be required. However, most commercial applications require a single knowledge engineer and one or more conventional software engineers. Most early rule-based systems were programmed from scratch with LISP or Prolog, but today the most common medium is a rule-based system shell or a programming environment or toolkit.

The use of tools such as programming environments and rule-based system shells has improved the productivity of knowledge engineers and has made rule-based systems commercially accessible. However, the success of a rule-based system still depends largely on the ability of a knowledge engineer to isolate expert information and to use a programming environment. Isolating expert knowledge continues to be a labor-intensive process for both the knowledge engineer and the expert.

16.3 Types of Rule-Based System Development Software

There are three principal alternatives for developing rule-based systems: a rule-based system shell software environment, a general-purpose programming language, and a programming language toolkit (Table 16.1). The primary difference is in the amount of knowledge-engineering experience required and in the amount of effort required to develop the rule-based system. The alternatives for developing rule-based system software range from the shell, which requires the least amount of programming effort, to the programming language, which requires the most.

Rule-based system shell: Rule-based system shells are so called because they are empty of any knowledge. Shells usually consist of four components: a knowledge base, an inference engine, a user interface, and a knowledge encoding facility. A shell may or may not include an interface with a traditional hierarchical or relational database.

Programming language: One of the limitations of shell systems is the lack of a powerful method for representing deductive thought. For this reason, it is desirable to use one of the powerful programming languages associated with artificial intelligence: Prolog or LISP. These languages

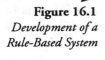

Figure 16.1
Development of a
Rule-Based System

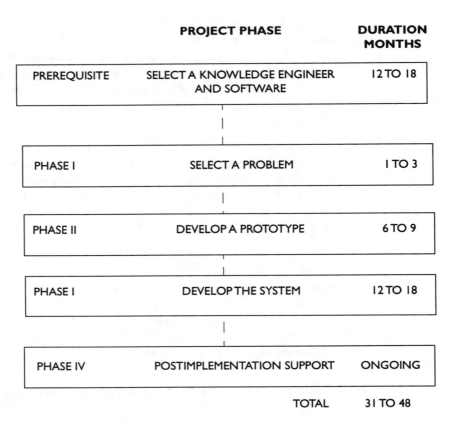

PROJECT PHASE		DURATION MONTHS
PREREQUISITE	SELECT A KNOWLEDGE ENGINEER AND SOFTWARE	12 TO 18
PHASE I	SELECT A PROBLEM	1 TO 3
PHASE II	DEVELOP A PROTOTYPE	6 TO 9
PHASE I	DEVELOP THE SYSTEM	12 TO 18
PHASE IV	POSTIMPLEMENTATION SUPPORT	ONGOING
	TOTAL	31 TO 48

lack a standard user interface or a run-time facility. If, for example, rules are encoded in Prolog, a user interface program must be developed to inspect their operation. As a result, languages such as Prolog and LISP tend to be extremely labor intensive and are less suitable to business application than are expert shells.

Programming language toolkit: Toolkits attempt to bridge the middle ground between rule-based system shells and programming languages. The facilities offered by a toolkit can vary across a wide range. They can range from extensive to austere. Depending on the facilities offered, toolkits can look similar to rule-based system shells, or they can be little more than a programming language. Ideal toolkits are a complete developmental facility that includes a programming language, a flexible way of representing and storing factual and judgmental knowledge, and an inference facility to solve problems easily. Such toolkits may utilize or work in conjunction with Prolog or LISP, but the newer toolkits are more likely to run on a personal computer and use languages such as C++ or Pascal.

Development of a rule-based system takes two and a half to four years if your organization starts cold with no previous experience (Figure 16.1). Can it be done in less? Yes. Is it likely? No.

16.4 Rule-Based System Shell

16.4.1 Origin

Many of the original rule-based system shells originated with rule-based systems that were devised to satisfy a specific application problem. The applications were stripped of their knowledge and altered for general use. The name *shell* originates as follows: shells are applications that are devoid of any knowledge—empty shells. Many of the newer rule-based system shells, however, are developed specifically as shells in an attempt to overcome some of the shortfalls of the original software.

The newer shells are typically either mainframe-based, server-based, or personal computer–based with an interface into mainframe or client-server databases. The server or personal computer–based systems far outnumber the mainframe-based systems. The cost of personal computer–based systems ranges from $100 to $6,000, whereas that of mainframe-based systems ranges from $25,000 to $200,000. Mainframe-based systems are more robust; they support multiple users, more rules, and larger knowledge bases.

16.4.2 Organization

A typical rule-based system shell consists of four components: a knowledge base, an inference engine, a user interface, and a knowledge-encoding facility. Shells are developed with languages such as LISP or Prolog, but it is becoming increasingly more common for them to be developed in C++ or Pascal for personal computer–based systems and sometimes even COBOL for mainframe-based systems. Rule-based systems no longer require specialized hardware, and it is now practical to use commercial programming languages.

Knowledge Base

A knowledge base is a collection of heuristic rules of behavior—the knowledge of good practice or good judgment that is common knowledge among the practitioners or experts in a field of knowledge. This collection of heuristic rules forms the base of knowledge and rules that experts use to solve problems. Sometimes an interactive editor is provided for developing the knowledge base.

Inference Engine

The inference engine is the computer software that replicates the logic or thought process of an expert. It is the compiler or interpreter that translates the base of rules in the knowledge base into executable rules. Accepting input from the user of a rule-based system and the knowledge base, the inference engine simulates the reasoning of the expert.

User Interface

The user interface is the computer software that allows the user of a rule-based system to enter facts and ask questions of the rule-based system. It is an executable system that allows the user interactively to apply the rules to the knowledge base. The interface with the system is in a natural language.

Knowledge-Encoding Facility

The knowledge encoding facility is the software used to acquire and encode the expert knowledge or rules of the knowledge database.

16.4.3 Advantages

Rule-based system shells are the easiest way to cast a prototype of a rule-based system. The knowledge engineer does not have to contribute anything to developing the interface between the rule base and the knowledge base. The knowledge engineer does not have to develop an executable system. This is especially important later because the executable system provides facilities that are common across most any rule-based system application. The execution-time system facilities include features such as provisions to do the following:

▶ Expand the meaning of a question

▶ Change the answer to a previous question or previous questions and propagate the effect through the session

▶ Volunteer information or answer questions before they are asked

▶ Inspect the knowledge base to see previous or derived answers

▶ Justify why a question is asked or why an answer is given

These common features are labor intensive to develop, and their presence accelerates formation of a prototype and development of a rule-based system.

16.4.4 Disadvantages

The principal limitation of expert shells is the limited power of their production rule system. For this reason, many rule-based systems are still developed with artificial intelligence programming languages such as LISP or Prolog. These languages lack the features of the execution system components and are not as suitable for prototypes as a rule-based system shell. However, the search mechanism, data structures, and interpretative nature of languages such as LISP and Prolog do make them better tools than conventional languages such as Pascal and C++. Programming environments or toolkits are available to mitigate some of the disadvantages of LISP and Prolog. When toolkits and shells are used in synergy, the result is the best of both worlds.

16.4.5 Selection Process

Selection of a rule-based system tool is a multiple-step process. First, the organization must be aware that the implementation of rule-based system applications is possible and that the results are valuable. It requires a commitment on the part of the organization to use the results. It requires that the organization be prepared to make a long-range investment in one or more knowledge engineers and rule-based system software tools. The investment in the development process is $2 million to $5 million.

The second step is selection of a knowledge engineer. Knowledge engineers are rare. Identifying the correct set of skills and selecting the correct person is difficult for the information technology group. In many cases, it is necessary to identify someone willing to learn the discipline and to make an investment in education. Both alternatives are risky, but the knowledge engineer is the keystone to the process of building a rule-based system.

The next step is selection of the rule-based system application. Because the technology is still quite limited, it is important that the correct application be selected. If an inappropriate application is selected and the process bogs down, the organization loses interest quickly. The earlier in the process that a failure occurs, the greater is the likelihood that the process will be abandoned. It is therefore critical that care be given to selection of the application.

At this point, the knowledge engineer selects a rule-based system development tool. The knowledge engineer is an expert who specializes in understanding the strengths and weaknesses of the rule-based system tools. On the basis of this understanding and the technical environment, the knowledge engineer selects a rule-based system shell or toolkit to implement a prototype system and eventually the complete system. In some cases, the experience gained from the prototype causes a change in the tools used for the final system. Table 16.1 lists some of the common commercially available rule-based system shells and rule-based system toolkits.

Table 16.1   *Rule-Based System Software*

Tool	Vendor	Platform	Price
Rule-Based System Toolkits			
Goldworks	Gold Hill Computers 36 Arlington Rd. Chestnut Hill, MA 02167 617-621-3300	IBM PC, GC LISP	$7,500
Texas Instruments Series	Texas Instruments, Inc. 12501 Research Blvd. P.O. Box 2909 Austin, TX 78769 800-527-3500	IBM PC/TI PC	$425 to $2,950
Rule-Based System Shells—IBM PC–Based			
EXSYS	EXSYS, Inc. 1720 Lusiana Rd., Ste. 312 Albuquerque, NM 87110 505-256-8356	IBM PC/VAX C	$395 $5,000
Levels PC	Information Builders 1250 Broadway New York, NY 10001 212-736-4433	IBM PC Pascal	$485
Nexpert Object	Neuron Data, Inc. 1310 Villa St. Mountain View, CA 94041 415-528-3450	MAC Assembler	$3,000
Copernicus & M1	Technowledge, Inc. 1910 Embarcadero Road Palo Alto, CA 94303 415-424-0500	IBM PC/VAX	$5,000 to $60,000
PC Easy & PC Plus	Texas Instruments, Inc. 12501 Research Blvd. P.O. Box 2909 Austin, TX 78769 800-527-3500	IBM PC/VAX	$300 to $3,000

Table 16.1 *Continued*

Tool	Vendor	Platform	Price
Rule-Based System Shells—IBM Mainframe–Based			
KBMS	Platinum Technology 404 Wyman St., Suite 320 Waltham, MA 02254 781-891-6500	IBM proprietary	$2,000
Application Expert	Computer Associates One Computer Associates Plaza Islandia, NY 11788-7000 516-342-6000	IBM/VAX, COBOL	$30,000 to $90,000
Expert System, Environment, Knowledgetool, and APLPIE	IBM Corporation (Local IBM marketing representatives)	IBM Pascal/APL	$60,000
S.1	Technowledge, Inc. 1910 Embarcadero Road Palo Alto, CA 94303 415-424-0500	IBM/VAX	$25,000

The skills and procedures required to develop a rule-based system differ considerably from those required to develop a commercial computer-based application system. The process of developing rule-based systems depends heavily on the skill of a knowledge engineer. The knowledge engineer performs the crucial steps of selecting the rule-based system application and selecting the rule-based system tools.

Another crucial element is selecting a willing expert. The correct person is the expert who is indispensable to the organization. The knowledge engineer and the expert work together closely; therefore, the expert and the knowledge engineer need to establish rapport. Experts tend to embrace the rule-based system. They are a part of the entire process: prototype development, system development, and performance evaluation. Persuading a nonexpert, however, to embrace a system is fraught with all the pitfalls associated with installing any new system. The key to success is to make the user part of the process.

It appears that the two most important aspects of building a rule-based system are the knowledge engineer and the choice of application. A knowledge engineer is a facilitator who understands rule-based system development and has the interpersonal skill to work with the expert, management, and the users of the rule-based system to select the correct tools and the appropriate application.

16.5 Implementing Knowledge-Based Systems

There are three prerequisites to implementing a rule-based system: a knowledge engineer, rule-based system tools or a rule-based system shell, and management commitment to the development of rule-based system applications.

16.5.1 Knowledge Engineer

As described earlier, knowledge engineers are experts who select rule-based system tools. A knowledge engineer typically identifies a problem suitable for solution with a rule-based system, isolates information from an expert, develops a prototype of the rule-based system, and in close cooperation with the expert develops a working rule-based system. The knowledge engineer is a facilitator who understands the process and the tools and who has the interpersonal skills to work with management, experts, and users. The knowledge engineer has the project management skills to identify an objective and bring it to a satisfactory conclusion.

16.5.2 Rule-Based System Shell or Tools

As described earlier, there are three principal alternatives for developing rule-based systems: a rule-based system shell, a more general programming language, and a programming language toolkit. The primary difference between the alternatives is the amount of effort required to develop the rule-based system and the amount of knowledge engineering experience required. The alternatives range from the shell, which requires the least amount of knowledge and effort, to the programming language, which requires the most (see Table 16.1).

16.5.3 Management Commitment

Rule-based systems are a whole new breed of business computer applications. Traditional business computer applications are oriented to automating the operational functions of a business: processing vendor payments, paying employees, maintaining inventory records, and maintaining and calculating bank balances. These software systems automate clerical functions. The rule-based system replicates the knowledge store and thought process of the expert—the electrical or structural engineer, medical diagnostician, geologist, or estimator. These systems are targeted at the previously sacrosanct professionals in the organization.

The application opportunities for rule-based systems are limitless. However, the selection process requires that management recognize that such applications are possible and that the results are both valuable and usable. Rule-based systems require a commitment from management to use the results. The technology is new to business, and rule-based systems require management to make a long-range investment in a knowledge engineer, software tools, and computer processing when a cost-benefit analysis is probably not possible.

The implementation process for rule-based systems is a four-phase process, as follows:

1. Select an application area

2. Develop a prototype of the system

3. Develop the system

4. Provide postimplementation support of the system

The implementation process requires a belief in the technology and the tenacity to make it work. It takes two and a half to four years to develop the first rule-based system application (see Figure 16.1) and an investment of one to five million dollars.

16.6 Select an Application

Selecting an application is probably the most crucial aspect of the expert development process. The technology, although not new, is still quite limited. If an inappropriate application is selected and the process bogs down, management quickly loses interest. The earlier in the process that a failure occurs, the greater is the likelihood that the process will be abandoned. If the first rule-based application fails, it will be far more difficult to get support for successive applications than if the same failure had occurred in the third or fourth application. It is critical that care be given to application selection.

Identification of an application includes five activities that precede the actual decision to begin development of a full rule-based system. These activities are equivalent to a feasibility study in commercial application software development.

16.6.1 Identifying an Application

The selection of a likely application begins with a review of the likely areas in which a rule-based system can be used. The most likely application areas require performance that depends on subjective, changing, symbolic, or judgmental knowledge. Clues to watch for when looking for knowledge-based system opportunities are as follows:

▶ A few knowledgeable people are spending a substantial amount of time helping others.

▶ A function requires large numbers of people because there is no single expert.

▶ Complex tasks require the analysis of a large number of variables.

▶ The competition excels because their performance is consistently superior.

▶ Essential, highly skilled human resources are not readily available.

▶ The variation between the best and the worst performance is wide.

Commercial rule-based systems seem to be most successful when they process knowledge in a narrow specialty. Other guidelines for success are to select problems that are neither too easy nor too difficult. An expert should be able to solve a problem in a period of one day to one month. Problems should be clearly definable, have outcomes that can be evaluated, and should not depend on common sense or sensory discrimination.

16.6.2 Finding a Willing Expert

The best person to work with the knowledge engineer to develop a rule-based system is an expert who is indispensable to the organization. More is required, however. The expert must be able to communicate his or her expertise and must be comfortable doing so. The knowledge engineer and the expert work together closely; therefore, the expert and the knowledge engineer need to establish a rapport. The availability of a willing expert is crucial to selection of an application and to development and implementation of a rule-based system.

16.6.3 Identifying an Approach

As the expert communicates knowledge to the knowledge engineer, the knowledge engineer evaluates and reevaluates the rule-based system tools available. The knowledge engineer determines whether the tools are adequate. A deciding factor in selection of a rule-based system application is whether new tools are required.

16.6.4 Cost-Benefit Analysis

Identify the costs involved with developing the rule-based system and balance the cost against the benefits. As a rule, choose projects that have the potential for high return because the likelihood of high cost and cost overrun is great for knowledge-based systems. If, as anticipated, high costs do materialize, then a high benefit will reduce the payback period.

16.6.5 Preparing a Plan

Once the application has been identified, a willing expert has been isolated, the development tools have been identified and agreed on, and there is a favorable cost-to-benefit ratio, the knowledge engineer can develop a plan for subsequent prototype and development phases.

16.7 Prototype System

Unlike other commercial computer-based systems, a rule-based system is preceded by a prototype system. The prototype is an abbreviated version of the rule-based system designed and created to test the design for the system and to actively engage the expert in the process on a small scale.

16.7.1 Learning the Application

In this step the knowledge engineer makes an intense effort to learn as much as possible about the application area through close interaction with the expert. The knowledge engineer teaches the expert to formulate judgments in terms of rules. To help formulate the problem-solving rules, the knowledge engineer formulates a series of cases and works with the expert to solve the cases step by step. Whenever possible, the reasoning process is translated into rules, and the rules are classified for inclusion in the prototype system. The goal of the knowledge engineer is to learn as much as possible about the application.

16.7.2 Performance Expectations

The knowledge engineer, while learning more about how the expert applies knowledge, begins to formulate the performance criteria for the prototype system. The performance criteria are the expectations for the system. The performance criteria consist in answering questions such as, Should the rule-based system reach the same conclusion as the expert regardless of the sequence of the questions? or, Should the rule-based system reach the same conclusion as the expert for a yet unspecified test case? Performance criteria focus the attention of the knowledge engineer on the precise performance conditions and final output that the rule-based system is expected to produce.

16.7.3 Selecting a Tool

As the knowledge engineer comes to understand what the expert does and how he or she does it, the knowledge engineer can assess whether the rule-based system shell or toolkit is adequate for the application. If the development software is not adequate, it is now possible to establish requirements and select new software.

16.7.4 Implementation and Testing

After selecting a software tool, it is possible to begin developing the prototype rule-based system. The knowledge engineer develops the prototype using a series of test cases. The knowledge engineer discusses each rule in the test case with the expert. This is a time-consuming and labor-intensive task for both the knowledge engineer and the expert. If the rule does not work, they revise it together and move on to the next. This procedure is followed for each additional case until the prototype is complete.

Once the prototype is developed to the satisfaction of the knowledge engineer, the prototype functions are tested on a wide variety of test cases. This testing allows the knowledge engineer to understand if the representations of the expert's knowledge are correct. It allows the expert to see how the system uses the information provided. By becoming part of development and testing, the expert becomes committed to the rule-based system-development process.

16.7.5 Planning Development

When the prototype operates correctly, the knowledge engineer can begin to plan the complete rule-based system. If certain aspects of the prototype are awkward, they can be corrected. On the basis of the prototype, estimates of the number of rules can be made. These adjustments and estimates, along with estimates of staffing requirements, financial considerations, and the time-line for implementation, can be calculated (Table 16.2). All of these aspects of the rule-based system can now be included in the development plan for the complete rule-based system.

Table 16.2 *Resources to Develop Knowledge-Based Systems*

Type of System			
Task	Small	Medium	Large
Number of rules	50–350	500–3,000	10,000

Table 16.2 *Continued*

Type of System			
Tool available	Probable	Probable	Maybe
Man-years to develop	.25–.50	1–2	3–5
Project cost (millions)	$.04–06	$.5–1	$2–5

From Paul Harmon and David King, *Expert Systems* (New York: John Wiley & Sons, 1985), 20.

16.8 Develop the Complete System

After the prototype system is tested to the satisfaction of everyone and the design and plan for the complete system are finished, development of the complete rule-based system can begin. The knowledge engineer and the expert expand the prototype into a complete rule-based system according to the specifications of the plan.

16.8.1 Development

A good rule is to throw out the prototype system and redesign the production system. The prototype typically has gone through so many revisions that it is best to stop and rethink the basic design. Most rule-based system tools support rapid prototyping, and the loss of the prototype is not usually significant. This is not a recommendation to abandon the development tool, but if serious prototype design problems are detected, this is the correct time to rethink the choice of development tool. As a result of development of a prototype, however, the knowledge engineer is now in a good position to develop the complete rule-based system.

16.8.2 Expanding the Knowledge Base

The most important task of the development phase is expansion of the knowledge base with the addition of a large number of new rules. These additional rules increase the depth of the rule-based system so that the system can handle subtler aspects of the test cases. The knowledge engineer and expert also increase the breadth of the rule-based system. They add rules to handle new subproblems or additional aspects of the decision-making functions of the expert.

16.8.3 User Interaction

In an operational status, a rule-based system operates by means of a dialogue between the rule-based system and the user. Considerable effort should be exerted to make the dialogue as easy and natural as possible. Attention should be given to phrasing and explanations. The user should be able to obtain as many details as possible about how the decision making is done. Graphics are valuable; they help the user follow the reasoning process of the system and can help sell its use.

16.8.4 Performance Evaluation

A good rule-based system shell or tool allows the expert or user to inspect how the rule-based system arrives at each answer. It allows the expert or user to walk through a case and determine why or why not a rule was executed, thereby isolating additional knowledge or rules that have to be added. Usually by this time, the expert can formulate and enter many rules without the assistance of the knowledge engineer. At this point, the knowledge engineer begins to transfer ownership and ongoing support of the rule-based system to the expert, making a smooth transition from prototype to production system.

16.9 Postimplementation Support

At this stage of development, the rule-based system is fully developed and tested. It is now time for the final evaluation of performance, integration into the day-to-day operation of the organization, and ongoing support and enhancement.

16.9.1 Evaluation

When the knowledge engineer, the expert, and the users are satisfied with the performance of the rule-based system, the system is tested against the acceptance criteria that were agreed on during the prototype phase. This is the time when other experts and users are invited to try their hand at running test cases. This process of running test cases continues until the performance criteria are met and all the experts and users agree that the performance is acceptable.

16.9.2 Integration

The rule-based system is now ready to be integrated into the day-to-day work environment of the organization. Integration means developing all the methods and procedures necessary to make the rule-based system work with the existing computer-based systems and manual procedures.

The first step in integration is to transfer the responsibility for use, maintenance, and expansion of the system to the expert, users, and system staff. The transfer is a particularly delicate process; the organization is dealing with new technology, a different type of user, and a new type of system. Experts tend to embrace the rule-based system. They have been a part of the entire process: prototype development, system development, and performance evaluation.

Persuading nonexperts to embrace the system is fraught with all the pitfalls associated with installing any new system. The key to success is to make users part of the process. Get their suggestions about how to make user interface easy. Get users excited about the potential, and ease them into the process. Make sure the rule-based system meets the performance expectations before users are forced to depend on this system. An early failure of a rule-based system makes future acceptance difficult.

The second step of the integration process is to interface the rule-based system with existing databases and computer-based systems. Rule-based systems may require information stored on other databases or computers as input into the rule-based process. The rule-based system also may have to be transferred to a more robust computer to improve performance or response time or to provide access to more users. These kinds of transfer activities vary from application to application. Consideration has to be given to these activities early in the process, because the interface to a database or transfer to a different computer can affect the choice of rule-based system development tool.

16.9.3 Production Support

Support for the rule-based system varies depending on whether the system is operated in the same environment as it was developed or is transferred to another computer system. Regardless, it is safe to assume that new knowledge and rules will have to be added in a manner that does not jeopardize the integrity of the operational system. A test environment is required. These changes and enhancements should not require the availability of the knowledge engineer. The process should be designed to allow the expert and users to maintain their own system. Allow for some support from system development staff for changes to the interface into traditional databases.

16.10 Conclusion

Although old in chronologic age, the development of rule-based systems is new to commercial information technology groups. The skill and processes required to develop a rule-based system differ considerably from those required to develop a commercial computer-based application system. The differences are the source of most failures. It is therefore important to highlight these as areas of caution.

The process of developing rule-based systems requires a knowledge engineer. Knowledge engineers are rare, and it is difficult for the information technology group to identify the skills required of a knowledge engineer and to select the correct person for the position. It frequently is necessary to identify someone who is willing to learn the discipline and make an investment in education. The knowledge engineer is the keystone of the entire rule-based system development process. Early in the selection and development process, give thought to how you will back up this person. Losing the knowledge engineer could put you back to square one.

Rule-based systems require a belief on the part of the organization that such applications are possible and that the results are usable and valuable. The technology is new to business, and it requires that the organization make a long-range investment in knowledge engineers, software tools, and computer processing when a cost-benefit analysis may not be possible. If belief and commitment are not there, the process is doomed to failure.

Selecting the application is another crucial aspect of developing a rule-based system because the technology is still quite limited. If an inappropriate application is selected and the process bogs down, management quickly loses interest. The earlier in the process that a failure occurs, the greater is the likelihood that the process will be abandoned. It is critical that care be given to selection of an application. Select application projects that have the potential for high return. The likelihood of a high cost or a cost overrun is great for knowledge-based systems. If high costs materialize, the high cost will be offset by a high benefit. An application with a very short payback period gives high visibility to rule-based systems and ensures their success.

The availability of a willing expert is crucial. This person should have expertise indispensable to the organization. The expert must be able to communicate his or her expertise and must be comfortable doing so. The knowledge engineer and the expert work together closely; therefore, the expert and the knowledge engineer need to establish a rapport. The expert is the second most important person in the rule-based system development process.

Rule-based systems are preceded by a prototype. However, a good rule is to discard the prototype system and redesign the production system. The prototype usually has gone through so many revisions that it is best to stop and rethink the basic design of the rule-based system. Most rule-based system tools support rapid development of prototypes, and the loss is not usually significant. As a result of development of a prototype, the knowledge engineer is in a good position to develop the complete rule-based system with a fresh perspective, and it is advantageous to do so.

The rule-based system operates by means of a dialogue between the rule-based system and the user. Considerable effort should be exerted to make the dialogue as easy and natural as possible. Attention should be given to phrasing and explanations. The user should be able to obtain as many details as possible about how decision making is done. Ease of use can ultimately spell the difference between the success and failure of a rule-based system.

Experts tend to embrace the rule-based system: they are part of the entire process. However, persuading nonexperts to embrace the system is fraught with all the pitfalls associated with installing any new system. The key to success is to make users part of the process; get their suggestions on how to make the user interface easy. Get the users excited about the potential and ease them into the process. Make sure the rule-based system meets performance expectations before users are forced to depend on the system. Early failure of a rule-based system makes future acceptance difficult.

Rule-based systems may require information stored on other databases or computers, or the system may have to be transferred to a more robust computer to improve performance or provide access to more users. Consideration has to be given to these activities early in the process because the interface to a database or transfer to a different computer can affect the choice of rule-based system tool.

Support for a rule-based system varies depending on whether the system is operated in the same environment in which it was developed or is transferred to another computer system. A test environment is required, and the process should be designed to allow the expert and users to maintain their own system with support from the system development staff.

It appears that the two most important aspects of building a rule-based system are the knowledge engineer and the choice of application. A knowledge engineer is a facilitator who understands rule-based system development and has the interpersonal skills to work with the expert, management, and users to select the appropriate application.

17

Computer Center Automation

The computer center is an area for reengineering. In most computer centers, the expense of the staffing is about 30 percent of the budget, whereas the hardware, software, and supply expenses are about 70 percent. With the increasing demand for computer capacity and computer center automation software, hardware and software expenses are increasing at a faster rate than the need for staff to operate the computer centers.

The objective of computer center reengineering is not expense reduction. The objective is *quality.* One of the obstacles to the expansion of information technology as a whole is a lack of confidence on the part of computer center users, organizational management, and even computer center staff that the technology can work. They do not believe that the computer center will be available when it is needed or that response time will be adequate to get work done. These groups of people have been conditioned to believe this from years of unacceptable quality. What has developed is a fundamental lack of confidence on the part of key groups of people that information technology in general and computer centers specifically can meet their expectations.

17.1 Quality

There are two ways to deliver a quality product or service. Quality can be inspected into the product or service or quality can be built into the product or service. In the first case, the product is made and then it is inspected for errors. When errors are detected, the product is reworked to correct the error or errors. If the product cannot be repaired, it is destroyed, and a replacement is produced.

When quality is built into a product, the process takes on a different perspective. The product is made, but the production effort is directed at identifying the source of error. When the source of error is located, it is permanently corrected. This sounds basic, but so often problems are identified and fixed but effort is not expended to isolate the source.

Computer centers are inspecting quality into their service. Functions have been created such as help desks, change coordinators, quality control, schedulers, operators, input-output control, production coordinators, and even job control language (JCL) specialists. These workers are all acting as inspectors. They are a human bridge that acts as an interface between the computer center user and the computer. This bridge is either at the front end of the process or at the back end. These workers are looking for errors either when the data is submitted or when the product is created.

Computer centers have become complex, and there is every reason to believe that they will become more complex. It is not uncommon for a computer center to have one thousand or more terminals, hundreds of concurrent simultaneous users, dozens of concurrent jobs, millions of on-line transactions, billions of bytes of on-line storage, thousands of tapes in its library, and millions of lines of print.

The result of this complexity is that there are billions of points of human interface between the user of the computer center and the computer. This translates into billions of potential errors or billions of fault points. Worse yet, these are recurring fault points. The fact that computer center personnel did one of these manual tasks correctly today is no assurance that they will do so tomorrow.

The problem is that computer centers are so complex it is not possible to inspect quality into the services provided. The solution to this problem is to build quality into the center by systematically identifying the fault points and permanently eliminating the fault points. Elimination of fault points is the definition of computer center automation, and it is essential to any reengineering project.

17.2 Implementing Quality

There are two ways to implement computer center automation: *lights out* and *problems out*. Lights out is the process of isolating equipment that does not require intervention and moving it into a dark room or unattended environment. Such equipment includes the central processor, disk drives, communication controller, and like equipment. Large computer centers have been doing this for a long time.

A second approach to lights out is clustering noncritical computer processing into a lights-out period and conducting unattended processing during that period. In this approach, noncritical processing is clustered into periods such as weekends or the graveyard shift. During this period, the computer center is operated without staff. If the work fails, it is left until morning or Monday, and it is corrected and rerun at that time.

Problems out, on the other hand, is the process of implementing tools and techniques that eliminate or reduce dependency on human intervention. The objective is not to black out space or time periods but to implement tools and techniques to reduce the fault points, the points of human intervention. As the points of human intervention are reduced, the amount of staffing is reduced. Lights out and problems out address the same issue in different ways.

17.3 Computer Center Automation Strategies

Three strategies are integral to implementing computer center automation.

17.3.1 Value-Added Data Handling

Eliminate all procedural steps that do not add value to the data entered into the computer or produced by the computer. Wherever possible, eliminate the bureaucracy or paperwork associated with interfacing with the computer center. In most cases, the people who intervene between the data entered into the computer center and the data produced by the computer center add no value to the data. They actually reduce the quality and timeliness of the product.

17.3.2 Automate All Manual Computer Center Functions

Install automated computer center management tools to eliminate the fault points produced by human intervention between the computer center and its users. Some amount of dialogue is required between the computer center and its users, such as scheduling, report distribution changes, and control parameters. There is no need for these to be manual.

17.3.3 Provide a Self-Service Environment

Provide an environment in which users can enter their own data, schedule their processing, and control the distribution of their output and so on. Provide an environment in which users have complete control over their data from cradle to grave.

17.4 Where to Build in Quality

Where can quality be built into the computing center? There are many opportunities, and some of the more important ones are addressed here.

There is no particular relevance to the sequence because the positive effect of accomplishing one as opposed to another differs greatly from one computer center to another. These opportunities are intended as thought provokers and are by no means a comprehensive list.

The first area to look at is automated computer center management tools that automate manual functions and eliminate failures due to human error. These software tools include the following types of software:

▶ Tape management system or automated tape library

▶ Automated rerun-recovery system

▶ Automated computer job scheduler

▶ Report management and distribution system

▶ Automated console response system

▶ Security system

For example, security software is extremely important. The computer center is returning control of its priorities to the users and needs to have a high level of assurance that it can access its data without affecting someone else. The computer center also needs a high level of assurance that someone is not intentionally accessing information he or she should not access. Many of these software tools are already installed in computer centers. The challenge is to seek software that can be administered by users of the computer center while avoiding software that requires dependence on central administration. These software packages and their attributes are discussed later.

Second, introduce quality into the computer center by implementing a physical plant monitoring system: equipment that recognizes failing computer or ancillary equipment, interruptions to application processing, or security breaches. It should provide automatic recovery or automatic notification of service support staff. Some aspects of a physical monitoring system are inexpensive and others are expensive. Regardless, such monitoring is available, and it is important to assume that it is necessary.

Identify recurring computer center problems, and set up a work plan to eliminate the source of the problem, not the latest occurrence of the problem. Remember, the computer center is establishing its creditability, and it needs to focus on the source of error. Use a computer job scheduling system—a software system that provides the ability for all users to directly schedule their own work. This includes the ability to schedule ad hoc work and to alter the schedule for routine work. Again, the objective is to remove human intervention between the user and the computer.

Eliminate control statements from batch jobs, and automate the process for end-user creation and submission when elimination is not possible. When it is not possible to eliminate control statements, an edit facility is required to help ensure that the process works correctly the first time. For computer center users who operate out of remote sites, this may be motherhood and apple pie, but for others, this can be a monumental task.

Introduce a JCL scan product to ensure that the computer job is correct before it is submitted into the computing environment. Again, it is important to remember that the computer center is establishing its creditability. If users have the ability to submit jobs, the computer center has to increase the likelihood of success on the first try.

Eliminate centralized data entry functions. It is an obsolete concept, and it makes the transition to real on-line processing difficult. During the interim, however, distributed data entry can become a transition to real on-line processing. Provide facilities for direct data entry either by means of an on-line data entry package or by means of distributing the terminals of a key entry system. On-line processing establishes a dialogue with the computer and widens the opportunity for a positive return.

Many computer centers still have a requirement for batch report balancing. Automate report balancing and control procedures, and return this function to the end-user department, where this kind of involvement has a chance of correcting the source of out-of-balance conditions. Automated report balancing eliminates manual handling and expedites distribution of reports.

Tape processing is a serious fault point. Although replacement media are available, such as an automatic tape library and optical disk, tape is a medium that will be with computing centers for a long time. Elimination of tape may be difficult at this time, but the dependence can be mitigated by means of reducing the use of tape processing. Computer centers can identify that tape is obsolete and that it is a roadblock to unattended computer center operation and consciously reduce its use. When tape is used, it will be a conscious deviation, and the computer center will be cognizant of the consequences. Nibble away at this medium.

Move toward eliminating hard-copy printing at the computing center. Encourage use of exception printing, remote printers, and electronic report distribution systems. Again, these techniques are not an end in themselves but are a bridge to real on-line processing. Eliminate hard-copy computer operation instructions. Such documentation is most likely obsolete. Automated tools should be self-documenting, and manual procedures should be eliminated. Remember, the objective is not to have anyone in the computer room to use it.

Install electronic mail and electronic form authorization. Neither of these tools is integral to unattended computer operation, but they do make the transition much easier. Electronic communication makes communication easier and quicker during the transition period.

Automate the job turnover process. Installing new jobs into production status is a considerable source of error in most computer centers. Moving programs into the correct libraries and changing JCL are labor-intensive and error-prone processes.

The importance of any one idea for implementing computer center automation varies from computer center to computer center. This list is not intended to be comprehensive. However, it does represent important areas to address.

17.5 What to Look for in Automated Products

In most cases, automation tools are already installed in the computer center. In other computer centers they have to be selected.

Where software is already installed, it may be necessary to modify the installation or replace the software to achieve the functions necessary for unattended computer center operation. For example, a scheduling system may not provide the ability for computer center users to schedule their own work. In this case, the function has to be added or the software has to be replaced in favor of one that can provide the function. Frequently, computer center automation software is installed as an automation tool for the computer center staff rather than for the computer center user. In such cases, it is necessary to dissolve central staff in favor of distributing the functions of the software to computer users. This is the human side of automation. In many cases, rebuilding organizations is a far more difficult task than selecting and installing software.

When software is not already installed, the computer center needs to identify the requirements and select the specific software necessary to achieve unattended computer center operation. The following primary software packages are central to computer center automation:

▶ An automated computer job scheduler

▶ An automated console response system

▶ An electronic report distribution system

These software packages address the three most labor-intensive and error-prone activities of the computer center: scheduling batch jobs on the computer, managing the operation of the computer, and distributing hard-copy output media. The following are secondary software packages and support packages:

Automated Computer Job Scheduling

CA-7	Computer Associates, Islandia, NY
CA-Scheduler	Computer Associates, Islandia, NY
Zeke	Altai Software, Arlington, TX
ESP	Cybermation, Markham, Ontario, Canada
Control-M	Fourth Dimension Software, Irvine, CA

Automated Console Operator

AF/Operator	Candle Corporation, Los Angeles, CA
Netview	IBM Corporation (see local representative)
CA-Opera	Computer Associates, Islandia, NY
WTO-Operator	Empact Software, Atlanta, GA
Auto Operator	Bool & Babbage, Sunnyvale, CA
Operaider	Computer Associates, Islandia, NY

Automated System Monitor

Omegamon	Candle Corporation, Los Angeles, CA

Report Management and Distribution System

WSF2	RSD America, Rockville Center, NY
RMDS	IBM Corporation (see local representative)
CA-Dispatch	Computer Associates, Islandia, NY
CA-7/Report	Computer Associates, Islandia, NY

Tape Management Systems

CA-1	Computer Associates, Islandia, NY

Tape Data Set Stacking Utility

TDSU	U.S. West, Bellevue, WA

Automated Rerun and Recovery System

CA-11	Computer Associates, Islandia, NY

Disk Space Abend Software

Stopex-37   Empact Software, Atlanta, GA

Security System

CA-ADC2   Computer Associates, Islandia, NY

CA/Top Secret   Computer Associates, Islandia, NY

RACF   IBM Corporation (see local representative)

Automated Report Balancing and Control

U/ACR   Unitec, Elk Grove Village, IL

17.6 Primary Software Systems

17.6.1 Automated Computer Job Scheduler

This software is installed to manage the routine, daily, batch computer-processing schedule. It is essential that the functions of this software be extended to computer center users. The objective is to provide computer center users with the ability to change the routine schedule or process ad hoc work without computer center intervention. Business organizations that purchase a departmental or small business computer or a turnkey system need to make sure this is an integral function of the operating software. The functionality of the automated computer job scheduler should include the following:

▶ Provide most users with the ability to schedule their own workload. The objective is not to support the computer center but to support the computer center user.

▶ Eliminate the need to submit paper documents to schedule or reschedule routine or ad hoc work.

▶ Provide the facility to submit job control parameters directly into jobs without any knowledge of JCL or without assistance from computer center personnel.

▶ Provide users with the ability to know the run status of their own work. The user needs to know whether something ran or did not. The last thing the computer center wants is hundreds of calls asking the status of a job.

▶ Provide the ability to see other systems and scheduled work. This aids in scheduling work that has cross-system dependencies and ensures that jobs will not be submitted when capacity or availability is not there.

▶ Provide the ability to model the production schedule, allowing computer center users a high level of confidence that their desired schedule can be met.

17.6.2 Automated Console Response Systems

The objective of a console response system is to eliminate all routine interaction between the computer operator and the computer. It is important to impress on hardware and software vendors that console traffic is viewed as both error prone and labor intensive and is therefore unacceptable. Yet these activities have become so ingrained in software and hardware that suppliers do not even realize they are designing or perpetuating this kind of activity. Let them know their objective is to eliminate the console!

An automated console response system should support the objectives of computer center automation. It is the tie that binds together the numerous software packages used to achieve unattended computer operation and is therefore the new quality assurance manager. An automated console system improves the quality of the service of the computer center by eliminating the human intervention between the application software systems and the computer and between the computer operation software and the computer. A console response system eliminates the human intervention required to operate the computer at all levels.

It is not necessary for the console response system to directly satisfy all requirements of an organization. In most cases, multiple software packages are required, and the console response system acts to integrate these software packages. The automated console response system ties them together into a fault-tolerant environment. Automated console response systems should provide the following functionality:

▶ Handle all routine console messages. Computer centers should try to eliminate all system messages either through software or through system modifications.

▶ Trap any system console message and provide an automatic response. Put pressure on hardware and software suppliers to eliminate these operating system activities. If the messages can be answered automatically, they can be eliminated.

▶ Perform all computer or master console operator functions. The lights on the console are gone, the hard-copy console is gone, and now it is time to get rid of the console.

▶ Automatically cancel and reset terminal and similar devices when a system "hang" condition is detected.

▶ Automatically balance the system workload when system thresholds are exceeded or system standards are violated. Computer centers have expected operators to balance workloads for a long time but have not provided the criteria for balancing. If the criteria can be established, the system can be balanced automatically.

17.6.3 Electronic Report Distribution System

Software is available for electronic management and distribution of hard-copy reports. This software directs reports in an output queue to a disk device rather than to a printer. Once on disk, the information can be retained for a defined period, viewed, and, if necessary, printed under the control of an end user. This is not a substitute for on-line query, but it is an outstanding intermediate step. It encourages computer users to think in terms of the information required rather than in terms of reports. Electronic report management and distribution systems should provide the following functionality:

▶ Enable the user to view reports on line, to administer their own report distribution, and to print exception reports locally or at the central computer site.

▶ Provide spreadsheet-like capabilities for formatting and reformatting reports. Most reports are not designed for an eighty-column screen; therefore some formatting capabilities are necessary for effective viewing of these reports.

▶ Offer the possibility to define logical reports and the capability of using implicit rather than explicit report description definitions.

▶ Offer retention and archival facilities for reports and thereby not only eliminate the need to print reports but also eliminate the need to rerun them when they are lost.

An effective way to implement the report management and distribution system is by developing a do-as-I-do attitude rather than a do-as-I-say attitude. Start to implement this product in the computer center: put all JCL, dumps, and all internal reporting on the system. In many computer environments, the largest single user of hard-copy reports is the computing center.

Begin user involvement by migrating large-volume reports that are used primarily for reference, reports that are periodically refreshed with up-to-date copies (for example, financial reports, lists of names and addresses, and marketing information). Start with users who are receptive to the technology, product, and approach. Get these users involved early in the process. Take them on site visits before the software is purchased and installed.

17.7 The Second Level of Software Systems

The automated computer-job scheduler, the automated console response system, and the electronic report distribution system are central to computer center automation. At the next level are four additional software systems: security software, automated rerun-recovery systems, automated computer monitoring systems, and automated problem notification.

17.7.1 Security Systems

Security software operates as an umbrella over the top of all the other computer center automation tools. Security software is a prerequisite for a self-service computing environment. It enables users to access their information and software without interfering with the integrity of other users or without relying on central computer center administration. The most common security software is RACF from IBM and Top Secret from Computer Associates.

17.7.2 Automated Rerun and Recovery Systems

Rerun-recovery software enables automatic restarting of batch jobs without technical support or database or computer center personnel assistance. Automated batch job restarting is crucial to unattended operation. It enables automatic housekeeping (for example, uncataloguing datasets, restarting tape management systems, and determining restart step), so the only intervention required is to correct the problem and restart the job. Batch jobs are within the control of end users; reliance on computer center staff for cleanup and restarting is unacceptable. Software is available to handle these conditions, and new applications should be designed with this as a requirement.

17.7.3 Automated System Monitors

Interactive computer system monitors have been available for a long time. This software provides the technical service staff and computer operators with the ability to monitor interactively the performance of the computer system. Within the software, thresholds are set for computer performance, and when the threshold is crossed, corrective action can be taken. This software allows computer operators to manage the computer. However, when the automated system monitor interacts with an automated console response system, conditions that exceed threshold can be automatically corrected through an automated response. The combination of the automated console response system and the automated system monitor offers the opportunity to automatically correct performance imbalances before they affect computer users. An automated system monitor typically has the following functionality:

▶ Provides the ability to define the parameters for normal computer operation, such as response time, use of the central processing unit, resource utilization, and elapsed time.

▶ Identifies abnormal processing and provides on-line diagnostic functions to isolate problems.

▶ Provides statistics for historical analysis of abnormal processing conditions and their correction.

▶ Identifies the status of all processing on the system with the flexibility to isolate and provides additional resources to specific, highly sensitive work.

▶ Allows the system monitor to pass messages to the console response system in response to abnormal work-load balance conditions. The console response system can take steps to correct abnormal workload-balance conditions on the basis of predetermined rules, frequently before an operator could even recognize they exist.

17.7.4 Automated Problem Notification

Security and environmental monitoring devices are available to monitor the vital aspects of the computer center in the absence of computer room staff. Such equipment can recognize failing equipment or intrusions and phone designated staff on an exception basis using voice synthesizers. The devices can be queried by cautious or inquisitive management.

A similar device is available for the computer. Messages are passed to a subsystem where they are logged and filtered. Messages that require no action are ignored, those that require a response are answered, and those that cannot be satisfied initiate a phone call to on-call support personnel. All messages are logged. When the computer center is unattended, such a device becomes indispensable to follow up on the software failures that are sure to occur in even the best-run computer center. Some computer centers that operate one or more unattended shifts do not respond to computer job failures; they let those jobs go uncorrected until the next staffed shift.

17.8 Other Automated Computer Operation Software

Achieving unattended operation requires that the power of the computer be used to manage itself. For a couple of decades or more, information technology experts have been applying their skills to managing the business. It is time to do the same for the computer center. This is a classic case of the cobbler's children going without shoes. There are many other areas in which automation can be applied to the computer center.

17.8.1 On-line Data-Entry Software

Centralized data entry is an obsolete function. Recent Association for Computer Operation Management (AFCOM) studies indicated that only 488 of the computer centers surveyed had a centralized data-entry function. In 1984 more than 90 percent of computer centers had a data-entry function, a decrease of almost half (42 percent).

The typical data-entry function operates something like this: information is written on an input document, the documents are batched, and the batches are logged and sent to data entry for key entry and processing by a batch system. The information is processed with the computer, and an exception error report is returned to the originator for correction. The process is then repeated for the corrections. In an on-line system the originator does not rewrite the source document but enters data into the system directly, correcting errors as they occur—a far less labor-intensive process. However, not all systems are on line, and a reasonable, low-cost alternative is on-line data-entry software.

On-line data-entry software provides the information originator the opportunity to enter data directly. The edit and update facilities are not equal to those of custom on-line update systems, but the software usually offers some logical editing, as of numerics and date ranges. These products also offer personal computer functionality with uploading and downloading capabilities and even stand-alone updating to diskettes. If the software is used in conjunction with a report management system, it eliminates the need to return exception error reports. Keymaster from TSI International, with more than 50 percent of the on-line mainframe computing data entry market, is the most common on-line data entry software package.

17.8.2 Automated Report Balancing and Control

Automate the report-balancing process. Banks, insurance companies, and other companies that do a lot of report balancing and have large staffs to accomplish it are moving in this direction. For the most part, this has been accomplished through in-house-developed software, but at least one purchased-software package on the market accomplishes automated report balancing: U/ACR from Unitec Systems, Inc., in Elk Grove Village, Illinois. Report-balancing software should provide the ability for computer users to define balancing rules and to change them as necessary. It should automatically check and balance reports when required.

Ten or more years of effort frequently are expended on the efficient design of application systems, and little or no effort is spent on automating the balancing process. An entire processing stream can be halted for hours or even days waiting for computer users to review and balance their systems.

17.8.3 Library Management

Library management should be performed by computer center users under the protection of a security package. Programming and technical support staff should move modules into production libraries. This presupposes an electronic signature and an audit trail. Remember that computer center librarians do not know what a new software module can do, only that the proper forms were provided and that they had proper authorization. Using the security system as the substitute for authorization, the computer center can allow programming and technical staff to maintain their own libraries. It is time for computer centers to take advantage of the security system the way computer center users are.

17.8.4 JCL Scan Utility

JCL continues to be a labor-intensive and error-prone activity. JCL is the source of a large portion of a computer center's interruptions and problems. Scanning JCL for syntax errors or conformance with computer-center standards should be part of building the computer center batch operation schedule, library maintenance, and production and test job submission. Syntax checking is part of the operating system. Some automated job schedulers include it as an integral part of their software, and stand-alone software is available for scanning JCL.

17.8.5 Disk Space Management

An alternative that is becoming more and more cost effective as a trade-off for tape processing is to substitute disk or direct access storage devices (DASDs) for tape as permanent or temporary storage. As a result of these and other uses, data stored on disk media is growing at a rate of 30 percent or more a year. This growth pattern has resulted in the increased use of disk management software to ensure that sufficient disk space is available, that it is used efficiently, and that its use is not dependent on human intervention.

17.8.6 Disk Space Abend Software

Disk space abend software stops space-not-available DASD abends during step initialization. These conditions are associated with disk-space availability and management and arise when the IBM MVS operating system is not able to satisfy space allocations for a new data set. These abends are found in even the best-run computer centers. Because abends are not part of the programming staff's area of responsibility, recovery from these conditions can place a burden on computer center, technical service, or database staff.

17.8.7 Tape Management Software

To achieve total computer center automation, it is necessary to reduce and eliminate the dependency on tape. If the computer center has a large tape inventory, it is almost mandatory that the computer center have a tape management system. Tape management software helps to improve reliability and reduce the direct labor associated with the use of this medium. Tape management systems make tape labeling a thing of the past. Tape management systems, such as Computer Associates CA-1 TMS, control the inventory and disposition of tapes.

Tape management systems are valuable tools for isolating the use and reducing the inventory of tape volumes. They should reduce the labor associated with tape handling, improve the quality of the retention process, and assist in identifying ways to reduce tape use. Tape is a data storage medium that is likely to be with us for a long time. Start reducing the inventory of tapes by no longer designing software systems that require tape as a processing medium.

17.8.8 Tape Data Set Stacking Utility

Eliminate the use of tape as a storage medium from existing systems whenever possible. Look for ways to reduce the numbers of tape volumes. Statistics indicate that 80 percent of all tapes use only a few inches or feet of the tape reel. Install software to stack multiple data sets on a single reel using software such as the tape data set stacking utility offered by U.S. West of Bellvue, Washington. Stacking data sets reduces access time to retrieve them, but it is likely that the tape will never be used again or that it will be used very infrequently.

Tape data set stacking software should be used in concert with tape management software. Many tape backups are used only in exception processing. Many of these backups use only a fraction of a tape volume. By stacking these kinds of tape data sets, the computer center can reduce the physical handling of tapes, reduce the volume of tape inventories, decrease off-site storage cost, and improve cost containment.

17.9 Benefits of Computer Automation

Because the objective of computer center automation is quality, the primary benefit is consistent, high-quality service. Computer center automation is a reengineering process that eliminates human error by removing human intervention from routine computer center operation. It eliminates recurring error-producing situations and improves the reliability of the entire physical plant. Computer service centers are in the *service* business, and their users expect consistent quality. That is just what computer center automation delivers.

Benefits are not limited to quality. There is increased flexibility. By means of standardizing and automating manual functions, unattended operation provides the ability to adjust rapidly to changing business needs. It improves the ability of the computer center to absorb additional workload with minimal environmental change.

Automation improves productivity by means of eliminating manual, repetitive functions and by allowing the computer center to emphasize the primary functions of the business, not only in the computer center but also in the user area. Remember, we are doing source data entry and source control, which eliminate paperwork, follow-up, control logs, and endless meetings. In many cases, the productivity gains in user areas are greater than in the computer center. It is an education medium. Automation increases the knowledge of the nontechnical staff and, when required, prepares them for an assignment in areas of information technology outside the computer center. Last, automation provides a less stressful and chaotic work environment for remaining information technology professionals, computer center users, and management.

Unattended computer center operation improves cost effectiveness. It reduces personnel expense through head count reduction, through reduction of benefit expenses, and through elimination of premium pay (overtime, off-shift, holidays). It optimizes the use of the computer hardware by allowing the computer center to use the computer hardware up to its million instructions per second (MIPS) rating and therefore maximizing resource utilization. It avoids expenses through improved reliability. Computer center automation focuses on the removal of fault points and therefore reduces software maintenance expense. It eliminates rerun expenses.

17.10 Obstacles to Achieving Computer Center Automation

There are two obstacles to achieving unattended computer center operation: *human* and *technical.*

17.10.1 Human Obstacles

The human obstacles are the most diabolical because they are extremely difficult to detect and even harder to correct. Many computer centers have yet to recognize that the unattended computer center is both possible and desirable. Where the recognition of possibility is absent, so is opportunity. Second, there are computer center professionals who do not believe that it is possible or desirable to achieve unattended computer center operation. This, of course, is a self-fulfilling prophecy. In reality, most vendors that offer midrange or departmental computers provide a computer environment that will run unattended. This is the computer center's competition.

17.10.2 Technical Obstacles

The second obstacle is technical. Although on the surface it looks more imposing, it is far less severe than the human obstacle. The most important technical obstacle is tape use. Although there are alternatives to tape, there are also ways of reducing its use. The per unit expense of DASD is being reduced, and optical disks are becoming commercially available. After a case by case analysis, use of these technologies can replace a large amount of tape use. There are automatic picking systems for cartridge tape systems that reduce the manual intervention required when tape is used. Other technical obstacles, such as operator intervention and hard-copy report distribution, are being solved or can be worked around.

17.11 Making It Happen

If the benefits are great but implementation is fraught with pitfalls, how does a computer center go about making computer center automation happen? The answer is my seven steps to computer center automation.

First, you have to believe that it can happen. If the computer center does not recognize that the technology has evolved to this point or it does not see the value in achieving the objective, then it will never happen. The first step is to attack this human element.

Second, make sure that everyone understands why it must happen. The objective of automation is quality. It is only through quality that the credibility of the computer center can be established. Make sure that computer center users, organizational management, and most important, the computer center staff understand why it must happen and buy into the process. It is important to understand that the competition for the computer center is departmental computers, and they already provide unattended operation. If necessary, error in favor of excessive communication.

Third, ensure that computer center staff members do not lose their livelihood as a result of making unattended operation happen. Implementing unattended computer center operation has a built-in requirement for training. Staff targeted for displacement need to be trained for a position of equal or better pay than the position displaced.

Fourth, be opportunistic. Unless the organization is in a growth mode, it is difficult to achieve the third step. As computer center turnover is experienced, treat it as an opportunity. Do not refill the position, look for an opportunity to change priorities and work on an aspect of the unattended computer center automation project that makes the position unnecessary. This approach makes step three easier.

Fifth, reinvest saved dollars in the hardware and software needed to implement computer center automation. The process is much more palatable to management if it is convinced the project is self-funding.

Sixth, as computer center personnel become available, provide opportunities that will use their time by having them participate in the implementation process. Reinvest the human resources you save in making computer center automation work. The staff loves it, and it is an opportunity to train them. Note the word *opportunity* again.

Seventh, treat the process as a project with measurable goals and target dates. Projects that are planned tend to happen, and targets tend to be hit.

17.12 Conclusion

The objective of professional information technology management is to promote and expand the use of information technology to achieve the goals of the organization. One of the major obstacles to achieving this objective is a lack of confidence on the part of users, management, and even computer center staff that the computer center can provide expected service, availability, and response time—that the computer center can provide high-quality service.

The problem is that computer centers have been attempting to inspect quality into their product. However, computer centers have become so complex that it is no longer possible to inspect quality into the computer center. The solution is to *build* quality into the computer center by identifying fault points and by eliminating the fault points. The definition of computer center automation is the removal of fault points.

Part 4

Reengineering Summary

18

Engineering Opportunity

18.0.1 Creation

Over the last twenty-five or thirty years, the most popular method for developing information systems has been new development, or creation. When information technology was first introduced, computer-based software systems were created as a replacement for manual systems. When technology changed, new systems were created to replace old systems, and as systems became older and inundated with problems, the natural solution was to create new systems. This creation has not always taken the form of custom development; it can include purchased software, purchased services, or turnkey systems. Regardless of the form it takes, it is creation.

The most common information technology development scenario, therefore, is creation. Creation starts with a statement of requirements or a problem statement that is translated into software development or software selection and finally into a working software system. Because most manual systems have been replaced with some form of automation, creation is now a result of a crisis in a software system, a period of turbulence that results from business, human, and technologic factors. During this crisis, the user organization has numerous options, but despite the reason, the result is usually the same—a completely new system is created.

By far the most successful approach to developing technology-based systems is creation. Any other form of supporting a change in requirements or an enhancement is frowned on as second class. Support personnel are not viewed as positively as development personnel. Further, computer users have been conditioned to seek replacement as the solution to changing requirements or the need for new functions.

18.0.2 Evolution

During the same time frame that creation became the pervasive mode of software development, software systems became increasingly more complex. This complexity increases the expense and the risk associated with replacing a software system. The alternative to this cycle of problem → creation → problem is to harness the change that is a natural part of all software systems and direct it toward the objective of the organization, thereby extending the life of the system. An evolutionary strategy improves productivity by focusing on the 20 percent of the features of a software system that result in 80 percent of the problems. It releases 80 percent of the effort to build new and enhanced features on the base of features that work.

During the last 20 years, the following three factors have affected the speed and direction of the evolution of computer-based systems:

1. No matter how good the technology, it has little chance of success if business conditions do not foster its introduction.

2. The technology has little chance of success if people do not embrace it.

3. The expectations and use of information technology have to correspond with the way technology actually evolves.

These factors are categorized as business factors, human factors, and technologic factors. Understanding the nature of these makes it easier to harness the evolution of systems.

18.0.3 Opportunity

It is important to remember that change is the norm, that the opportunity for change exceeds the capacity to absorb change, and that some change has a higher return than other change. These characteristics imply that organizations continually have high-return opportunities to implement information technology available but that these opportunities are camouflaged by many other less valuable opportunities. An innovative organization is the one that has the facilities to seek out and implement high-return opportunities for information technology change.

Most successful innovations in information technology exploit the change condition. Therefore, the very source of information technology opportunities is change. Focusing on this change is equivalent to focusing on opportunity. The change provides an opportunity to enhance existing technology, extend its life, or create new value. The person most qualified to achieve this goal is the chief information technology officer. The chief information technology officer has a base of experience, a management perspective, and the ability to implement change that is unequaled in the organization.

The keys to this opportunistic approach to information technology are first, to create an environment in which change, not success or failure, is rewarded. Second, to develop an opportunistic approach to the selection of information technology change. And third, to systematically extend the life of existing software investments until opportunities are identified.

18.1 Reengineering Software Development

Successful migration from creation to opportunism is based on three-step reengineering. First, establish an overall computing architecture that defines the business, technologic, and human directions of the organization. Second, establish a set of strategies for implementing an evolutionary approach to software system development. Third, create and foster change.

18.1.1 Architecture

The increasing number of innovative solutions to information requirements cannot be ignored. Information technology is akin to a symphony in which hardware, software, and turnkey solutions are the instruments. The architecture is the orchestration of these instruments. On the basis of the objectives of an organization and the availability of solutions, the composition of the orchestra changes.

Organizations need to build as much flexibility as possible into their system architecture, recognizing the value of past successes and leveraging them with the potential of new technology. This is not a simple task, but the harmony derived from orchestrating the rich variety of alternatives derived from strategic planning can be rewarding to an organization.

18.1.2 Strategy

It is relatively easy to conceptualize setting a direction for the evolution of an existing software system. Evolutionary systems are typically viewed as directing the maintenance and enhancement of existing systems. Operational analysis is used to identify the requested maintenance and enhancement. Improvements are specified, and a direction is established for the software system. Implementation is achieved through a series of small projects, sometimes called *chunks*. As changes are requested, they are tested against this direction for conformance. The organization becomes comfortable that the changes are moving the software systems in the desired direction.

Establishing a direction for a new software system is a different matter. There is no history for the design. As a result, it requires experience, intuition, and fuzzy logic to determine a direction. Timing also plays an important role in this process. Identifying the portions of the software system that have to be completed first and establishing a sequence of events help clarify the direction. If a new database is required, identifying the data elements and designing maintenance and reporting procedures helps to identify future features. Experience with similar applications or insight into the experience of others is beneficial in establishing direction.

Assume that the direction is changing. As portions of the new system are designed, other portions become clear. Learning is gradual, and users cannot accurately specify system requirements until they see them. Assume that it is necessary to change earlier designs as directions change. No one is clairvoyant, and allowing room for software system improvement ensures a greater chance of success than trying to identify every feature of a software system. It is usually easier to improve or modify an existing software system than it is to specify all of its features with no prior knowledge.

18.1.3 Reengineering

The operational analysis and reengineering techniques described thus far are directed at returning creditability to the much maligned process of software maintenance. By harnessing change, it is possible to direct the natural process of change toward achieving organizational objectives. However, maintenance is not the only way software systems can evolve: software systems can evolve through creation. Software creation and reengineering are not contradictions in terms, nor are they mutually exclusive. It is both possible and desirable to create an evolutionary system, a system that is easy to reengineer at a later date.

Systems that are easy to reengineer are developed by segmenting projects into small pieces, or chunks, that can be developed and evaluated quickly by computer users. Get the product out quickly, and try it out with the computer user. The small chunks become prototypes that give the computer user a chance to change before large investments are made. Small chunks allow software products to be tested and implemented quickly before barriers are developed. Chunking incorporates all the principles for successful evolution: it is easy to modify; learning is gradual; users see the results of requirements; improvements are encouraged; and high-return functions are isolated.

A good rule is that a chunk should result in a project of six months or less with a usable product delivered in that time frame. After the chunk is complete, future improvements are included in another chunk. There is no limit to the number of chunks, and theoretically successful evolution could go on forever.

Continuous development does not imply that development of a software system must receive constant labor commitments. There can be periods when the software system becomes dormant, and no improvements are made. During these periods, the evolution of other software systems may have a higher priority. Remember, the software system must grow, or it will die.

18.2 Automating Software Development

Automation of software development and computing center operation is integral to the process of implementing evolutionary software systems and directing the evolution of existing software systems. This automation requires substantial rethinking of the way software is developed and processed. Quality is essential. Automated software development using computer-aided software engineering (CASE), object technology, and rule-based system technology is integral. Computer center automation is mandatory for high-quality service in complex computer centers. The outcome of these activities is increased dependence on automation. This requires increased emphasis on computer security.

18.2.1 Quality

An obstacle that inhibits the rapid expansion of information technology is inability to quickly create high-quality, low-cost software that meets the expectations of computer users and operates flawlessly without human intervention. Software is still developed manually, a slow, tedious, and laborious task. The obstacles are complex and legitimate, and as a result, little has been done to automate the process. Yet the return on an investment in quality is immense—a software product that meets the requirements of the computer user the first time with a reduction of effort up to 50 percent.

The solution requires a belief that quality is achievable and a commitment to make it happen. If information technology professionals do not accept that flawless software can happen, it will never happen. Everyone must understand why quality has to happen. The first step is to achieve a commitment to quality and a belief that productivity can be improved. Make sure that computer users, organizational management, and most important, the information technology professionals understand why quality must happen and that they buy into the process.

Look for the source of error and correct it. Automate as many aspects of computer development as possible. Use object technology, CASE technology, rule-based systems, and fourth-generation languages (4GLs) whenever possible. Transfer much of the software development process to computer users. Every automated tool that reduces human intervention in software development improves quality, and every action that reduces the need to communicate specifications for software from users to computer professionals improves quality.

Reinvest the dollars that you save from improved quality in the hardware and software required to automate software development. Reinvest the labor saved in the process of improving quality. The entire process of improving quality is easier to sell to all involved when it is self-funding. The entire process is an opportunity for in-service training to develop new techniques and, more important, new attitudes. Financial return in terms of improved revenues or decreased expenses will follow.

18.2.2 Object Technology

Software development has always been expensive. The dream of software developers is to obtain results for lower cost and in less time. The search for tools to accomplish this objective has produced database management systems, query systems, screen development tools, 4GLs, graphic programming aids, and code generators. The ultimate dream, however, is to find ways to avoid programming altogether. The best way to not program is to reuse existing code.

A key part of the attraction of object technology is that once an object is created, tested, and found useful, it can be cloned and used repeatedly. This has the potential to save software developers untold time, because it saves them from reinventing the wheel.

Reuse allows mistakes to be reduced substantially. Construction of an application from tested, reused parts lessens the possibility of errors in the parts and relegates testing to the design and assembly of the correct objects. To attain meaningful levels of reuse, a strict design and architectural approach to building and assembling objects must be established.

18.2.3 CASE Technology

Another factor that inhibits expansion of information technology is the high cost of software development. It continues to be difficult to develop low-cost, high-quality software. Software systems require flexibility, yet the process of developing these systems is so complex that it requires rigid process control. Establishing requirements and translating them into designs, computer code, and operational procedures is a frustratingly slow and laborious manual process. Therefore, the software development process is rigid, and this rigidity is manifest in the design of the software system.

The development process is error prone. Specifications are almost always incomplete. Requesters do not understand their needs until they actually see samples, and the opportunity for translation error is astronomical. Furthermore, information technology is alien to most business executives. It is difficult for them to conceptualize how they can best apply technology to business. Conversely, information technology is so complex that most computer professionals become proficient at the expense of achieving insight into business. The result is an environment in which business executives understand their requirements when only they see the end result and computer professionals are not likely to add a business perspective. Under these conditions, it is likely that a system design will be modified. The business environment is not stagnant, which increases the need to modify previously developed software.

The laborious and error-prone aspects of software development make the software rigid and difficult to change. An ever-increasing proportion of software development labor is expended on maintaining previously developed software because of the limited scope of understanding of businessmen and computer professionals. The solution is to automate the process of software development by creating a highly flexible software development environment or CASE. Over the past two decades, numerous solutions have been proposed to correct the rigidity of software development. Computer languages have evolved from machine level code to 4GL, and purchased software was introduced, as were turnkey systems that entailed inexpensive small computers and personal computing.

18.2.4 Rule-Based Systems

Another alternative for automating software development is to use rule-based systems. Use of rule-based systems is the discipline in which business professionals are most likely to come in contact with artificial intelligence skills. For purpose of this discussion, artificial intelligence is equated with rule-based systems.

Experts solve difficult problems, explain the solution, learn from problem solving, explain the relevance of the solution, and possibly most important, are capable of knowing when they do not know something. A rule-based system, like a human expert, gives advice by drawing on its store of rules and requesting information specific to the problem under consideration.

The incentive for rule-based systems is contained in the attributes of knowledge. Knowledge is perishable; its longevity is tied to the expert. Expert knowledge is scarce and difficult to accumulate, pass on, and use. Expert knowledge often is vague, inconsistent, and widely distributed over a number of widely dispersed experts. As a result, rule-based systems are used to preserve, clone, and apply knowledge. Rule-based systems pass on knowledge to another generation of experts or users, who encourage its growth. Rule-based systems attempt to make knowledge more precise and systematic and to collect it into a knowledge base.

Rule-based systems provide the benefit of making knowledge readily available. A rule-based system is impartial in its decision making, and it has total recall. It provides the opportunity to share knowledge over a large user base, and it expedites routine decisions. Rule-based systems conserve valuable experience in an organization and can act as a tutor to pass this information to trainees.

Rule-based systems require knowledge engineering. In the past, knowledge engineering required immense amounts of human labor and more computing than was readily available. From a business perspective, both human involvement and computing resources were expensive, making the entire process impractical. In light of current investments in rule-based systems research, the tide has turned in favor of rule-based systems. There are opportunities to address business operations that were beyond the reach of computer professionals.

18.2.5 Computer Center Automation

Another obstacle to expansion of information technology is a lack of confidence on the part of users of computer centers, organizational management, and even computer center staff. They do not believe that the computer center will be available when it is needed or that response time will be adequate to get work done. These groups of people have been conditioned to believe this on the basis of years of unacceptable quality. What has developed is a fundamental lack of confidence on the part of key groups of people that information technology in general, and computer centers in particular, can meet their expectations.

Computer centers are inspecting quality into their service. They created functions such as help desks, change coordinators, quality control, schedulers, operators, input-output control, and production coordinators. The workers are all acting as inspectors. They are a human bridge that acts as an interface between computer center users and computers. The workers doing these functions are inspecting for errors either when the data is submitted or when the work is produced by the computer center.

Computer centers have become highly complex, and there is every reason to believe that they are becoming increasingly more complex. The result of this complexity is that there are billions of points of human interface between users of the computer center and the computers. This translates into billions of potential errors or billions of fault points. Worse yet, these are recurring fault points. The fact that computer center personnel do one of these manual tasks correctly today is no assurance that they will do it correctly tomorrow.

The problem is that computer centers are so complex that it is not possible to inspect quality into the services provided. The solution is to reengineer the center by systematically identifying the fault points and by permanently eliminating them. Elimination of fault points builds quality into the computer center.

There are three strategies to implement computer center automation, as follows:

▶ Provide value-added computing. Value-added computing eliminates the procedural steps that do not add value to the data entered into the computer or produced by the computer by means of eliminating the bureaucracy or paperwork associated with interfacing with the computer center.

▶ Provide a self-service environment in which users can enter their own data, schedule their processing, and control the distribution of their output. Provide an environment in which users have complete control over their data.

▶ Automate all manual data-center functions by installing automated computer center management tools to eliminate the fault points created by human intervention between the computer center and its users.

Automated computer center management tools are central to achieving computer center automation. In many cases, automation tools are already installed in the computer center. When the software is already installed, it may be necessary to reinstall or replace the software to achieve the strategies necessary for computer center automation.

Computer center automation software frequently is installed to automate the computer center staff rather than to improve service for computer center users. In such cases, it is necessary to dissolve central staff in favor of distributing the software functions to computer users. This is the human side of automation. In many cases, rebuilding organizations is a far more difficult task than selecting and installing software.

When software is not already installed, three primary software packages are usually central to the computer center automation: an automated computer job scheduler, an automated console management system, and an electronic report distribution system. These software packages address three of the most labor-intensive and error-prone activities of the computer center: scheduling batch jobs, managing operation of the computer, and distributing hard-copy output media.

There are two obstacles to achieving computer center automation: *human* and *technical.* The human obstacles are the most diabolical because they are difficult to detect and even more difficult to correct. Many computer centers have yet to recognize that automation is both possible and desirable. When the recognition of possibility is absent, opportunity is absent. Second, there are computer centers that do not believe it is either possible or desirable to achieve computer center automation. This is a self-fulfilling prophecy. Actually, many client-server alternatives provide an unattended computer environment. This is the computer center's competition.

The second obstacle is technical. Although on the surface it looks more imposing, it is far less severe than the human obstacle. The most important technical obstacle is tape use. Although there are few alternatives to tape, there are ways to reduce and eliminate its use. The per unit expense of a direct access storage device (DASD) is being reduced, and optical disks are becoming commercially available. Mass storage devices and automatic tape libraries also are available. After a case-by-case analysis is performed, these technologies can be used to replace a large amount of, if not all, tape use. Other technical obstacles such as operator intervention and hard-copy report distribution are being solved or can be worked around.

18.2.6 The Security Umbrella

The goal of information technology is to provide information and information processing in support of organizational objectives. Rapid advances in information technology, increased need to process large quantities of information, and greater availability of computing has resulted in the need to secure this same information. In support of this need, a series of security procedures are usually developed to circumvent the risks associated with increased access to computer-based information and information processing. These procedures are used to maximize protection from areas of vulnerability. The procedures minimize the aspects of security that inhibit the use of information processing and the distribution of information while maximizing security, integrity, and privacy.

Management plays a key role in security by ensuring that an organization is adequately secured through a series of prudent checks and balances. For corporate officers and other management, such as data-processing management, there are legal implications in exercising prudent security management, including the safeguarding of computer facilities, computer-based information systems, and information vital to the organization. Numerous court cases in which disgruntled shareholders sued corporate officers solidified this prudence-management concept into a standard called the "prudent man rule." It requires that officers and other agents discharge their duties with the diligence and care that an ordinary prudent person would exercise under similar circumstances.

The specific conduct required to manage and protect information assets varies depending on the circumstances of any given organization. When little or nothing productive is done in connection with security of information technology, the objectives of the organization are placed in increasing jeopardy. With extensive reliance on computers, management can hardly ignore the need to evaluate security risk. Although 100 percent security remains elusive, a great many policies, procedures, and practices are possible to narrow security risks. An audit of policies and procedures is a common practice in most organizations. However, assessment of policies and procedures for risk is far less common. The following simple three-step risk-assessment procedure isolates areas in jeopardy and therefore reduces security risks:

1. Perform diagnostic procedures to assess and evaluate the level of risk associated with a potential security exposure.

2. Rate the effectiveness of existing checks, balances, and protection measures.

3. Prioritize corrective measures to address high-risk areas and to avoid adverse effects should a potential hazard materialize.

Having accomplished this three-step risk-assessment procedure, management implements the corrective measures and audits for compliance. Management routinely repeats the assessment to evaluate the ongoing level of risk associated with security measures.

Security assessment is a systematic method for assessing jeopardy to computer centers and computer-based information systems. It enables management to take immediate steps to deal with information technology security by (1) evaluating risk, (2) establishing programs to minimize risk, and (3) correcting or minimizing security risk.

The effectiveness of security assessment depends on the steps taken by management to ensure a free exchange of information throughout the assessment. The assessment requires the cooperation of the specialists within the organization, and it requires that management communicate its determination to conscientiously execute and follow up on the security assessment.

18.3 Conclusion

The success of reengineering software systems is based on the human aspects of information technology. Creating new software systems is the solution of choice because it has demonstrated itself to be a durable, if not the most effective, approach to developing and maintaining software systems. Information technology professionals and computer users alike have become comfortable with it.

Software support and enhancements are viewed as less desirable than creating new software. Yet most benefits are derived from building on the installed base of software systems. Furthermore, information technology professionals and computer users need to recognize that most of the benefits from computer projects are derived from a small number of functions. The real opportunities are derived from enhancing existing systems.

Architectures, plans, and strategies are required to redirect the established strategy of recreating systems when a system crisis occurs. The critical success factor for harnessing all aspects of change is the human factor, not the technologic factor.

Automation tools are available to automate computer centers and the software development cycle. Reengineering development does not require automation, but it is enhanced and accelerated by automation. Reengineering development does require an acceptance of the principles behind the approach. The key to success is to make computer users and information technology professionals understand the advantages of a reengineering approach to system development and to have them buy into the concepts.

Engineering Enterprise Computing

Enterprise computing is an achievable opportunity. Tools are available to achieve the different functional aspects and to implement interoperability between distributed systems, client-server technology, UNIX-based platforms, and personal computer local area network (LAN) clusters.

In many cases, the obstacles to the realization of enterprise computing are more organizational than technologic. So new paradigms must be established for both users of information technology and central information system organizations. The following techniques have been effective in moving toward this goal:

Economies of scale: Consolidation and reengineering of applications can yield considerable cost savings. In some cases this involves some outsourcing.

Information-driven applications: Mainframe databases for basic business accounting and mission-critical applications are combined with client-server systems to realize new high-productivity applications, such as decision automation, and incorporating technologies such as rule-based systems, voice technology, and imaging.

Core competence: This business model enables users to leverage key strengths and skills and to define new roles for centralized information technology.

Alternative development approaches: To respond to changing business demands on information technology, organizations must develop new approaches to both mainframe, personal computer LAN clusters, and client-server applications development. For example, properly used computer-aided software engineering (CASE) strategies and object technology can meet user needs more effectively and reduce the need for later changes by tying applications to business processes. Reengineering can similarly improve the flexibility and performance of applications, while changes in project management procedures, programmer organization, and other factors can yield substantial benefits.

Service business model: The development of value-added services to support distributed users dictates that the information technology operation adopt the service-business model. This requires more flexibility in the content of services as well as changes in pricing, packaging, and delivery mechanisms. It also requires proactive information technology marketing to interface with, and sell new services to, internal and external customers.

19.1 Creating an Architecture Vision

Creating a strong, sustained linkage between a computing architecture and a process is a constant challenge in large organizations. Process reengineering is meaningful only if it promotes an organization's strategy. Embedding the corporate vision in each process makes the vision vital to the success of the process. The key activities in developing process visions are as follows:

1. Assess existing business strategy. Strategy is a set of long-term directional statements on key aspects of an organization. Vision is a detailed description of how a process should work in the future. The former must exist before the latter. Strategies should include all aspects of the organization's operations (financial and otherwise) and should be measurable, long-term, inspirational, and distinctive to the industry or organization.

2. Consult with process customers. It is important to remember that process customers can be both internal and external to the organization. Asking for customer input generates new ideas, demonstrates a desire for a close relationship, and may require customers to change their behavior for the process to work.

3. Benchmark performance targets and seek examples of innovation. Benchmarking helps define objectives for process innovation and can help identify key attributes that the process should have. Organizations can study other organizations that are known for their process refinements, even if those organizations are in another industry.

4. Formulate process performance objectives. Process objectives include the overall process goal, the specific type of improvement desired, the numeric target for the innovation, and the time frame in which the objectives are to be accomplished. Objectives should include both general process functionality and the goals of change.

5. Develop specific process attributes. Attributes constitute a vision of process operation in a future state. These qualities can be as general as describing the extent of employee empowerment in the process, or as specific as defining the number of employees used for it.

Overall, the visioning process asks several questions such as, "How could we do things differently?" It also leads to an initial vision statement that includes the following:

▶ Key characteristics (How will it work?)

▶ Performance objectives (How well will it work?)

▶ Critical success factors (What things have to go right?)

▶ Potential barriers (Why might they fail?)

19.1.1 Understanding and Improving Existing Processes

Understanding the current processes is an essential element of process innovation. Organizations look to these tools and techniques to play a role in finding improvements. Process diagrams such as flow charts and cost build-up charts are among the most useful of these tools. They can reveal bottlenecks or unnecessary steps in a process that would otherwise be overlooked.

None of these traditional improvement techniques can consistently yield radical process innovations. Although they may share characteristics with process innovation, all the techniques begin with the existing process and are intended to yield incremental change. None addresses the envisioning, enablement, or implementation of across-the-board changes. They are most appropriately used to complement the components of the innovative approach described herein.

19.1.2 Designing and Implementing the New Process and Organization

The design process involves a group of intelligent, creative people who review the information collected in the steps mentioned earlier and create a new system based on the stated objectives. This effort usually takes less time than the process of gathering information. There are techniques for facilitating data acquisition, but the success or failure of the design phase rests solely on the members involved. The key activities in designing and developing a prototype of a new process are as follows:

1. Brainstorm design alternatives. Brainstorming involves any facilitation method that encourages all group members to throw out ideas. This activity does not have anything to do with analysis. It is often the most

outrageous ideas that at first seem impossible that lead to a more reasonable, truly original solution.

2. **Assess feasibility of alternatives and select the design.** The team members involved in this phase should keep the objectives of the effort in mind when they select the most promising alternatives. A cost-versus-benefit analysis is not enough to choose the best design alternative. Issues such as nonfinancial benefits, though it is difficult to quantify specific value, may be the most important aspects of a plan to reach the organization's desired objectives.

3. **Develop a prototype of the new process design.** Developing a prototype is a way to simulate and test the operation of a new process. Often a new process can be applied to a single department or business unit of a firm, provided that the "host" unit reacts consistently with the firm as a whole. The results of not developing a prototype of a new system can be disastrous. Even if the new system is far superior, employees can develop resentment to operating in a way with which they are unfamiliar or a way that has unproved results.

4. **Develop a migration strategy.** A full, immediate cutover to a new process may be difficult or impossible for a large organization. It is essential to plan a phasing in of a new process, especially if it involves interaction with external forces (suppliers, customers) that may not share the firm's desire for change.

5. **Implement the new organizational structures and systems.** Many organizations that are structured on product lines or functions have a hard time assessing the big-picture results of a large-scale system-innovation effort. For this reason, it is vital to the success of the effort to have tools for evaluating results before the system is implemented.

19.2 What the Experts Advise

What does all this mean? How does an organization translate all this information into a meaningful computing architecture? A study of senior information service managers suggests the following guidelines for reengineering technology:

▶ Do not rush to migrate from legacy systems before fully analyzing the costs.

▶ Fully replacing legacy systems is expensive and time-consuming. A hybrid approach of new development, rehabilitation, and replacement is more practical.

▶ Use metrics to classify legacy systems on the basis of relative business value and soundness of technology. Then treat them accordingly.

▶ Reuse everything possible, particularly the business-specific logic code.

▶ Reuse legacy code if it dramatically shortens implementation time for the new system.

▶ Reexamine and reengineer work processes before overhauling legacy systems.

▶ Be aware that packaged applications may be viable only for standard, stand-alone processes.

▶ Be aware that political pressures weigh hard on the side of maintaining the status quo.

▶ Be aware that pockets of technology bigots attempt to sway decisions on the basis of the seductiveness of their technology rather than on sound business cases.

▶ Expect friction with users whose enhancement requests cannot be fulfilled during the migration.

▶ Be aware that the cost of resolving maintenance backlog may not be as high as the lost-opportunity cost of not doing it.

▶ Persuade pessimistic users by demonstrating the value that the reengineering effort will add for them. Leave the decisions in the hands of the users.

19.3 Conclusion

If information service organizations are to continue to play an active role in the effort to control costs and generate revenues, then software system reengineering needs to be included as part of the overall enterprise computing architecture.

To make more information available in less time, information service organizations implement a variety of proprietary technologies, develop new systems, and add capabilities to existing ones. The amount of system integration, development, and maintenance activity required to accomplish this leaves them with little time to properly care for the base of aging legacy systems.

By definition, legacy systems are usually more than seven years old. They may or may not be mission critical, use outmoded or different proprietary technologies, have poorly structured program code, have ineffective reporting systems, and use system and human resources inefficiently. To further complicate these systems, the original design and development teams have changed, leaving the current support team without a complete understanding of the detailed operation of the system. In other words, legacy systems are usually the systems that everyone fears and no one wants to support.

It is common for legacy systems to be in a state of disrepair and suffer from the use of outmoded technologies and years of changes at the hands of different information service personnel using different programming styles and formats. For many organizations, these application systems age with few, if any, improvements to the program structure, complexity, or hardware and software technologies. Frequently, new systems are easier to use, more flexible to modify, and operate more efficiently than the legacy system. Unfortunately, no staffing is applied to bring legacy systems up to standard.

The tide is turning, and emphasis is being placed on expense reduction and improved financial performance. Information service budgets are being cut, business processes and computer systems are being reengineered, application systems are moving away from centralized computer centers and rehosted in operating divisions with departmental computers, and computing is being outsourced or downsized to client-server technology.

When the expense of maintaining legacy systems is evaluated, it is increasingly apparent that management must seriously consider system reengineering as an integral component of cost containment and business process reengineering.

The increasing popularity of business process reengineering has placed greater pressure on information service departments to keep pace with similar system reengineering projects. Companies are maintaining and repositioning their legacy systems to make them more cost-effective, competitive, and easy to use. This frees resources to support activities associated with the larger issue of business process reengineering.

Appendix

Selected Readings

Bakker, Robert T. *The Dinosaur Heresies.* New York: William Morrow & Company, 1986.

Beard, Charles A. *An Economic Interpretation of the Constitution of The United States.* London: Collier McMillian, 1986.

Deming, W. Edwards. *Out of Crisis.* Cambridge: The Massachusetts Institute of Technology Center for Advanced Engineering Study, 1986.

Drucker, Peter F. *Innovation and Entrepreneurship: Practice and Principles.* New York: Harper & Row, 1986.

Eldredge, Niles, and Gould, Stephen Jay. "Punctuated Equilibria: An Alternative to Phletic Gradualism." In *Models in Paleobiology,* edited by T. J. M. Schopf, 82–115. San Francisco: Freeman Cooper, 1972.

Garvin, David A. "Competing on the Eight Dimensions of Quality." *Harvard Business Review* 6 (November/December 1987): 101–9.

Gibson, Cyrus F., and Nolan, Richard L. "Managing the Four Stages of EDP Growth." *Harvard Business Review* 1 (January/February 1974): 76–88.

Ginsburg, Sigmund G. "The Five Major Roles of an Outstanding CEO." *The President* (June 1988): 78.

Isenberg, Daniel J. "How Senior Managers Think." *Harvard Business Review* 6 (November/December 1984): 81–90.

Jacobs, Jay, ed. *The Horizon Book of Great Cathedrals.* New York: American Heritage Publishing Company, 1968.

Kanter, Rosabeth Moss. *The Change Masters: Innovation & Entrepreneurship in the American Corporation.* New York: Simon & Schuster, 1983.

Kull, David. "The Aging System Saga." *Computer Decisions* (January 1989): 42–47.

Mayr, Ernst. "Evolution." *Scientific American* (September, 1978): 47–55.

Mendelssohn, Kurt. *The Riddle of the Pyramids.* New York: Praeger Publishers, 1974.

Miller, Howard W. "20 Tips for Unattended Operations." *Datacenter Manager* (March/April 1989): 54–59.

———. "Achieving Unattended Operations." *Enterprise Systems Journal* (April 1991): 63–68.

———. "Altering the Status of the Help Desk." *CMG Australia Journal* 8 (May 1992): 27–31.

———. "Assessing Your Security Risk Index." *Technical Support Magazine* (January 1989): 35–40.

———. *The Automated Computer Job Scheduling Guide.* Byfield, Massachusetts: Massachusetts Information Technology Institute, 1991.

———. "Automated Computer Job Scheduling Systems: How to Select and What to Expect." *The Computer Operations Manager* (March/April 1989): 12–25.

———. "Automated Disaster Recovery." *Contingency Journal* (January/February 1991): 22–26.

———. "Automated Operations: The Tape Escape." *Technical Support Magazine* (July 1989): 93–96.

———. "Automatic Problem Resolution." *The Computer Operations Manager* (January/February 1991): 13–19.

———. "Automatic Report Balancing and Control." *CMG Australia Journal* (August 1991): 19–23.

———. "Automatic Report Balancing and Control." *Technical Support Magazine* (November 1991): 49–54.

———. "Automating the Computer Center." *Technical Support Magazine* (March 1989): 44–49.

———. "Automating Storage Management." *CMG Australia Journal* (February 1992): 17–21.

———. "Automation at Boston University." *Inside Operations: The Candle View* (March 1990): 1–4.

———. "The Chief Information Officer as an IS Architect." *Information Executive* (Spring 1989): 31–35.

———. "Client, Network, and Server Imaging Technology." *Technical Support Magazine* (December 1995): 16–20.

———. "Client-Based Electronic Report Distribution." *Technical Support Magazine* (August 1995): 24–27.

———. "Client/Server Poses New Challenges in Disaster Recovery Arena." *The Computer Operations Manager* (July/August 1996): 12–16.

———. *The Client/Server Sourcebook.* Byfield, Massachusetts: Massachusetts Information Technology Institute, 1995.

———. "Client/Server Network Security." *Technical Support Magazine* (January 1995): 14–18.

———. *Computer and Network Security.* Byfield, Massachusetts: Massachusetts Information Technology Institute, 1996.

————. "Computer Center Automation." *Cause/Effect* 15 (Winter 1992): 45–46.

————. *Computer Center Automation Implementation Techniques.* Byfield, Massachusetts: Massachusetts Information Technology Institute, 1991.

————. "Computer Center Environmental Monitoring." *Technical Support Magazine/Special Report: Contingency Awareness* (November 1991): 29–32.

————. *Computer Disaster Recovery Contingency Guide.* Byfield, Massachusetts: Massachusetts Information Technology Institute, 1988.

————. *The Console Automation Guide.* Byfield, Massachusetts: Massachusetts Information Technology Institute, 1990.

————. *Console Automation Implementation Techniques.* Byfield, Massachusetts: Massachusetts Information Technology Institute, 1992.

————. "Console Automation Reduces Security Risk." *Technical Support Magazine* 6 (August 1992): 24–29.

————. "Creating an Evolutionary Software System: A Case Study." *Journal of Systems Management* (August 1990): 11–18.

————. "Designing an Evolving Information System." *Journal of Systems Management* (August 1991): 9–12.

————. "Developing Information Technology Strategies." *Journal of Systems Management* (September 1988): 28–35.

————. *The Disaster Recovery Source Book.* Byfield, Massachusetts: Massachusetts Information Technology Institute, 1992.

————. "Disaster Recovery Planning." *Journal of Systems Management* (March 1986): 25–30.

————. *Downsizing and Client/Server Computing.* Byfield, Massachusetts: Massachusetts Information Technology Institute, 1993.

————. "A Dozen Client, Server, and Network Performance Options." *Technical Support Magazine* (August 1996): 24–28.

————. "An Economic Interpretation of Data Processing Growth." *CMG Australia Journal* (December 1990): 21–28.

————. "Eight Areas to Automate Operations." *Corporate Computing* (February 1993): 90.

————. "Electronic Communication." *Technical Support Magazine* (February 1992): 37–40.

————. *Electronic Data Interchange.* Byfield, Massachusetts: Massachusetts Information Technology Institute, 1992.

————. "Electronic Data Interchange." *Enterprise Systems Journal* (February 1991): 92–97.

————. *Electronic Mail System Alternatives.* Byfield, Massachusetts: Massachusetts Information Technology Institute, 1992.

———. *The Electronic Report Distribution Guide.* Byfield, Massachusetts: Massachusetts Information Technology Institute, 1990.

———. "Electronic Report Distribution." *The Mainframe Journal* (September/October 1988): 74–81.

———. "Electronic Vaulting." *Contingency Journal* (November 1989): 10–17.

———. "Electronic Vaulting." *Contingency Journal* (January-March 1990): 8–14.

———. *Electronic Vaulting: A Special Report.* Byfield, Massachusetts: Massachusetts Information Technology Institute, 1991.

———. "End Users Drive Benefit Analysis." *Computerworld* (10 August 1987): 59–62.

———. *Evolutionary Systems.* Byfield, Massachusetts: Massachusetts Information Technology Institute, 1989.

———. *Expert System Technology.* Byfield, Massachusetts: Massachusetts Information Technology Institute, 1993.

———. "Expert Systems and Systems-Managed Storage." *CMG Transactions* (Fall 1992): 19–24.

———. "Exploiting Console Automation." *Inside Operations: The Candle View* (July 1989): 4–6.

———. "Exploiting Console Automation." *POSPP Report* P-53B-9, PII 0902.13, (June 1989).

———. "Exploiting Console Automation." *Datacenter Manager* (September/October 1989): 32–37.

———. "The Future of Unattended Computer Center Automation." *The Mainframe Journal* (September 1989): 61–70.

———. "Guest Editorial." *Technical Support Magazine/Special Report: Automated Operations* (August 1991): 4.

———. "Hardware and Software Negotiating Tips: More Than Just Reading the Fine Print." *Technical Support Magazine* (July 1995): 22–25.

———. *How to Automate Your Computer Center: Achieving Unattended Operations.* Wellesley, Massachusetts: QED Information Sciences, 1990.

———. "The Human Side of Automated Operations." *The Computer Operations Manager* (January/February 1989); 36–44.

———. *Image Processing System Guide.* Byfield, Massachusetts: Massachusetts Information Technology Institute, 1994.

———. "Implementing Mainframe Based Expert Systems." *Technical Support Magazine* (October 1989): 66–70.

———. "Implementing Unattended Computer Center Operation." *Technical Support Magazine* (September 1988): 24–31.

———. "Improved Security Tactics Through Computer Center Automation." *Computing Solutions* (December 1993): 22–24.

————. "Information Technology: Creation or Evolution?" *Journal of Systems Management* (April 1991): 23–27.

————. "The Information Technology Cost Containment Checklist." *The Mainframe Journal* (March/April 1988): 75–95.

————. "The Leaning Tower of Technology." *Information Strategy: The Executive's Journal* (Spring 1989): 17–21.

————. "'Lights-Out' Versus 'Problems-Out' Automation Strategies." *Inside Operations: The Candle View* (September 1990): 2–4.

————. "Mainframe-Based Expert Systems." *Technical Support Magazine* (October 1989): 66–70.

————. "The Manual Side of Unattended Computer Center Operations." *Technical Support Magazine* (August 1989): 28–42.

————. "Microfiche Replacement Alternatives." *Technical Support Magazine* (December 1992): 6–12.

————. "The Need for Quality in Computer Center Automation." *Enterprise Systems Journal* (September 1991): 83–86.

————. *Object Technology.* Byfield, Massachusetts: Massachusetts Information Technology Institute, 1996.

————. "Opportunism: Nine Steps to a Better Information System." *Chief Information Officer Journal* (Summer 1990): 24–30.

————. "Planning the Unattended Computer Center." *CMG Australia Journal* (June 1991): 20–24.

————. "Planning the Unattended Computer Center." *Technical Support Magazine* (March 1992): 12–17.

————. "Planning for Unattended Data Center Operation." *The Mainframe Journal* (January/February 1988): 10–87.

————. "Practical Console Automation." *Datacenter Manager* (September/October 1990): 24–27.

————. "Project Management: A Structured Framework." *System Development Management* 35-01-25 (1989): 1–15.

————. "Project Management: A Structured Framework." *System Development Management* 35-01-25.1 (1993): 1–16.

————. "Quality and Unattended Computer Center Operation." *Technical Support Magazine* (May 1990): 40–45.

————. "Quality Software: The Future of Information Technology." *Journal of Systems Management* (December 1989): 8–14.

————. "The Rationale For Unattended Computer Center Operation." *Computer Associates DIALOG* (May 1989): 1–15.

————. "Re-Engineering the Computing Center." *Technical Support Magazine* (October 1996): 36–39.

———. "Removing Computer Center Barriers." *Technical Support Magazine/Special Report: Automated Operations* (August 1991): 9–14.

———. "Rethinking Computer Center Design." *Technical Support Magazine* (April 1989): 41–71.

———. "Selecting Artificial Intelligence Software." *The Mainframe Journal* (August 1989): 44–80.

———. "Selecting CASE Technology and Software." *The Mainframe Journal* (July/ August 1988): 63–66.

———. "A System Erector Set." *Information Strategy: The Executive's Journal* (Winter 1988): 22–26.

———. "Three Management Considerations for Unattended Operation." *The Computer Operations Manager* (January/(February 1990): 13–64.

———. "The Tie That Binds: Automated Console Response." *Technical Support Magazine* (September 1988): 24–31.

———. "Unattended Computer Center Implementation Strategies." *CMG Australia Journal* (August 1990): 33–37.

———. "An Unattended Computer Center Operation." *The NACAS Journal* (February 1993): 14–17.

———. "Unattended Computer Center Operation at Boston University." *CMG Australia Journal* (February 1993): 24–28.

———. "Unattended Computer Center Operation at Boston University." *Journal of Systems Management* (April 1993): 8–42.

———. "Unattended Computer Center Operation: 50 Questions and Answers." *The Mainframe Journal* (April 1989): 58–89.

———. *Unattended Computer Center Planning*, 10th anniversary edition. Byfield, Massachusetts: Massachusetts Information Technology Institute, 1995.

———. *Unattended Computer Center Planning Guide.* Byfield, Massachusetts: Massachusetts Information Technology Institute, 1989.

———. *Unattended Computer Center Source Book.* Byfield, Massachusetts: Massachusetts Information Technology Institute, 1995.

———. "Understanding CASE Technology." *The Mainframe Journal* (May/June 1988): 44–47.

———. "The University of Automation." *The Computer Operations Manager* (September/October 1993): 13–21.

———. "Unraveling the Purchased Software Dilemma." *Technical Support Magazine* (June 1989): 50–53.

———. "Upgrading Computer Center Automation." *Technical Support Magazine* (April 1993): 23–29.

———. "User Job Scheduling." *Technical Support Magazine* (November 1991): 29–23.

————. "Value Added Print Reduction." *Technical Support Magazine* (November 1990): 58–64.

————. "Value Added Tape Elimination." *Technical Support Magazine* (April 1992): 8–15.

————. "When 'New' Is Not 'Improved'." *Computerworld* (15 September 1986): 71–74.

Nolan, Richard L. "Managing the Computer Resource: A Stage Hypothesis." *Harvard Business Review* 4 (July/August 1973): 399–405.

Nolan, Richard L. "Managing the Crisis in Data Processing." *Harvard Business Review* 2 (March/April 1979): 115–126.

Wroblewski, Adam, and Cupoli, Patricia Dymkar. "Evolutionary Approach to Data Management." Journal of Systems Management, (July 1988): 24–31.

Yaffe, Jerry, "External-Internal System Design." *Journal of Systems Management* (July 1988): 20–23.

Other Books from Digital-Press

Designing and Developing Electronic Performance Support Systems
by Lesley A. Brown
1996   250pp   pb   1-55558-139-0

Microsoft Exchange Server V5.0: Planning, Design, and Implementation
by Tony Redmond
1997   728pp   pb   1-55558-189-7

Migrating to the Intranet and Microsoft Exchange by Randall J. Covill
1997 250pp   pb   1-55558-172-2

Software Implementation Techniques, 2ed by Don Merusi
1995 608pp   pb   1-55558-134-X

TCP/IP Explained by Philip Miller
1996   450pp   pb   1-55558-166-8

X.400 and SMTP: Battle of the E-mail Protocols by John Rhoton
1997   206pp   pb   1-55558-165-X

. . . .

Feel free to visit our web site at: http://www.bh.com/digitalpress

These books are available from all good bookstores or in case of difficulty call:
1-800-366-2665 in the U.S. or +44-1865-310366 in Europe.

E-Mail Mailing List

An e-mail mailing list giving information on latest releases, special promotions, offers and other news relating to Digital Press titles is available. To subscribe, send an e-mail message to majordomo@world.std.com.
Include in message body (not in subject line): subscribe digital-press